Cultural Pluralism as a
Social Imperative in Education

Cultural Pluralism As a Social Imperative In Education

Research for Change

by

Renée A. Davis, Ph. D.

VANTAGE PRESS
New York / Washington / Atlanta
Los Angeles / Chicago

Published by Vantage Press, Inc.
516 West 34th Street, New York, New York 10001

Manufactured in the United States of America
Standard Book Number 533-04555-X

Library of Congress Catalog Card No.: 79-57152

To my parents, who gave me
the foundation on which to build

Contents

List of Tables   ix
List of Figures   ix
Foreword   xi
Acknowledgments   xiii

I. Cultural Pluralism as a Social Imperative in
   Education   1
         Problem   1
         Introduction   1
         Background   4
         Role of Scientific Research in Education   7
         Education, Schooling, Purpose, and
                American Tradition   12
         Common Prejudices, Abuses, and the Great
                American Dream   16
         Jargonese and Terms That Confuse   22
         Dearth of Theories for Educating for a
                Culturally Pluralistic World   26

II. The Study   30
         Purpose   30
         Nature of the Study   40
         Methodology   44
         Assumptions and Context   46
         Scope and Limitations   49
         Theoretical Basis of the Study   51

III. Literature Review 59
  Introduction 59
  State-of-the-Art Survey 64
  Summary of the State of the Art 64
  Compensatory Education: Is It Educational
    Reform? 73
  Compensatory Education as Cultural
    Conditioning 74
  Analysis of Deficits as Cause for Poor
    Performance 78
  The Emergence of Valuing Diversity 82
  Multicultural Education 94
  Three-Pronged Components in the
    Theoretical Base 101
  Summary 117

IV. The Theoretical Model 121
  Prelude 121
  The Universal Culture Affective
    Theoretical Model 126
  Basic Components Defined 129
  Organization and Relationships: Maxims
    in the Universal Culture Affective
    Model 131
  Postulates by Components 134
  Principal Concepts by Components 141
  Universal Culture Affective Model 141
  Assumption 145
  Universal Culture Affective Model
    Construct 145
  Hypotheses 150
  Universal Culture Affective Model
    Paradigm 151
  Conclusions and Recommendations 155
Notes 157
Glossary 181
Bibliography 189
Index 219

List of Tables

Table 1.   Federal Officials Contacted in Bureaus and Divisions   65
Table 2.   Professional Contacts (Nonfederal and Academic)   66
Table 3.   Document Search Systems   67

List of Figures

Figure 1   UCAM components (theoretical model)   128
Figure 2. Culture change due to diffusion   133
Figure 3. Difference between the traditional and UCAM sphere of influence   143
Figure 4. UCAM construct   150
Figure 5. Culture (matter-energy continuum)   154

Foreword

Dr. Davis's in-depth analysis of social diversity and social struggle—and her recommendations for teachers and administrators to lay the foundations for a greater acceptance and respect for cultural differences—will be widely read.

Although the book is heavily researched and carefully documented, the author's concern for people of all backgrounds is never rendered dry or academic. It is up to the educational institutions to carry the ball from here—and to take the initiative in preparing us all to live in social harmony with one another.

—Jonathan Kozol
June 3, 1980
Boston, Massachusetts

Acknowledgments

This book is the published and modified version of my Ph.D. dissertation. I want to take this opportunity to publically acknowledge the people who helped me in various ways during my long journey, at times quite intense in the research, the writing, and the technical requirements at Walden University.

First I want to thank Roy Fleischer and James Robinson. They both understood and permitted me the peace of mind and the time when it was crucial to pursue the tedious research and writing while I was engaged in full-time work. Their interest made it possible for me to increase my professional growth and to potentially influence education in some significant way.

To Dr. Matthew Wakatama, my research advisor, I thank him who went beyond the call of duty to facilitate my strong inclination to tackle a very difficult subject in a non-conventional view. He encouraged me to plow ahead taking whatever direction that came regardless of the current opinions in the educational field.

Thanks to Dr. Sadie Grimmitt, who read and commented on the document.

A very special appreciation to Dr. Robert Bentley, who was not only a supportive reader but trusted my professional integrity and let me know it.

Without my dependable colleagues, Carol Berk and Diane Gerras, the last moments of editing the manuscript wouldn't have been possible.

And to Tina, Tina Janey-Burrell, whose strength sustenance, and belief in me championed my efforts as a woman supporting women's efforts, as a professional and confidant.

I must also thank Fletcher Pence, who not only cheered me on as I worked on my Ph.D. research but provided me with some important resources.

And lastly, my thanks to Betty Kulleseid, Maggie Albrecht, Jim and Anne McWilliams, long-time friends who always believed in me.

Cultural Pluralism as a
Social Imperative in Education

Chapter I

Cultural Pluralism as a
Social Imperative in Education

Problem

There has been an absence of consciousness, interest, and focus on all levels of education and in American society, in general, which promoted or enhanced concepts of acceptance and deference for cultural differences among the various indigenous social groups.* Lacking was a theoretical model that provided the assumptions to educate personnel and children to respect diversity. Children from all ethnic groups have the right to be assured an authentic education that takes into account the cultures from which they come and to be educated to live potently in a culturally pluralistic world.

Introduction

Without the examination of culture's role in the lives of individuals from disparate groups, without observation and knowledge of how cultures differ, without understanding the universality of cultural dynamics, there has been no incentive

*At all times when "America" is used, it refers to the United States of America.

1

for people to grasp the antecedents and consequences of differences. This has led to little motivation for learning about how one's own cultural background influences one's own behavior, values, and judgments about others, thereby having perpetuated little or no interest in learning about how other cultural groups believed, behaved, and made judgments. No viable bases have existed for developing the kinds of approaches to cooperate with and to accept the behaviors and beliefs of people from divergent cultural groups. The dilemma in seeking effective solutions to societal problems has been attributed to inadequate identification of consequential interrelated and overlapping social factors. Also, the ideology, traditional biases, and functions emanating from the respective social science professions have not been recognized to the degree necessary to create the systems for positive acceptance of diversity. Barriers have resulted due to the confusion about the various meanings of democratic ideals. One example was related to the concept "Freedom for All," as the substance in which all nationalities had equal opportunity in the common institutions. This has been a contradiction in historical and current practices. Selected groups have been systematically omitted from full participation. In addition, all those factors that governed the highly complex technological society have been further complicated by a resistance to change.

Educational planners often had little awareness of the cultural manifestations in each of the social groups in which the changes were expected by the preferred group. There has been no theory or a premise for establishing the consequences comprehensively created by the highly industrialized democratic structure within the frame of reference of historical ideology and for the treatment experienced by groups that were not permitted in the mainstream of American society. Since the attitudes held and settings provided by the dominant group have not been explicit about functions of different ethnic communities, it has contributed to obstacles to mutual understanding.

The challenges facing the nation were both critical and

complex. Most authorities acknowledged that the overwhelming magnitude of such problems as energy, food, poverty, unemployment, inflation, education, technological growth, etc., needed global solutions. It was clear that improvements in the promotion of intercultural relations must be addressed by educational institutions. Knowing that "culture" essentially was made up of values, concepts, and interpretations of the world (reality), it could function as a common bond among cultural groups. Cultural cooperation was basically human cooperation, and it had an inherent value that transcended other functions such as politics, economics, and education. Having the knowledge, insight, attitude, and feeling of respect for the particular orientations of involved cultures could serve to facilitate more open and respectful responses to the variety of human transactions. Cross-cultural relations could have narrowed the ethnocentric monocultural outlook that generally underlies conflict among groups. More flexible options for parity of acceptance and mutual respect needed to be developed for intercultural encounters.

From the cultural anthropologist's view, education was seen as cultural transmission. Beginning with preschool through the secondary grades, existing curricula represented different sets of concepts about which certain segments of the community received certain types of education. These assumptions were based on the presuppositions made about the background and potentiality of these groups, the criteria having been "one model American." The type and quality of service provided in poor inner-city schools did not match those of the affluent suburban schools.

The problem of this research could not be simply stated because it was multifaceted and there was yet to be developed a comprehensive view of human behavior. The forces that impinge upon it stemmed from a number of interrelated influences that included historical events, the impact of the sociopolitical beliefs held by the founders of the American democracy, the economics of slavery, the beliefs held by the preferred group about the inferiority of black and native Americans, the subsequent momentum created by economic growth during industrialization, the social and political conditions of immigrants, the events leading to and during the civil rights movements, and to the rapid development of sophisticated technology that was now a forceful competitor in the labor market. The various levels and dimensions of the problem could not be understood through the significant interrelated ingredients or components as reflected within this American historical, economic, social, and educational framework. An awareness of the epistemology in the examination of the components necessarily became the basis for critical elements in attitudes and expectations. These basically simulated historical doctrines continuously persisted in hampering a fair analysis of the behavior and beliefs of particular groups. Valid solutions became virtually impossible. Ethnic groups were affected by characteristics of educational programs depending on the assumptions made about them. The problem of this study was unsettling because of disordered and overlapping determinants. The need to have a philosophical base for an education to acknowledge and appreciate cultural pluralism was the foundation on which authentic education for American children rested. The need for preparing children to live effectively in a multicultural world was imperative. In order to grasp the substance of the problem, one had to be alert continually to the component contingencies and synergistic connections; namely, the role of scientific research in education, schooling, and the American tradition, common prejudice, abuses and the great American dream, the function of terms and confusing jargon, and the lack of philosophical principles that enhanced culturally pluralistic education.

Background

Society, Socialization, and Reality

The evidence was mounting leaving little doubt that highly industrialized nations had serious social problems that needed immediate attention. The crises in contemporary life were clearly divided into two reciprocal realms. The most obvious and discernible pertained to the physical environment, that is, resource scarcity and the size of the population. The other, much more ethereal, less visible, and probably more lethal, humankind itself—how people treat people. The human desire for expanding individual capacities and the inclination for exploiting others, no matter what the motivation, has led to the kind of social institution in which some groups were permitted to "have" while others were not considered worthy of the same advantages. Relationships between and among human societies were effected by the nature of the communication, in other words, the culture. In the final analysis, the economy, politics, social and educational problems and their interconnections could not be solved through physical or technical means because they originated with people. Current predicaments, pressures, frustrations, and conflicts among incongruous groups had been accumulating over centuries. Any human society existed through consensus among its members and included values, goals, and the ways one could attain them. People of the "chosen" group through their organizations, structures, and cultural patterns have exhibited a tenacious capacity for inflicting cruelty and human suffering rather than having the will to change their concepts, beliefs, and values about those they regarded as "unequal." Under these circumstances (ethnocentrism) their social behavior was not considered "irrational" since the individual cultural context provided the "reality" or meaning for dealing with the world.

Things are quieter in the ghettos now because the rhythm of black life is in a quiet phase—they are taking a breather. . . . But the major and continuing source of frustration exists because the many gifts and talents of women, black people, Indians, Spanish Americans, and others are not only unrecognized but frequently denigrated by members of the dominant group. It is the corrosive daily and niggling frustration, the inability to communicate or to establish meaningful relationships that is so soul-shrinking.

The cultural and psychological insight that is important for man to accept is that denying culture can be as destructive as denying evil.[1]

Knowledge about the rules of nature contributed to human endeavors whether life facilitating or life destroying. To know nature, on the one hand, was to be able to describe what had happened, not what should happen. Humanity's rules, on the other hand, were different in that they prevailed only because human beings agreed that they should exist. In addition, human beings had the tendency to bestow nature with a purpose and this varied from culture to culture. Studies in cultural anthropology revealed it has been a universal phenomenon for human beings to explain why they exist and, in addition, to give special meaning to it. It has been explained that it fulfilled a social and psychological human need.[2]

In American society, social organizations, educational institutions, and the general population have had little sound knowledge or positive attitudes for accepting authentic cultural diversity. Some of the causes were due to the nature of the fragmentation in scientific investigation, the interdisciplinary competition in the social sciences, and traditional social attitudes. There has been no ideological basis for the larger society to internalize relevant concepts and information stemming from cultural anthropology. Also, there were no viable institutional means to respect members of various cultural groups. Anthropology studied every aspect of human behavior, environmental conditions through comparative exploration, and searched for universal phenomena. Its influence in education has been negligible. Rather, the social sciences have reflected historical views, customs, and expectations of the dominant group consistent with America's social and political history. Thus, left ignored and misunderstood have been the cultural values and behaviors manifested by diverse ethnic groups that have sought to adapt to dominant values. An "American" has been defined through an indigenous national or "civic" perspective. Cultural anthropologists subscribing to theories of cultural relativity asserted that every human being was born into an environment defined by a culture and that it has been impossible to completely erase one's past culture.[3]

The problems for those Americans who came from non-dominant heritages were further exacerbated by the scientific community that governed research methodology in their attempt to be "purely objective." There has not been a complete appreciation or the acknowledgment of the concept that culture permeated every thought, decision, and human act. This concept was implied, however, in the definition of "science" itself.

Role of Scientific Research in Education

Research was faced with having to handle confounded conceptualizations in the attempt to understand the variety of interrelating factors in learning about the nature of humankind and in ways of applying findings to solve social concerns. Little effort has gone into recognizing derivational and methodological problems both in the process and theory in the scientific study of human groups. One problem related to complex issues when researchers of one sociocultural background studied the behavior and/or beliefs of groups from different sociocultural backgrounds. A second problem was revealed in research design. The way any investigation was organized was based on cultural definitions. The kind and the meanings given to the taxonomy influenced the interpretation of findings and carried with it numerous complicated cultural implications. The generalizations inferred by conclusions reached by scientists, a third concern, were dependent upon how, what data were collected, and the assumptions underlying them. Other cultural factors too numerous to detail here influenced the thinking approaches and particular foci practiced in research. The validity of theory might have been called into question when generalizations did not take into account the kind of global interacting issues pertinent at each phase of a study.

In American scientific study of social problems, the goals of conventional, experimental, and psychometric paradigms that strived to achieve full "objectivity" were based on arbitrary agreement, based on certain values, thought to be "scientific truth." This concept, however, was limited in scope, though not recognized as such. The "objective data" gathered to date have contributed little to revelations about the complex problems confronted by these studies since each raised other disjointed questions. As a matter of procedure, it has been expected and recommended that "further study" of particular elements be done. Furthermore, the findings that emerged from this "classical" approach did not provide sufficient integrated information to develop holistic theoretical constructs for application to the myriad situations generated by the dynamic encounters. This was especially applicable to heterogeneous interactions between and among diverse ethnic groups.

> The aim of "objectivity" in social science may well be a red herring. More realistic goals might include the establishment of a reliable data base and the articulation of biases which could affect the validity of data reports.[4]

As a consequence of experimental and psychometric approaches, the probability of formulating erroneous theories about a particular cultural group's behavior or misinterpreting their values had been dangerously real. A biased mode could place the investigator on the wrong track. In other words, to disregard the total cultural context in any phase in conceptualization in the field of human inquiry would be a serious matter because the field of education has relied more and more on research for application and evaluation. Certain characteristic generalizations had been used for policy decisions to be transcribed into educational models. For example, the recently resurrected debate of "intelligence"—that is, genetic versus environmental influence—had confused the issues that determined social policy.[5] The emerging interest from the cross-cultural and interdisciplinary research in social psychology, psychiatry, and the cross-cultural and intercultural communication professions have been instrumental in exploring other scientific paradigms.

Discussion

Researchers and methodology generally ignored or disregarded the configurational context manifested in culture for one reason or another. Cultural anthropologists who subscribed to theories of cultural relativity asserted that every human being was born with an environment defined by a culture and that it was impossible to erase completely one's past culture.[6] Generic concepts and hypotheses that permeated how problems were defined, that is, "truths," "facts," "objective data," and other highly precise terms (in which "measurement" was mandatory), have not taken into consideration the personal cultural influences and the dominant criteria that determined the content and context of conclusions. Scientific inquiry historically stemmed from conditions created, based on concepts and theories of homogeneity and assimilation goals set by the dominant cultural group. Past events assume a special meaning in shaping other cultural phenomena. Within this framework, terms such as "logic," "objectivity," "facts," and "reason" are the values held by a group. Value assumptions are an integral component, though often unstated when examining criteria, the data, in reporting and interpretation of findings in studies of social groups. "Reality" was made up of values. Therefore, these scientific terms (add "reason," "rationale," "exact," "logic," and others), if associated with a special meaning, that is, "scientific truth" as absolute and not related to the culture in which it had been identified, were curiously "unscientific" and reflective of a lack of culture sense.[7] To put it another way, "reality" should be considered within the historical and cultural confines of role, functions, structure, and those other characteristic elements in which the concept "culture" has been by definition. These variables have not been internalized holistically or employed in society's ideologies, including the scientific world. Wolfgang Kohler maintained that value and insight were at the very essence of human mental life.

It is quite as important to realize that the meaning of "objective" in the phenomenal field has no direct connection with physical existence outside the physical organism. We tend to call such properties of our phenomenal environment objective as have a counterpart in the physical environment of the organism.[8]

One example of the cultural element that perpetuated highly selective values and priorities was myths.[9] The transmission of myths throughout time has played an essential role in introducing and carrying out a culture's customs, traditions, and overall view of the world. Myths developed very gradually, and they tended to become culturally ingrained long after configurational contexts—which made them once useful—were no longer applicable and valid. Myths were generally unconscious beliefs and since they have not been perpetuated as a conscious effort, they have been held tenaciously as "fact." The White House Conference forum on "Myths of Education" stated

The curriculum, objectives, and structure of our present educational system are largely products of another age—responses to the needs of a society immersed in the rapid transition from rural/agricultural to urban/industrial life styles. . . .

Much of our educational system has failed to meet the challenges presented by this rapid transformation. We believe that our educational myths severely inhibit effective response to the pressing demand for better education of all children. We believe the confrontation of these myths or false assumptions is the first prerequisite to reform. Too long have our children been learning *in spite of*, rather than because of, our well-meaning but often misguided efforts; it is imperative that we reverse this trend.[10]

The concept (myth) of the "disadvantaged," for example, was a result of the cultural construct promoted by social scientists who researched educational methods on selected populations (currently called "minority groups").

The United States was made up of groups of immigrants and migrant peoples, in a sense paralleling the history of humankind, moving in search of compatible environmental conditions. In the American picture, since its inception as a nation, such experience resulted in cultural discrimination. Subsequently, it was structured into the political system when legislation sanctioned prejudice toward selected nationalities and religions.[11]

The existence of a complete American culture was a concept developed after the First World War. It required all who lived in the United States of America to become assimilated into the dominant culture, excluding only black Americans and native Americans who have been historically considered more inferior than the immigrant.

The political ideological "culture deprivation" hypothesis of the 1960s was developed on the premise that differences in educational achievement (through test scores) of the poor was due to their "deficit" backgrounds. During this period, the idea of "minority group" was still used. However, the ethnic groups essentially changed. Black Americans and other "minority" groups were compared with middle class children, usually white Anglo-Saxon, through I.Q. and other achievement measures. These measures purported to be "scientifically objective." It was still believed that the reason that children of minority groups did poorly on standardized tests was due to their "deprived" homes. The political origins and the conditions surrounding immigration showed how neatly a concept like "disadvantaged home" could be "logically" assumed. It was consistent within the perspective that evolved. It continued through the educational system in the United States by developing "compensatory" programs. The Anglo-Saxon model, as dominant, was and still is the "cultural" orientation that prevails in standards of conduct, belief system, and values related to schooling.

Education, Schooling, Purpose, and American Tradition

Education's purpose in America has been influenced by several themes. First of all, it has been expected that the educator's responsibility was to understand humankind, to provide the fundamental knowledge, to teach the basic skills while transmitting "values" to children.[12] Second, schooling has been the significant vehicle to instill the "national culture." It provided the foundation for a social balance and promoted the values defined by the dominant society to contribute to the stratified economy. Third, decision makers in educational systems also voiced the goal that the function of formal schooling lay the groundwork for lifelong learning. Fourth, industry viewed the responsibility of public schools to provide certain skills to prepare future citizens to live in the technological world and to participate in the economy in some fashion. Fifth, parents believed that to go through school (at least high school) was the path to a higher status and for obtaining a higher income in the open competitive economy. Martin Carnoy argued that schooling was not the "liberating" means many seemed to believe, nor was it the school's role; rather, it served the function of domination, control, and perpetuation of an inherent unequal and unjust structure of production and political power.[13] Dehumanizing experiences for some groups occurred in this complex structure—through stratification, power conflicts, economic and social competition. It has been almost impossible to separate the concepts of distribution of wealth and market and services changes from political organizational aspects concerned with the management of all those elements within the system. The allocation of scarce resources and services in societies has been but one factor in attempting to solve survival problems. Anthropological evidence suggested that when food production and technology advanced to the development of the "city" and centralized "states," conflicts became more serious between peoples of differing cultural groups. "War," for example, has been prevalent only in the last 10,000 years.[14] Many anthropologists believed that with the evolution of state level structures, "war" was waged for the desire to control economic resources and perpetuation of an inherent unequal and unjust system of production and political power.[15]

Discussion

The reality from which educational principles, methods, and goals stem has been the ethnocentric monocultural philosophical view and its political determinants. The United States has been a heterogeneous country encompassing many subgroups, while at the same time homogeneity has been considered essential for maintaining the political philosophy of social equality and democracy. During colonial days, public education was carried out by families. The family was the unit responsible for socializing the child. If a child was not "well provided for," the parish (the community) took on the responsibility. The standards were the prevailing mores and morality of the times.[16] As industrialization grew, and society became more complex, public education was considered to be the vehicle through which the idea of democracy, literacy, and the route out of poverty were possible. The common belief during this period persists, which persists, was that the goals of public schooling ought to instill the ideas in individuals to adjust to a particular work function on various ranges of the ladder to fit into an industrial society. Also, public schooling served to keep the "neighborhood" free from unemployed youth. In short, the main responsibility of educators was to teach the kinds of skills in which economic productions have been maintained. Assimilation of all cultural groups into a model American continued to be a major function of public schooling with the noted exceptions of peoples of color (and other "minorities"). As the nation expanded further in its diversity during the period sometimes referred to as "the new society," the heterogeneity caused conflicting messages—the backward poor would be educated and shaped into a uniformly productive middle class—within the pervasive doctrine of the superiority of the Anglo-Saxon culture. Cubberly stated,

> Our task is to assimilate these people as a part of the American race, and to implant in their children, so far as can be done, the Anglo-Saxon conception of righteousness, law, order, and popular government, and to awaken in them reverence for our democratic institutions and for those things which we as a people hold to be of abiding worth.[17]

Seymour Itzkoff reported that Benjamin Franklin was doubtful about the differences. He felt it was important that all newcomers be Americanized, as they presumably were a threat to democratic ideals. "Toward this end, they would be forced to adopt the English tongue and, possibly, the Protestant religion."[18] The role of schools to this day has been to facilitate homogenization into a singular cultural "American style."[19] These inscriptions were deeply rooted and to legitimately question their validity would raise feelings of unAmericanism.

In American society, as Colin Greer pointed out, public schools have been the places where poor immigrant children eventually could learn to become affluent citizens of the nation.[20] He showed how, through the late nineteenth and early twentieth century, public schools failed poor children and actually forced large numbers out of school. The "new pluralism" movement of the 1970s had attempted to expose the fallacy of assimilation belief.[21] The reality of the "unmelted ethnic" and the rise of minority voices demanded acceptance, respect, and opportunities previously denied.[22] However, the education rhetoric continued to purport to prepare children from all ethnic groups for "equal" opportunities.*

Based on this philosophy, educational decisions were founded upon standardized criteria. Measurements and statistical scores have been the primary method for judging "poor achievement," "low reading scores," "dropouts," illiteracy, and the like. The education researchers and test developers (who have evolved into a rather large business enterprise) continued to ignore their own ethnocentric biases.[23] In addition, versions of studies on "genetic inferiority" that reappeared as the dominant ethnocentric view reinforced covert attitudes, prejudice, and outright discrimination. As implied in the component of the problem dealing with research itself, the assumptions, methods, and conclusions became cyclical, that is, shaped by political views, the priorities of legislation, and administrating agencies making funding choices. The prevailing theory of the 1960s maintained that "deficits" existed in these poverty-stricken subgroups that could be remedied by prescriptive educational content. And, as has been pointed out in another component, these "deficits" have their foundation in dominant codes—one model American. Scientific knowledge has not been sufficiently debated on ideological merits other than socio-eco-politico positions of the stratification system in the United States.[24] Since formal education in the United States has been dependent on the economic, political, and class-status issues, the control of one democratic class over another has been at the very core of its philosophy. Martin Carnoy argued that social mobility through personal, material, and moral standards fostered through schooling was purported to counter social inequities; however, it had not occurred in reality.

The educational system was no more just or equal than the

*As evidenced by the need for the legislation on Affirmative Action, Civil Rights, Equal Employment Opportunity. Five court cases during 1952-1955 (schools in Sumerton, South Carolina; Farmville, Virginia; Topeka, Kansas; Wilmington, Delaware; and Washington, D.C.) and decision of Brown versus Board of Education, May 17, 1954.

economy and society itself—... because knowledge itself is "colonized." Colonized knowledge perpetuates the hierarchy structure of society ... Those who supported schooling as a means to mass mobility wanted either to perpetuate the myth to support the social structure unchanged in their own interest or, as "disintegrated" academics, were themselves colonized sufficiently to accept the system's rules for limited self criticism.[25]

Obviously, schools did not only develop work related skills in isolation. They transmitted "culture" and those values that guided children into different social roles. Those in tune with the economic, social, and political institutions (dominant members) were rewarded. There was no evidence that mass education distributed on the basis of stratification and income equalized the distribution of income and wealth.[26]

Common Prejudices, Abuses, and
the Great American Dream

The American society's traditions and expectations, which governed individual and group behavior underwritten at the behest of the dominant group, have been a source of frustration, anger, and more recently conflict for the poor and "minority groups."[27] As noted earlier, schooling has been seen to be the social institution that prepared the individual for ethical and material improvement while enabling social mobility. It was thought that these elements merged into a strong national economic establishment, patriotism, and harmony so that the country could compete effectively in the industrialized world. It was important to recognize the link that schooling had to the larger social and economic structure as well as the principles of American democracy because it basically caused resistance to necessary changes. From "freedom of oppression," in England, during the colonial period to the assimilationist ideology during the industrialization era, this mixture of ideologies became embodied in the "American Dream."[28] The great dream itself, historically, was a political rarity since it symbolized the hopes of a homeland for diverse groups in which life itself would be enriched, regenerated, and potentially more satisfying for all Americans.[29] Colonial thinking encompassed the goal to create a social and political order in which potentially everyone could achieve while being accepted by others regardless of the circumstances of birth or status. Coming from white European traditions and belief systems, the "founding fathers" had not recognized their own ideas and opinions about the worth of nonwhite non-European groups. The articulated values, through the Constitution and Bill of Rights, as designed, were meant to be enjoyed by the "accepted" preferred groups. Women from any cultural group were not esteemed at all. Native Americans, black Americans, and Asian Americans were not yet considered "equal" in intelligence (by their test scores). In general, the genetic factor rationale has been replaced by the "disadvantaged background" due to the "minority" status of these groups. The decade of the 1970s was embroiled in this struggle, and the class-action litigation on the use of I.Q. tests ended in the California courts.[30] Concerns of this nature led to the enactment of the Equal Rights Amendment (ERA).[31]

The criteria for the standardization models stemmed from the socio-cultural concepts already stated. School personnel viewed themselves as having the responsibility to accentuate sameness as a major standard for judging success without the awareness that such terms as "race," "disadvantage," "I.Q.," "achievement motivation," were the sociocultural classifications characteristic of dominant white middle-class American society. Proponents for standardization emanate from the "scientific education," which stressed specific content, minimum requirements, and normative tests, which came into vogue during the rise of "scientific objectivity" and measurement movement during the nineteenth century.[32] This testing approach, adopted by most schools and proliferated during the 1960s, further led to a philosophical stance in which efficiency (through behavioral objectives and performance contracts) has conflicted with humanistic theories (which emphasize curricula based on human needs consistent with the diversity of the population). A counterreaction during the civil rights movement began to raise consciousness about the "dominant criteria" and "equal educational opportunity standards" for judging school "success." Assumptions made by measurement theory and scientific principles included concepts that the majority of Americans had similar perceptions of reality and that certain characteristics of individuals such as the physical, mental, or personality were normally distributed throughout the population. And while intervening variables were recognized, there was no comprehensive explanation about the nature of them, for example, emotional needs, learned behavior patterns, cultural context, and so on. Public education's emphasis on subject content and values without full recognition or provision for differences in cultural orientation, known by anthropologists to have a deep impact on the goals and accomplishments of subgroups, preserved the deficit approach to education.[33]

More recently, a thrust for "accountability" as a means to assist in making educational decisions through (scientific) evaluations has become an integral part of many programs.[34] The "evaluator" has been influential and has legitimized the concept of the "disadvantaged" for intervention techniques. The most common evaluations replicated experimental research design stressing standards to be reviewed on predetermined criteria.[35] The most common method of evaluation was based on goals established beforehand, their plan, judging whether implementation was representative of the plan, and whether the desired goals were actually in operation. While on the surface these standards appeared "logical," they nevertheless implied that the practice of educational programs had clear specification in those areas. In actuality, it was rare when staff had agreed on or shared goals or that the method to quantify "good achievement" was unambiguous. In addition, to try to measure "true implementation" was more idealistic than real.[36] Here again, a careful analysis of the ambiguities, par-

adoxes, ambivalences, shortcomings, and social injustices revealed the identical sociocultural basis for frustration, tensions, and pressures that culminated in the events of the 1960s.
The exaggerated claim about the importance of "race" continued to "scientifically prove" that one social and/or economic
group was more or less genetically able might have been a
moot point after all.

> Alarming, because racial dogmas have been made the basis
> for inhumanly brutal political philosophies which have re-
> sulted in the death or social disenfranchisement of millions
> of innocent human beings; exaggerated, because when the
> nature of contemporary "race" theory is scientifically ana-
> lyzed and understood it ceases to be of any significance for
> social or any other kind of action.[37]

The belief that research was "pure" or "absolute," especially
when it did not examine its own motives, methodology, or inclination, was ethnocentric. It was possible that this "blind-
ness" to monocultural values might be interpreted as an
avoidance for taking the responsibility to change attitudes and
direction in those systems that have enjoyed success and high
status.

> Science and engineering produce "know-how"; but "know-
> how" is nothing by itself; it is a means without an end, a
> mere potentiality, an unfinished sentence. "Know-how" is
> no more a culture than a piano is music . . . To do so, the
> task of education would be, first and foremost, the trans-
> mission of ideas of value, or what to do with our lives. At
> present there can be little doubt that the whole of mankind
> is in mortal danger, not because we are short of scientific
> and technological know-how, but because we tend to use it
> destructively, without wisdom. More education can help us
> only if it produces more wisdom.[38]

The absence of focus and interest to enhance and promote

cultural diversity or multicultural education demonstrated the failure to accept authentic pluralism.[39] Forces of the last decade indicated that education could no longer rely on past ideologies, past expectations, or past values to meet the current needs and to prepare children to live effectively in their future.[40] Education has been more than factual dogma. Values penetrated the being and they acted as mediators created by cultural groups for adapting to the physical and social environment. There was no doubt that the nation formulated a remarkably different social and governmental system; however, class and racial oppression have been pervasive.[41]

Discussion

This component identified institutional racism as a part of the overall fabric of education in American society. It has been common for teachers and school psychologists to identify the "underachiever" (usually the poor "disadvantaged") and the "overachiever" (usually the "advantaged" white middle class). The "ideal" American (student) has been considered to be one who did not differ from anyone else. In short, schools viewed themselves as having to accentuate "sameness" as a valued goal.

Children who "fail" to meet the achievement expectations and/or who have not acted in the manner prescribed by the school authorities were thought to have the source of those problems "within them." It has been that which the child did not have or know that has been perceived to be the "learning problem." The compensatory education movement proliferated during the 1960s made the assumption that there was something wrong with the child's family environment. Educational programs were funded to intervene to correct some of the conditions, at various times called "deficits," "weakness," and/or "low-achievement motivation."[42] Former terms that described "their problem," such as "socially disadvantaged," "culturally deprived," "culturally deficient," were being replaced by the term "culturally different." This term crept into the "field" as a result of the efforts to provide an alternative approach for attempting to meet "poor minority group" children's cultural needs.[43] Esther Hovey examined the research on the relationship between ethnicity and early academic success and the rationales of several ethnic groups for education of their young children. The implication was drawn that all American children reflected cultural group diversity. She suggested that early childhood programs should relate to the ethnic characteristics "taken from the abstract." The studies noted came from the compensatory field.[44] The connotation, however, has been around the concept of compensation and for all to fit into the larger group's standards.

Historical events revealed underlying values and beliefs that lead to actions for or against some social groups. These beliefs were considered "truths." While the "American Dream" has been the underlying goal that determined the aspirations of different groups who came to America as immigrants, the peoples of color were treated according to "beliefs" about their inferiority. Many of these beliefs have persisted. Those "truths" and their related manifestations over periods of time became the "reality" in which a group was guided in thought, action, expectation, and were considered acceptable, correct. They were perceived, then, as "natural." Public policy in education contributed to the concept that there was something wrong with the backgrounds of some groups.[45] A variety of legislation reflected the widely accepted notion that certain groups were "problems" to society and that their children failed and dropped out of schools because "they" came from disadvantaged homes.

The Anglo-Saxon model influenced and set the tone for the views, hypotheses, and conclusions of social scientists as they sought solutions to the schooling problems of the poor "minority group" children.[46] In concept and in practice, federal legislation preserved the "inferiority" concept—the child entered the system with handicaps.[47] While the notions of the 1960s did not explicitly refer to an inherited inferiority, as was felt during the immigration period, a functional "inferiority" has been indicated. The vestiges of genetic inferiority remained through the use of I.Q. scores.[48] Other subtle messages lingered on through identifying the "victim" of environmental deficiencies.[49]

The civil rights movement plunged ahead, making a bit of progress, only to be hampered by the I.Q. inferiority theory advocates, adding fuel to the justification of inequality.* The four-volume report prepared by the Huron Institute for the Department of Health, Education and Welfare characterized the thoughts on childhood "disadvantage."[50] It is still considered a valid concept by experts in the field. The influence that these researchers have had on federal funding policies leads to popular misconceptions about the failures of minority groups. The struggle continued in the Supreme Court—before institutional discrimination could be turned around, situations like the Bakke Case cried "reverse discrimination."[51]

Jargonese and Terms That Confuse

Increasing pressures have resulted in "new programs" to respond to bilingual, bicultural, and desegregation concerns.[52] Education in the United States was controlled in two ways, one through statutes and the other by administrative decision. The first source included legislation, state and federal constitutions, court and administrative regulations. A second source was where decisions were the means to interpret statutes and create "common law." This source included court decisions but also those policy decisions made by federal, state, and local administrative agencies. The term "multicultural education" has crept into educational jargon. There has been widespread confusion over terms used to denote the status of diverse social groups (minority, ethnic, racial groups). The lack of systematic theories for promoting education that prepared children to live

*Great march on Washington led by Martin Luther King, 1963; the Civil Rights Act of 1964; the Voting Rights Act of 1965; the War on Poverty, 1964; the National Welfare Rights Organizations are but a few examples.

in a culturally pluralistic society took its toll in major national problems. It was difficult to discard old beliefs, comfortable attitudes, traditional theories, and mores discussed in the previous sections. Anthropologists have shown that every human group classified objects in the physical and social environment. And categories effected major cultural concerns while language determined the world view.

Discussion

Words like "class," "minority," "ethnicity," "race," "culture," and "mainstream" enjoyed meanings that were either highly personal (judgments) or they tended to imply thoughts and values unarticulated. Certain words gained popularity that became emotionally laden. The terms "poverty" and "minority," for example, tended to refer to nonwhite or those people who spoke languages other than English. Individuals from "minority groups," no matter what income bracket, became associated with poverty. The term "minority" perhaps inferred a special meaning related to a political stance. During this era, it generally referred to black Americans, Native Americans, Asian, and Hispanic Americans. "Poor" and "minority" virtually have become synonymous. To add to the confusion, "ethnic group" had taken on a "minority" connotation. This indiscriminate use of terms was common in the research literature. Esther Hovey, for example, reported a higher correlation between "ethnicity" and test scores for children who took standardized tests. Here "ethnicity" was equated with social income class. Middle class was equated with the dominant group, and so on. This portrayed an underlying assumption such as achievement varies among different cultures. This broad generalization was made, first, that *achievement* referred to school academic performance, and second, on culturally dominant criteria accepted in public education. The standard stemmed from middle and upper income groups who had easy access to upward mobility in the economic system. "Achievement" as a concept could imply other characteristics, such as the quality of a sculpture; it could imply how compatible a person is with "other" ethnic peoples, how cooperative one is, and so on. Agreement as to its value was the point. Throughout the work, biased assumptions and misuse of terms were found, such as "ethnic groups" meant dominant, and "middle-middle, upper middle class" indicated a white Anglo-Saxon Protestant orientation. There's no explanation about what is meant by "stimulating environment" to help children "achieve" in school and work. In certain sections, "ethnic groups" mean "minority groups." Other confusing concepts appear based on the researcher's cultural orientation. Examples may be found throughout the research literature especially in the field of compensatory education and disadvantage.[53] To use the concept of ethnicity calls into question one's patriotism, that is, to be thought of as an "ethnic" is to cast doubt on one's view as an "American." Implied is that one has given up one for the other. "Minority" now refers to those particular subgroups that have gained political notoriety.[54] It used to refer to the immigrants who were the target for being molded into the model "American"—Irish, Germans, Italians, Poles, Frenchmen, Finns, Swedes, Danes, Slavs, Greeks, and on and on. "Culture," especially in educational realms, has come to mean "material culture"—the artifacts or certain rituals traditional within groups; the food, music, "heroes," holidays, and art expressions.[55]

The term "minority" assumed another dimension in the political arena that logically referred to the opposite of the "majority" used to reach consensus. In reality, the "majority" tended to mean the "dominant" group representing a particular income class/caste holding certain standards in which only those "ethnic" white groups were permitted and accepted into the political system. Therefore, the confusion between the terms "majority" and "dominant" spilled over into the educational world. The term "mainstreaming" was consistent with educational goals but was of deep social concern to nondominant groups and their self-identity.[56] This term had a political connotation because the ingroup permitted (some) other groups into the regular system. The 1970s brought about some awakening in recognizing provincial behavior and attitudinal bias of school content. The ethnic studies movement was an attempt to modify curricula content by "mainstreaming" certain historical information through courses in history, social studies, and geography. The approach was one of including subject matter from "minority ethnic groups." It did not infer equity among all subgroups.* From "logic" came the tendency to rely on language as the means to take for granted "self-evident" values. The repeated use of terms in language presupposed culturally selective meanings that resulted in their believability or "truthfulness." As Nieburg noted, the conclusions from the works of Alfred Whitehead, Bertrand Russell, Rudolph Karneys, I. A. Richards, Ronald D. Laing, Noam Chomsky, and others raised some doubt attributed to current scientific paradigms influencing how terms were used.[57] The Report by the National Center for Educational Statistics used "race" as a classification according to self-identification.[58] In one chart, the classifications of ethnic origin/descent and language characteristics included: "Selected Europeans other than Spanish, Selected Asians, Blacks and others."[59] A table of estimated populations listed age and race, "White, Black, and other races."[60] These muddled terms were typical of the proliferation of euphemisms such as "increase learning motivation," "correct injustices," "gain positive self-image," and "be prepared to enter the job market." Derangements in terminology influenced the degree of clarity of issues. The common thread, however, was that values and criteria were the very foundation on which educational planning proceeded. Recent distinction was made in the debates about the validity of testing and the cry for "culture fair" (or free) tests. Since these tests tended to be nonverbal or a translation into languages other than English,

---

*Handicapped persons fit into this general category. Federal and state legislation have mandates for "mainstreaming" children. One example, see the Head Start Economic Opportunity and Community Partnership Act of 1974, which requires at least 10 percent preschool handicapped children to be in regular classrooms.

what remained ignored and misunderstood was the theory of the culture boundness of all concepts in any social group.

"Race" has many meanings and definitions depending on who makes it: the historian, the psychologist, the sociologist, or the geneticist. Differences in "racial" characteristics are found within and among different ethnic groups reemphasizing the impact of the evolutionary imperative in human nature. Montagu argued that the biological differences of race were too unimportant "to justify in making them the pretext for social discrimination of any kind."[61] Equality of opportunity in any social endeavor was not in conflict with genetic differences. The "scientific arguments" about "race" that interfered with the development of social, economic, and educational reform perpetuated the "dangerous myth." Montagu further suggested that the use of the term "race" was the witchcraft of our time.[62]

Dearth of Theories for Educating for a Culturally Pluralistic World

The need to recognize the importance of cultural commonalities and distinctions and their roles in learning was lacking. Educational institutions had not accepted the responsibility to help children, their parents, and the community to develop attitudes and concepts necessary for a global view. Educational foundations in the American experience needed a new and improved function that prepared its future adult citizens for living comfortably and respectfully in a society made up of diverse cultures and the economic structure. It was consistent with its historical and ideological goals. Since the United States was a microcosm of the world, such a metaphor assumed that diverse cultural resources were positive as well as a "fact of life" that no longer could be ignored. The need was to affirm the pluralistic nature of the American population, and the boost in morale would provide new impetus for building cooperation and reducing conflict.

A shift away from the deficiency theories (of disadvantaged peoples) was slowly forming to the recognition of the imbalance of social and political power among competing groups (which, of course, affected education). It was the democratic way to have issues like "unequal opportunity" be the impetus for applying political pressure, conflict, and litigation by certain ethnic groups to force schools to accommodate a handful of social groups. A natural outcome was the anger and frustration of "other groups" continuing the struggle for positive status. Crisis-oriented programs such as ethnic studies, bilingual education, and multicultural education programs tended to modify the traditional content-product approach so characteristic of public education. This singular isolated material artifact procedure did not lend itself to understanding, nor did it take into account the values, attitudes, beliefs, and knowledge of the deep aspirations of respective ethnic/cultural groups. This competitive mode did not provide a foundation for harmony, cooperation, or adequate recognition to advance "racial" and cultural relations.

A theory for the education for cultural pluralism needed to be developed so that teacher preparation and other interrelated programs could be established. An analogy could be made with psychology of learning, that is, just as it was important for educators to know child growth and development theory in working with children and their parents, similarly it was crucial to have them have "culture sense" or insight into the dynamics of culture for developing programs that produced the knowledge and feelings for social balance and convivial relationships.

Discussion

Theories of education did not regard cultural pluralism as part of the theoretical base in public schooling. A major concern became the neglect of an authentic education for some groups and another was that it did not contribute to a sympathetic cross-cultural coexistence among and between groups. A third problem was linked to the racial and ethnic conflicts and crises that arose due to the neglect of the reality of built-in competition.[63] It debilitated energies and wasted human resources. The literature in cultural pluralism considered the apathy as undemocratic.

Pointed out earlier, education built its curricula and its systems on the concept of conformity. Schooling functions ranged from maintaining homogeneity in colonial times, to the nineteenth-century assimilation goals, to the dual system of the sixties in which the poor "disadvantaged" and "minority" children were given compensatory education while white middle-class children were treated in a different mode. According to the Huron Report, four major objectives influenced the use of public funds for children in American life: (1) as preparation for later life, (2) to teach skills necessary in the economic system, (3) to indoctrinate patriotism, and (4) to provide a controlled setting for children to free parents to work.[64] It has also had the connotation to limit child labor.

Since the sixties, public appeal has been to "equalize" education. Schools translated this concept into subject matter, assessment instruments and teaching methods in patterns of standardization. The availability of educational opportunity still has been equated with outcomes from I.Q. and achievement test scores.[65] The disparities among particular "minority" subgroups compared to the white middle class were brought into focus when low scores were found on standardized tests. Efforts reappeared to close those gaps in the forms of designs to meet special needs of ethnic groups without violating the dominant national educational system.[66] However, the problem remained that children were not prepared to live in a global world in which differences were accepted and skills in intercultural communication were not developed, especially since there were emerging threats to survival.[67] However, since conceptual changes for the educational environment came from outside the sytem, decision makers did not ordinarily recognize the impact of their own (dominant) values on groups other than their own. Challenging the one model American concept, multicultural education supporters have come from outside political pressures. Educational thinking from within the field itself had minimal or no influence on systemic changes. The role of the educational decision makers was reactive rather than proactive, responding to a "public" (dominant) philosophical view. In short, the philosophy, the values, and the goals for the most effective means to educate children were determined outside the domain of educators, especially since education became so complicated in attempting to meet multiple goals. Because public education was thought to be the means through which the citizenry was exposed to economic, moral, and social responsibilities, a participatory role as part of the democratic system was seen as significant.[68] This component of the problem, then, stated that a predetermined system administered inhibited innovation and growth in theoretical paradigms except within given content/process parameters. In this last decade, the dialectics for building philosophical foundations had been within the narrow confines of the "public frame of mind."[69] Teacher training institutions, in the name of "reality" (and their dependency on federal funds), did not attempt to prepare educational personnel for that role, either.

Chapter II

The Study

Purpose

The purpose of this study was to develop a theoretical model that can be used by educational systems to promote cultural diversity and whereby criteria could be extrapolated to serve as a foundation for designing educational programs at all levels of development.

The ethnocentric view has been responsible for the failure of traditional education and of the dominant society to respect and appreciate cultural diversity.[70] Traditional education, up to the present juncture, had assumed that the preparation of children for their adult lives, through the schooling process, transpired through building upon past mores and custom. Educational goals and curricular approaches were, therefore, constructed on the concept of conformity. This was logically consistent with assimilationist theory.[71] Public education, a historically unique phenomena in the United States, has been seen as the institution through which literacy, the route out of poverty, and democratic ideals would be transmitted to its inhabitants. The American public tended to surmise that all eligible children go to school. Apparently, this was a false assumption according to data reported by the Children's Defense Fund.[72] Almost 2 million children between the ages of seven and seventeen either never got into the schoolroom or had been thrown out! Historically, an implicit conflict in educational values existed, though not recognized as such. Was one of the school's goals to "equalize" or to "maximize" education for all children—and did "maximize" mean to be based on the individual's cultural and individual learning potential? Publicly, the appeal was to "equalize" education. The school system translated this concept into a pattern in which the process, subject matter, assessment tools and procedures were standardized (based on the melting pot ethic).* Thus, conformity had been considered endemic to learning. Unfortunately, these two opposing forces, as practiced, symbolized a kind of magical thinking when the causes of "school failure" were attributed to certain social groups. The fact was that school content and teaching practice fostered "sameness" as the major criteria for judging "school success" without recognition and provision for understanding or taking into account individual differences as manifested in various cultural orientations. This has been fully neglected. Standardization had a deep impact on how "minority group children," for example, were judged through the educational system.[73]

These children are legion. They are the non-English speaking children who sit uncomprehendingly in classrooms conducted in English . . . or who have been placed in suitable classes where they do not learn. They are the poor white children in Portland, Maine, or Floyd County, Kentucky, from whom little is expected and for whom less is hoped. They are the black children in Canton, Mississippi, whose teachers call them dumb . . .

These children expressed . . . attitudes of indifference ("Nobody cares if I leave") . . . ("Jap") ("Nigger"); . . . ("What can you expect from these project kids?") . . . These atti-

*The Melting Pot, a play written by Israel Zangwill that became a stage success in the early twentieth century. The protagonist was to personify the American Dream in which all ethnic differences would disappear. From this process a unique person would evolve by the merging of ethnic differences or by a synthesis of the ethnic elements of the adopted land. Americans embraced the play willingly since it incarnated the ideology of the times.

tudes, so unquantifiable but so pervasive, probably contribute more to children leaving school than many of the more overt legal, illegal and extra legal exclusionary policies and devices . . . It almost seems that some school personnel have forgotten that helping and educating children are the reasons they are employed. Instead, smooth administration and efficiency have become the end, rather than the means to a decent education and schools where children learn and grow.[74]

This study could not detail the phases and consequences in American history when assimilation permeated all the activities from each of the ethnic groups who came to the United States from other countries. Nor has this study addressed the hardships encountered by the newcomers during the early nineteenth century when the industrialization period flourished. It has not been possible to point out the myriad of relevant social, economic, and political conditions, within the respective contexts, that had a profound effect on the groups that were already living on American soil such as the Native Americans or the black Americans who were forcibly brought to this country. Suffice it to say that the "ideal" American has been and still is considered to be one who has not differed from anyone else. And, that the schools have had the responsibility to accentuate the idea of "sameness" or "conformity" as the valued goal.

This study was concerned and challenged the concepts and theories that presumed defects in either the mentality or behaviors of selected ethnic groups in American society. These groups, called "minorities," varied throughout different stages in American history. This study was also concerned with the dilemmas presented and the endless confusion of the underlying messages conferred when national policy using democratic principles and the scientific concepts of culture were parleyed within political ethnocentric terms.[75] When the science of cultural anthropology developed the concept "culture," significant data pointed to ways that order and organization could be understood within variation. At least three aspects penetrated the concept that synergistically held the concept of an eminent metaphor for social harmony and for full acceptance of all ethnic groups. First, cultural phenomena were universal, that is, all human societies developed a culture using similar characteristic elements that defined its humanity. Second, all cultures were coherent and could be understood through their structures, the scope of which ranged from universal patterns to specifically evolved patterns that identified unique entities (ethnic groups). Third, culture was a creative human endeavor. It was an extension of collective human feelings, ideas, and efforts. These properties in the concept, combined, made the understanding of differences within universals, in the human species, possible.

Under these circumstances, each life style could be comprehended as unequaled and, thereby, could be perceived as worthy of acceptance and respect since it evolved through the experiences of those who developed it. Acculturation has been the means through which cultures perpetuate themselves. In spite of the uniqueness of each group, the phenomena were intelligible worldwide. These scientific data have philosophical connotations. In general, they've been neglected, ignored, contained, and/or contaminated by "logical conclusions" reasoned by social scientists, philosophers, and public policy. Humanistic realms have been omitted. The problem section of this study isolated at least five components relating to this evaluation: the role of scientific research in education, American traditional schooling, the effect of the American dream on the newcomer, the role of jargon and terms that confused, and the lack of a theory that enhanced a culturally pluralistic education.

The prevailing socioeconomic forces, the interaction of the world's social system, the aftermath of the civil rights movement, and the present political administrative thrust for "human rights," from the "logical" view, it could be argued, should be applied to the scope of educational goals. Global perplexities such as the ecological pressures, that is, the consequences of excessive tensions on the biological harmony in nature (over-fishing, deforestation, overgrazing, pollution, loss of crops, etc.), combined with rapid accelerated change brought about by technology, affected the total society.[76] It also placed educational institutions in a dilemma.[77] Its goals have been unclear and its problems severe.[78]

While anthropologists may have been committed to relativistic and pluralistic ideologies, they had not had much of an impact on the American social or politico-emotional life. For the most part, they had been employed in universities enjoying the reputation of studying exotic "primitive" societies. Exceptions were found, when studies were made on complex societies and subcultures. In America such changes had begun when the government, after the Second World War, hired anthropologists when international understanding was a critical political concern, especially when relationships with developing countries were at stake. Later, the controversy concerning pragmatic aspects arose when "modern problems" such as "poverty," "violence," "ghetto living," "civil rights," and "educational opportunities" were researched. However, there has yet to be substantial influence or "felt" appreciation from the distinct perspective that cultural anthropology has made outside the academic institution. Apparently, this situation might change. There was interest and the impetus provided by a new newsletter—its first issue was October 1978, entitled "Practicing Anthropology: A Career-Oriented Publication of the Society for Applied Anthropology." Its purpose was to serve as a means to encourage alternative employment away from the academic ordinarily not thought of by anthropologists.[79]

There was little doubt that cultural differences among social groups in a society exerted powerful contingencies in every conceivable aspect of life.[80] It was impossible for a human being to leave his or her cultural determinants at "home" with the family or with the given ethnic group outside and away from the educational process or, for that matter, any other human act.

It is probably true that no other professional group in the

United States daily faces the human and practical problems associated with cultural diversity so intensely as do classroom teachers, counselors, principals and others who work directly with students in schools. This situation is not going to change.[81]

Dangers that affected life itself have recently maintained exposure not publicized in the past. Newspaper headlines conveyed messages about the physical threats in the daily existence of life—aerosol spray cans destroying ozone layers in the atmosphere, food additives and food coloring, which potentially caused cancer, and drugs, whether used by "abusers" or as recommended by physicians for medical treatment, that could alter the brain waves. These revelations consolidated into the more usual unending news concerning violence, angry confrontation, and frustration stemming from political, economic, and social conflict alone would warrant significant change in educational goals and practice. However, socioeducational theories that elicited concepts such as "deprived homes" as the cause of "school failure" continued to be accepted by the scientific community, which, in turn, influenced the "educational experts." This hypothesis nourished too many misconceptions flowing to the general population; for example, about the intellectual capacities of certain groups. The "success-failure" debates could be attested to by the processes involved in formulating and passing legislation in respect to compensatory programs.[82] In general, federal programs were geared toward the goals to prepare children to assume an economic role in adult life and to assimilate children into the "American" national character, made up of shared beliefs and values of the dominant group.

In the very same sense, pedagogical theory must surely derive from a conception of economics, for where there is division of labor within the society and an exchange of goods and services for wealth and prestige, then how people are educated and in what numbers and with what constraints on the use of resources are all relevant issues, the psychologist or educator who formulates pedagogical theory without regard to the political, economic, and social setting of the educational process courts triviality and merits being ignored in the community and in the classroom.[83]

Public policy, at the federal level, as was shown in the "Discussion" section, "Education, Schooling, Purpose, and American Tradition," in the problem, contributed to the idea that something was wrong in the backgrounds of selected ethnic group ("minority" and/or low-income). It also perpetuated the widely accepted notion that certain groups of people were problems to society, that is, children who failed in school did so because they came from "disadvantaged backgrounds."[84] See the metaphor, developed by the writer, in Chapter IV, page 121.

The idea of the home environment as "advantaged" or "disadvantaged" has been thought to be central to a child's "success" and had been defined by researchers and school personnel, as had been noted in other sections of this study. This concept, moreover, also previously stated, evolved from quantitative research methodology, which measured children's academic performance using criteria primarily limited to the "three R's," children's behavior in the classroom, "motivation learning" and its relation to self-image (usually tested in terms of the child's attitude to the school). Findings were then translated into "conclusions" based on the collected scores from cognitive and affective measurement tests.[85] The reliance on measurement as a determinant of that quality, which avoided the margin of "error" or did not distort "fact," namely, "scientific truths," had been a perplexing predicament indeed. This was a flagrantly unscientific assumption since there had been the pervasive tendency, by social researchers, to disregard the dominant value codes implied in theoretical constructs and the role of bias.[86] At times, researchers did not bother to define in precise terms what was assumed, or they misused terms.[87]

Within all of the above concerns, their generic connotations and significant exigencies, the urgency for change was paramount. Educational institutions needed to have a base to develop new (different) assumptions, new (other) expectations, and to promote the values that corresponded with the needs created by transitional times and to articulate the emerging needs of the future.[88] Educational systems needed the philosophical foundation to be responsive to the diverse requirements of society comprised of numerous ethnic groups.

Of late, at all levels, there has been some motivation for bilingual, bicultural, and multicultural educational programs. The circumstances for such programming, however, came as the aftermath of pressures from "minority" groups for "equal educational opportunity," intermixed with their repudiation of both the cultural and generic "deficit" models as explanations for school failure.[89] The nature and scope of federal and state mandates and those resulting from Supreme Court decisions engendered hastily put together programs that came under the rubric of multicultural education.[90] Federal legislation in the area of ethnicity in America was divided into categories. One category pertained to those schools that were in culturally mixed communities. Another category was for meeting the special needs of non-white ethnic "minorities" whose primary language was not English. Until the Ethnic Heritage Program in 1972, Congress paid no special attention to studying American ethnic/cultural or "racial minority" groups in elementary or secondary schools. "Racial" balance was not unconstitutional. Legislation was to eliminate "racial" segregation.

Legislative provision for meeting the needs of diverse ethnic groups and their cultural implications could be divided into bilingual education or legislation for specific groups such as Afro-Americans or Native Americans. Thus, the intent had been for "equal educational opportunity" for nonwhite and non-English-speaking groups. The National Defense Act of 1958, which encouraged international studies, was enacted to promote foreign policy. As of January 1978, thirty-two states (including the American territories) had some kind of educational provisions for certain aspects of multicultural curricula, nineteen states had some policies for specific ethnic groups, twenty-one states required bilingual education, three states required Native American studies, and one state required curriculum areas in Spanish-American and Italian-American studies.

Bilingual bicultural legislation had been the response to accomplishing "equal educational opportunity," that is, the legislation phraseology referred to civil rights rather than "ideological" direction for educational goals. Ethnic studies or multicultural education legislation allowed, encouraged, and, in certain states, required instruction about ethnic/cultural groups and usually included women's studies. In some states, advisory councils, resource centers, and other groups concerned with multicultural education were permitted. Some states required in-service and/or a change in teacher certification. Educational laws had been designed either to promote U.S. foreign policy or to enable school desegregation and racial imbalance on the domestic scene.[91]

Ideological incentives have not been effective nor, apparently, has the time been taken to clarify assumptions, discuss broad issues, or develop concepts for theoretical explorations to meet different needs of ethnic groups except within the framework of bilingualism. As the emotional and precarious fervor and flurry of crisis-oriented programs became dissipated due to prevailing political priorities, the validity of cultural pluralism in education was endangered. The need was urgent for an educational theory that provided a holistic orientation determined and generated by the properties that make up the culture concept to be incorporated into the very foundation for imparting knowledge. Also, it was important to enhance such attitudes. This "culture sense" was salient, especially since education reflected the times and, if for no other reason than to reduce social conflicts.[92]

There had not been a systematic attempt at developing conceptual bases that esteemed the universality of cultural dynamics as part of the theoretical integral social "whole" within educational realms. This was not to say that sporadic attempts have not been made. They had, but they addressed "some" minority concerns. Also, it was not to say that there was an absence of a "democratic" ideology, rather that the premise for educational philosophy had been politically induced along the dominant ethnocentric dimension. This was particularly obvious in the bilingual bicultural movement. Change was inevitable, and educational institutions could take on the responsibility to play a significant part in increasing an awareness of the importance of cultural aspects in learning—life itself. Education could provide the wherewithal toward helping children and their parents to develop a world view that admired and appreciated variety (values) and contrasting beliefs, customs, life styles without a "who is better than" approach. It was not possible to accomplish this task through the traditional content-product orientation characteristic of public-school teaching. The celebration of "different" holidays, singing of songs in "foreign" languages, preparation and eating of "unfamiliar" foods for the sake of "tasting" other cultures did not assure understanding, acceptance, or even tolerance of "others." It was entirely possible, with the American "mass communication psychology," to have a negative effect by stereotyping such groups. Traits and expressions of life style, through distinct experiences, tended to become unconscious (sometimes called deep culture), therefore isolating "material culture," for study from the total context was an example of a lack of "culture sense." The necessary positive connections were missing.

Effective change denoted a change in priorities to revolutionize education to meet future needs. The writer agreed with the humanist Fred Polak,

Unflinchingly, we must return again and again to the cardinal question: why and where did these systems of great thinkers go awry? If we succeed in separating their true and false statements, there is no reason, even less an excuse, not to try anew. The main objection that could be made against all existing theories in this field is that they all derive from their predictions of the future from past-present segments of the time-flow. However, I am convinced that a well-

founded diagnosis and subsequent prognosis can be made
and justified *only* if the segment of the time-flow labeled
"future" is also included as an independent and co-deter-
mining entity.[93]

The purpose of this study was to provide the framework, the
model, the criteria for a new socioeducational ethic—a set of
propositions—an educational principle that would determine
new fashioned rules of "public" behavior—changed patterns of
values as a national stance—regulated by a humanistic affirmation, which moves beyond the current unfounded biased
assumptions which certain politically identifiable groups who
have had to resort to, such as expedient and dramatic strategies, to reach political figures and then demand acceptance and
respect for their "cultures." When particular gains were made,
other ethnic groups felt threatened. In short, to use the culture
concept, to have culture sense, would make a qualitative per-
mutation in knowledge and the behavior paradigm.

Nature of the Study

Introduction

The sociocultural and behavioral sciences were character-
istically much more perplexing and intricately dynamic than
the physical sciences. A major social science problem has been
the lack of a methodical means for contrasting the inherent
complicated sets of variables of one phenomena with that of
others. Since the Second World War, an approach called general systems theory had developed into a science that supplied
rules, concepts, maxims, and other abstract frames of reference
for the study of the various kinds of systems.[94] In general,
systems theory was based on two maxims that served as organizing the analytical elements of a system. First, that structure determined its function, and, second, the function and the
history of inputs determined the responses of the system. There

is the tendency of individual disciplines, such as psychology, sociology, politics, and economics, to promote competing postulates, each promising to interpret the same phenomena. They often do so without exploring other constructs from different disciplines. This situation needed to be replaced with a holistic approach. Systems theory and its related field of inquiry, systems analysis (structure, function, control, regulation, dynamics, synchrony, organization, change, and so forth), offered a methodology that focused on the common bases of different social systems in their totality rather than on the analytical reductionist approach common to the physical sciences.[95] For the most part, reduction to parts from a larger system had been initiated by social sciences research. The human sciences, after all, encompass the psychological, biological, sociological, political, economic, anthropological, and all those other happenings that resulted from developing organisms or open systems.[96] Systems theory drew from the structure of "wholes," utilized isomorphic properties as the analogy and foundation on which to develop theoretical models or, to borrow Thomas Kuhn's concept, paradigms.

> . . . I mean to suggest some accepted examples of actual scientific practice—examples which include law, theory, application, and instrumentation together—provide models from which spring particular traditions of scientific research. . . .[97]

Thus, a method existed that provided the common abstract underpinnings and skeleton for studying the gestalt of living systems—for the individual or for collectives—applicable, that is, on different levels.

Since "wholes" could be examined by their structures, then models such as those hypothesized in sociopolitical domains (cultural pluralism, for example), cultural anthropology (cultural relativism and relevant sociological constructs), and education (humanistic theory or open education) were amenable to analysis and suitable for synthesis of a model as proposed by this research. To put it another way, "wholes" could be called systems; systems could be studied, analogies, and metaphors could provide the abstractions for selecting pertinent properties, or concepts for developing constructs, postulates, hypotheses, laws, and metatheories.[98]

No natural history can be interpreted in the absence of at least some implicit body of intertwined theoretical and methodological belief that permits selections, evaluation, and criticism. If that body of belief is not already implicit in the collection of facts—in which case more than "mere facts" are at hand—it must be externally supplied, perhaps by a current metaphysic, by another science, or by personal and historical accident.[99]

Because this research was concerned with the gestalt and culture as the organizing force in the life of individuals and social groups, more needed to be said about the concept of "holism." It has been pointed out that social science research methodology is primarily motivated by experimental design that exploits a mechanistic view of human behavior. Humankind, metaphorically, has been likened to a "complicated machine" whose "parts" can be taken apart (physiologically and psychologically) and then explained in terms of those parts.

Thus, we have at base the concept of "system," of elements in mutual interrelations, which may be in a state of "equilibrium," such that any moderate changes in the elements are counter-balanced by change tending to restore it. It is the conception that has been taken over almost unchanged by many contemporary sociologists . . . The idea of society as a "system" of interrelated parts with a *boundary* [emphasis added].[100]

Cultural anthropology had been inspired by the idea of "wholeness" as the guiding concept even though general culture and unique culture were recognized in the continuum.

Cultural anthropologists ordinarily pursued the commonalities in human behavior—the universality—those patterns revealed in all cultures while at the same time heedful of the non-erasability of each specific distinguishable way of life. In unique culture, the content of life style, of that which is particular to a particular group, for example, language, kinship patterns, artifacts, or world view, was observed and recorded. In the context of the "holistic perspective," Clyde Kluckhohn explained that "no culture can be isolated or characterized by even the most exhaustively correct enumeration of its parts" and that "there is some notion of hierarchy among components of a culture."[101] Within every culture, then, there is general culture and unique culture that, on the "whole," cannot be understood without taking into consideration the total context (and cannot be comprehended by their parts alone). This led to the question What was a holistic system?

The system itself was the "whole organization," that is, the type of connections in a given whole makes the difference. It is distinguished from an aggregate where the parts were added. The quality of the parts were irrelevant but the way parts were arranged or distributed; their positional values comprised the concept of "wholeness." The concept "fruit" could be used as an analogy for further clarification. Fruit was a general term that described a generic category within the classification of (the concept) food. Apples (a concept that had been accepted as having the quality of appleness), if placed in a bowl, became an aggregate—a bowl of apples. These aggregates, if peeled, sliced, and cooked (the parts having been "rearranged" and changed), were no longer apples, although appleness was still qualitatively accurate. It—the apple ("whole")—had an entirely different form. The organization of the whole was affected by the relation (change) to that whole. "In a system, the members were from the holistic viewpoint, not significantly connected with each other except with reference to the whole."[102] Or to place the analogy in a cultural context, the structure of a social system, the Jewish culture, for instance (the elements that have been organized in a particular way), could only be identified and recognized by its totality (the ethnic Jewish heritage) and could not be recognized by its individual customs, patterns, beliefs, world view, and so on, for example, the eating of pork was forbidden or that the "creator" made a "man" and from this "man" took a rib and then made a "woman." These parts (of culture) do not, in themselves, identify a "Jew."

Buckminster Fuller's concept of synergy ("which means behavior of whole systems unpredicated by behavior of any of its parts taken separately . . .") could provide a concept for a revolution in educational thought.

> We must commence education with the inventory of all known, i.e., all as yet discovered, generalized principles and proceed from that whole to the realization of special cases. This calls for the elimination of all specialization, with generalists in limited period plunges-in-depth to special case studies and applications of the omni-interaccommodative generalized principles.[103]

Methodology

This was a two-phased study designed to develop a theoretical model utilizing the concept "culture" as the basic maxim and catalyst for cultural pluralism as the foundation for education. Systems theory and systems analysis provided the frame of reference for reviewing and studying complex phenomena involved in the interactions among sociocultural groups for an education for cultural pluralism. Model development, a subcategory of theory building, offered the conceptual referents for constructing the philosophical principles on which acceptance, respect, and enhancement of culturally pluralistic formulations and contingent systems were viable in the real world. In short, a macroeducational theory was created. The methodology for this research included:

Phase 1

1. Identification of criteria
   A. Review of current theories in cultural pluralism taken from the sociopolitical and educational perspectives.
   B. Review of cultural anthropology, especially cultural relativity and social-psychological theory.
   C. Review and selection of theoretical and functional elements in humanistic education and related open systems.
2. Selection of criteria and metaphors from cultural pluralism (including political and historically related aspects), social systems (including sociological literature), and humanistic education (including psychological literature and learning theory).
   A. Synthesize isomorphisms (the common bases of various systems).
   B. Structure new wholes (systems) suitable to the new model system.
   C. Identify the type of connections in the whole and the arrangements of those parts for a holistic model (paradigm).

Phase 2: The Model

A. Basic terms are defined.
B. The elements of the principles and their interrelating connections are identified.
C. Deduce postulates.
D. The construct is developed.
E. The hypothesis is formulated.
F. The paradigm is framed.

Assumptions and Context

The result of this research, a model for an education founded on the cultivation of cultural pluralism, could generate attitudes for policies and educational programs consistent with the advocated diversity and lacking in existing educational models. In any society, but especially in a complex society such as the United States, both belief (values) and attitude of its peoples cannot be overstated. The student of cultural anthropology knows full well that the content of any culture's heritage, that is, custom, tradition, traits, and so on, is governed by the particular world view marked for acculterating its members. When "life-way" became an integral part of the cultural configuration, anthropological theory became an important means toward understanding human behavior. Attitudes are precursors of behavior. Attitudes tend to reduce a wide range of relationships. They can be negative or positive and are different from the beliefs that may be associated with them.[104] Matthew Wakatama's study, for example, showed how children's attitudes changed when educational activities took this into account.[105] Bias and expectations that influenced outcomes and general conclusions have been well documented.[106] In the long haul, any attempt at educational criticism and reform serves social and political ends. In other words, pedagogical theories, as this research hypothesized, by necessity, will affect every tenet in the social life of individuals and groups. That is to say that interaction among subcultures in the society could be either harmonious or in some state of conflict. The more technological a society is, the more education needs to become aware of and utilize the knowledge *and* the feelings which humans have related to their total contexts. Functions, roles, responsibilities, and values change as societal phenomena impact on people. Therefore, one assumption made by this study was that a heterogeneous nation, made up of various distinct social (ethnic) groups, given their respective cultural systems and unique interests, would be provided the means to accept, respect, and function comfortably in more than one culture. And no one culture would be considered better than any other. Schools, as one of the significant social institutions, would recognize, value, and accommodate to the diversity of the real world. This postulate, that a future in which society is united by respecting and valuing cultural difference would replace the preferred/unpreferred doctrine that currently exists, was derived from conceptualization of the anthropological, social, and educational theory and advocates of a multicultural democratic society. It has not been possible to employ qualified adults for every linguistically or culturally different child in every program, nor has it been possible to teach about every ethnic group supported by the "multiethnic" and "ethnic studies" proponents. It is possible to have "culture sense"; it is possible to understand and educate in such a way as to enhance pluralistic images as a valued goal and accept human beings within their own cultural preferences.

Assumptions

It was assumed that such a model yielded the theoretical framework through which the educational system could be responsive to any and all ethnic groups.

It was assumed that the highly competitive situation among ethnic groups (and poor groups) would now have the basic philosophy for developing a means for participating in the democratic process regardless of particular cultural heritage. People from divergent backgrounds could be brought together to plan ways for understanding and communicating and to work out mutual concerns. This would be radically different from the crisis-oriented issues, which would bring together only certain groups (parts) of the community in temporary coalitions to bring to bear political pressures. After selected tasks were accomplished ("compromised"), each group continued in the stereotypic competitive model because the "system" forced the "preferred/unpreferred" attitude. The "pie" was just too small to be cut fairly among all ethnic groups in the American population. Alternatives are warranted.

It was assumed that the burden for transmitting this new (societal) value and for implementing formal and informal settings was most important and most appropriate for the educational institution as the vehicle for application of the proposed model.

It was assumed that this model would serve to open the door for informed questions in educational policies and practices. The most relevant questions were not only in areas of "new knowledge," although they would be framed in a "new" context. Questions that seriously and "unpolitically" examined the conventional phenomena were salient. Also, questions about what was said and what was actually done, needed to be aired. The credibility gap was becoming more and more critical at this point in history.

It was assumed that when the "role" of values took the central place in understanding differences, when its functions were internalized and when universal characteristics were recognized, then causal "scientific" explanations would change and would influence other social endeavors, such as "mental health," "testing," and the heredity versus environment debates. The locus for theory and practice as humanistic relativistic philosophy would affect changes in all social encounters.

It was assumed, however, that this model would support all ethnic groups, at least not just diversity based on concepts of social, race, or bilingual standards.

It was also assumed that the goals derived from this model would enhance a more harmonious concern with solving problems by establishing open lines of inquiry and communication.

It was assumed that if the concept "cultural diversity" became widely accepted as an epistemological "truth," it would provide the basis for mutual cooperation rather than conflict confrontation among groups and classes for solving social problems in a complex society. At least the "social problem" would have other meanings, therefore, solutions.

It was further assumed that an education that advanced affirmative attitudes about cultural pluralism was the relativistic mode, which was, in accord with the multicultural population of the United States of America, "healthier" and more "real," more practical, and more relevant than to continue to have all schools be uniform and for a universal education to strive for conformity across diverse values and needs through standardization. Thus, it was held that cultural diversity in education was an ethical matter as well as a scientific postulate and needed to be the philosophical basis through which the educational needs were met to enable society's members to function meaningfully as contributing competent adults in a technologically complex society.

Finally, it was assumed that a "new discipline" could be created that encompassed the art of, science of, and philosophy of process and content within the pluralistic framework.

Scope and Limitations

Most of the discussion on cultural pluralism and multicultural or ethnic diversity in educationally related matters had little regard for theoretical reflection. The preference was usually given to ways of invading curricular subjects.[107] Confusion and misunderstanding resulted from attempts at providing hypothetical recipes while trying to describe society in its heterogeneity and simultaneously advocating for social change. As prescriptions, target groups were identified to receive "remedial treatments," that is, areas for intervention were specified, and kinds and the forms for the intended modifications were precisely mapped. As descriptive of American society, discriminatory practices affecting "minority group children" (including both past immigrant experience to the current inequities) or schooling functions were promoted.[108] Justification was further supplied for necessary reform, which had roots in democratic pluralism and in theories of plural societies.[109] As advocates for social change, political issues that led to confrontations among subgroups and between "minority" and the dominant group were illustrations, and the potential harmonious relations that could result from comparative and cross-cultural orientations were promoted as solutions to clashes among ethnic groups in complex societies.[110] This research disclosed the critical role that cultural patterns had in the lives of groups for public scrutiny. Cultural patterns were the profiles of the dominant values created by a given group for the purpose of contributing to the coherence for the interactions among its members. It defined the quality of the group—its uniqueness. This research also pinpointed the disagreement with the quantitative-measurement approach to understanding and evaluating social phenomena. It emphasized that a valid comprehension of the quality of human experiences could be accomplished only through a holistic humanist view as to the "nature of humankind," through culture. Anthropologists have identified the organization of traits, in culture, as being the integrating principle at the basis of normative behavior.[111] Thus, being cognizant of human conditions or the total environment was crucial to the hypothesis. Because "quantitative" methodlogists permeated the scientific, bureaucratic, and other social experiences, there seemed to be little doubt that it had become an integral aspect of the covert culture in America. Evidence cited in numerous sections of this research characterized the effect that industrialization has had on the relationship among social groups. It seemed inevitable that quantification was highly valued as the outcome of technological progress with mass production, mass communication, and mass consumption defining the American experience. As stated in previous parts, the social sciences adopted techniques that emphasized efficiency, highly precise specifications, correlational methodology, and so on. The "dominant" professional and scientific world reinforced and perpetuated quantitative evaluation as being superior to any other.[112]

Cultural patterns then upheld particular ideas (values), and their expression served to reinforce those existing patterns. It was the contention of this study that the tacit notion that characterized American education (and society in general) was dualistic in nature. It was the superiority-inferiority syndrome in which the "superior" group was expected to "carry" and manage the "inferior" or "disadvantaged" groups, which, in the final analysis, sanctioned oppression.[113] Because American cultural traits and patterns that promoted double messages were profoundly ingrained, humanistic solutions to complex issues, raised by this study, seemed possible only in the light of a radical transmutation in basic ideological foundations, assumptions, and concepts. Dualistic thinking supported an either-or mentality, an all-or-nothing thinking. Typical examples were: superior-inferior, civilized-primitive, good-evil, right-wrong, smart-stupid, genetic-environmental, black-white, fact-fiction, developed-underdeveloped, home-school, and so forth. The literature in comparative cultural anthropology did not confirm that the either-or concept was universal.[114]

The Model

The universal culture affective theoretical model provides appropriate components to develop policies and curriculum options in education. It is capable of generating concepts and theories that can lead to changing policy and to the development of guidelines for the early childhood years through college age students.

Theoretical Basis of the Study

The Permeating Principle

This research was governed by the supposition that human behavior could be understood and entirely explained in terms of culture. An individual learns to feel, think, believe certain ways, and aspire to those things that are sanctioned by a given culture. One's food, likes and dislikes, eating customs, sleeping hours, waking routines, sexual life, the meaning of friendship, political and economic patterns—every way of life—are dictated by the culture into which that person has been socialized. The concept "culture" does not have a single definition, nor can it be explained in simple terms. Alfred Kroeber and Clyde Kluckhohn listed at least 164 definitions in seven different categories.[115] Despite different emphases, there has been general agreement that culture is learned, that it is inculcated (habitual), that it is social, ideational, adaptive, integrative, and satisfying.[116]

Culture can best be understood from the specific evolving form it takes (a recognized way of doing things according to rules), defined specifically by each group rather than by a general definition. "Society" and "culture" are often used synonymously; therefore, it was necessary here to make a distinction between them. Since sociocultural phenomena is contingent upon both the organism's biological and environmental factors, it is often difficult, if not impossible, to separate them out. For example, the need to eat for survivial is biological; the eating of hamburgers is cultural. Social and cultural practices can be distinguished within the larger context. "Society" (social life) is made up of groups, a collection of persons implying some unifying relationship. Thus, families, classes, communities, states, and other similar entities make up the larger configuration, the society. Different groups of interrelated individuals make up the society. The acquired beliefs, traits, habits, tools, values, and those behaviors that emanate from them, comprise culture. Society and culture coexist, but each can be demarcated. Therefore, distinctions need to be recognized as ongoing elements of a complex phenomenon but related only through association. Culture shapes human behavior (on individuals personally and individuals in a cohesive group) and has been considered the "product" of a human society.[117]

Theoretical Determinants of This Research

Having stated the primary assumption as culture that interpenetrates every part and parcel of humanity, the theoretical basis of this study has drawn on concepts from within three major pedagogies and related disciplines: first, cultural relativity derived from cultural anthropology and its close alliance with social psychology; second, drawn from sociology, principally the concepts of cultural pluralism and allied sociopolitical aspects; third, humanistic education and related aspects of educational anthropology and similar open systems.

Why select from these disciplines rather than from either psychology, sociology, or even learning theory in education? Anthropology, first of all, had direct application to formal education through the concept of groups—groups of children, groups of teachers, groups of parents, administrators as a group, and so on, and, further, the subcultures that derived from those roles and specializations. Second, anthropology was interested in salient ways and means by which ideas, processes, and knowledge have been subsumed in enculteration, and, therefore, analysis was also applicable to formalized learning.* Third, anthropology has been basically interested in understanding diversity of skills, knowledge, and, therefore, provided the base for synthesis—a further advantage stemming from analysis. These elements distinguished it from other social sciences in the study of phenomena. The anthropological field itself promoted an eagerness and willingness to examine and make use of essential information from other disciplines. The transcultural nature and the propensity for fine details provided an atmosphere in which the data became the object of knowledge. Fourth, the empirical transcultural setting of the "field methodology" had both an intrinsic as well as an extrinsic quality. The intrinsic dimension resulted in personal growth for the observer, and the extrinsic aspects referred to the "objective data" gathered. That is, the person was surely influenced by the particular cultural experience as well as by the "new" information collected and learned. And last, but most characteristic of anthropology, was the interest in the holistic means to understanding the particular aspects of a society.

*For brevity, the writer means "cultural" anthropology whenever the word "anthropology" appears in this work.

53

Attention in this study will be paid to cultural transmission, change theory, value acquisition, and other dynamic properties related to the subject at hand.

Brief Historical Antecedents

In order to provide a wider perspective, a brief background on cultural anthropology is worth noting at this point. The anthropological concept or definition of "culture" in its ethnographic meaning inferred the *whole* complex of events and matters (such as beliefs, knowledge, law, ethical standards, custom, traits, and any other potential practice) established by a group that was articulated by Sir Edward Tylor in 1871 and was still a useful definition.[118] The term was later employed by other ethnologists, but with a "new" focus on the pluralistic nature of cultures, thus replacing the previous emphasis on the study of specific customs and specific institutions within a culture.[119] This pluralistic and relativistic idea had influenced anthropology for about fifty years when universalistic theories began to take shape. A distinction was made between social anthropology and the comparative study of "social structure"; ethnology and cultural anthropology; and the study of culture in the historical and comparative mode. Basically, there have been two anthropological theories: one, the theory of "culture patterns," and the other, the theory of "social structure." Pattern theory postulated that individuals and groups created culture and interacted with them (patterns), as well as with the environment. Social structure theory has been focusing on a system or network of social relations and their functions as they acted on persons and groups.[120] Both of these theories were holistic and universal, covering every aspect of culture and society.

Consistent with the move away from the study of distinct culture was also the shift away from the exclusive study of their material and external manifestations. In other words, there was less of an interest in discrete culture traits and more of a concern for a definition of culture that is more abstract and conceptualistic. Behavior and material products studied in the previous period provided the raw data that were thought to be a part of a construct; however, those manifestations themselves are now no longer thought to be constituents of culture. The "new" ethnographers, ethnoscientists, ethnolinguists, and structuralists agreed on the conceptualization that cultures have been basically abstract structures. The patterns, norms, regulations, and criteria inherent in social relationships and artifacts were the constituents of culture.

As a theory, cultural relativism must be realized as multifaceted, first as an approach in ethnology and social anthropology, second as a theory and philosophy (that is, as theory, it was culturally deterministic and as a philosophy it explained cultural relativity), third, as a prototype for evaluation of value systems (morality, politics, aesthetics), and fourth, as a means (attitude) toward change.

As methodology, the cultural relativity proponent viewed and evaluated sociocultural phenomena from the orientation of the members of the given group under study—from their particular social context. Ethnologists reported information from the viewpoint of the culture being observed. This act naturally led to the observer's participation in what was being observed.

All anthropologists are in agreement on the values of the method . . . and the relative objectivity required to report and interpret data . . . There is considered disagreement in the use of the methods of impersonal objective functional evaluation.[121]

Cultural relativity, as a philosophy and theory, stated that *reality* for human beings was culture bound. Humankind created symbols, and all human experience was mediated through culture, which occurred through the enculturation process. Culture was the phenomenon that humans used to adapt to the world and was a fact of human experience through which conditioning was established by the culture.

As evaluation and verification of values, cultural relativism recognized that all values, morality being one, for example, had particular functions. Values have been the products of a culture, and these varied according to the style and concerns of each society. Judgments have been culturally determined and satisfy human needs. All value systems, it is believed, have equal validity. Therefore, the cultural relativist has been interested in the concept of ethnocentrism.

Sociocultural reform or change could be the means of applying the theory of cultural relativity to solving social problems. In this respect, a distinction needed to be recognized between the fact and the ideal value of cultural relativity. While the coexistence of disparate groups had often taken the path of rivaled encounters, due to a myriad of causes, the theory of cultural relativity as a potential for harmony was also possible. For all ethnic groups to exist with equal status in a culturally pluralistic society could be made "real."

> Cultural Relativism involves tolerance based on skepticism of universal, objective standards of value as well as of the progress. The comparative studies of cultures has made us conscious of the degree of uncritical ethnocentrism, but has also provided us with materials and the incentive to transcend the limitation of both cultural relativism and ethnocentrism through the pursuit of scientific truths concerning facts and values.[122]

Ethnicity

The use of the term "ethnicity" has been growing. It has been often misunderstood and popularly depreciated.[123] Therefore, it was worth pausing, briefly, to examine the concept and its relationship to culture. To begin, the terms "culture" and "ethnicity" came from anthropology and sociology, respectively. Even though common elements existed, each discipline developed its concept from a different perspective. Anthropologists were generally identified with studying "primitive" or less complex peasant societies while sociologists had directed their attention to urban complicated modern environments. As anthropologists begin to study the more complex urban settings and as sociologists take more of an interest in cross-cultural approaches, including studying abroad, it may be possible to link the contributions of both schools of thought into a valid comprehensive knowledge base about the "nature" of human beings and their societies.[124] Ethnic categories were generally founded on the social perceptions of language, nationality, religion, and particular physical attributes shared by a group of people. The term was used to distinguish groups from each other in industrialized societies. Ethnic classifications were cultural constructs, and they varied depending on the specific society and often functioned to define social roles. It was a structure for the interaction among peoples.

In the United States, for example, ethnic minorities had their origins in the various immigrant groups (Irish-Americans, Jewish-Americans, Italian-Americans, etc.), some of which, through the course of time and the process of assimilation, have been mainstreamed into American life for one reason or another, although others maintained separate closely knit enclaves. Ethnic minorities generally fell into a particular economic class at a particular time, as implied earlier. In America, they organized political groups for the purpose of improving their image, enhancing their identity and living conditions. An ethnic group can be thought of as a network of intricate direct and indirect relationships among members of a group bound together by a cultural heritage. The "cultural heritage" made up the group's shared history, kinship organization, language and dialects, ideology, world view, descent relationships, and all the symbols that expressed sociocultural differentiation and bonding.

The middle of the 1950s, inspired by the reexamination of the "melting pot," "Americanization" process, integration concerns, and "racial" confrontations, found the beginnings of an interest in the seeds for the "new pluralism," expressed in the early 1970s. Carlton Qualey suggested that ethnic history in the United States stemmed from emigration and immigration adjustments made by different groups to the new land.[125] Ethnic "nationalism" developed as a direct result of the American experience.

> ... most of the immigrants to America did not come with any strong notions as to nationality ... Most of these peoples were villagers, with attachment to a village district ... Nineteenth-century nationalist movements in Europe were of the middle and upper classes; they did not much affect the farming classes ... The one thing that attracted people together was similarity of language ... Gradually the terminology became generalized into major ethnic language groups ... Soon came the burial societies, the fraternal societies, the singing groups, the athletic societies, the insurance organizations and ultimately the political clubs.[126]

The movement toward diversity was the outgrowth of the humanistic respect for cultural pluralism. Ethnicity has been a compelling and persistent phenomenon.

> Furthermore, the ethnic entity would appear to possess most of the necessary ingredients ... provides for both congenial primary interaction and secondary activity especially in the important areas of politics where ethnic organizations tend to be active ... considering that the political process reaches to the very heart of the alienation problem.[127]

Extensive research is needed in order to assess accurately and understand the impact of contemporary ethnicity on American society as a whole. If a theoretical construct is to become possible, it must be based on further insights into the clarification of the behavior patterns and values that influence the kind of decisions which individuals and groups make to order, organize, and structure their lives in a highly technological and complicated society.

Chapter III

Literature Review

Introduction

As in ages of equality no man is compelled to lend assistance
to his fellow men, and no one has any right to expect support
from them, everyone is at once independent and power-
less . . . His independence fills him with self-reliance and
pride among his equals; his debility makes him feel from
time to time his want of some outward assistance, which he
cannot expect from any of them because they are all impo-
tent and unsympathizing.[128]

Americans tend to think of themselves as living in a nation
in which human rights are considered universal ideals. The
quandary in America's political and economic structure is its
contradictions. Among the ideals, values, and practices has
been the idea of assimilation, which permeates the process for
developing a national character while traditional politics exploited ethnic differences.[129] It has not been possible to explore
fully the ramifications of the political and economic milieu in
which Americans were driven to accumulate material possessions or of contemporary society's deep engrossment in raising
standards of living. However, it was useful to compare modern
urban cultures with simpler societies for the attainment of a

59

perspective on the progressively complicated social problems since it affected educational matters.

Cultures that have been called "primitive" generally tended to produce only those qualities of those items that have been thought necessary in an allotted time frame. This consistency between the group's wants and their manufacture, during a specified period, contributed to a society's cohesiveness. The items to be exchanged were known to all the members and to those who produced them. Neither were interested in increasing the market through any kind of persuasion or advertisement.

> On the whole he has a relatively firm demand and he is content to be underemployed at his craft if it does not keep him busy. There is, thus, a traditional and relatively stable relationship not only between production and material needs, but also between production and psychological ones: The craftsman does not try to invent new products to sell or to exchange, nor to convince his customers that they require more or better than they are accustomed to . . . there is an implicit understanding that wants and production shall remain unchanged . . .[130]

The implicit notion of satisfying established desires when contrasted with the boundless consumer society that typifies industrial societies brings into view baffling and intricate questions that command perplexing solutions. Akin to this "primitive" quality of producing only enough of what has been needed was the standard for a property ceiling. "Most primitive societies are provided with intuitive limits on how much property may be accumulated by one person, and the variety of ways in which primitive society compels people to rid themselves of accumulated property is almost beyond belief."[131] The concept and the value placed on the unlimited amassing of material strikes at the very core of the competitive structure and its resultant stratification. These material gains have been basic to the American national character. Cultural traits, such as the accumulation of wealth, competition or dreams of a "quick buck," built into the fabric of social organization created rivalry and conflict between the haves and have nots. It has been an essential function of American structure. "This capacity to use culture against himself may yet overtake man and destroy him while he works on his ultimate problem—learning to live with himself."[132] Since culture is an invention of the human species, the most profound task for human beings has been to "learn" how to live with the variety of sociocultural groups that make up humankind.

Education, in America, has been canonized with hope and idealizations of a free and open system for children from all socioeconomic levels and cultural backgrounds. The ideals have been that all persons would be provided with the skills for self-realization, social mobility, and compelling incentives for social change. The spasmodic gains that some ethnic groups have made in political and economic realms have generally resulted in politicized splits, often with social disruption rather than in favor of closing gaps. Part of the problem was that upward mobility has been somewhat evident in some ethnic groups. The recent "cultural" consciousness inspired by challenging discriminatory practices has rendered the monocultural ideal as untenable. This "new pluralism" came in the wake and context of the civil rights awakening, the black militancy, the increasing material expectations of the affluent society in which advantages seemed less possible for many. Added to this milieu was the "backlash" of the "white ethnics" who had been bewildered by the myth of the meltability of immigrant traits (carefully examined in previous sections of this study). The evidence has been growing, confirming that the cultural traditions survived despite the ideology and incentives for a singular American model. The competitive ethnic cultural conflicts produced by the socio-eco-political structure had a direct effect on schooling.

Education has to face a number of choices. One, just what traditional alternatives need to be made, another, which values should be reinforced and what forms of cultural adaptation should schools take?

Traditional education has been likened to a factory: mass

production, specialization of labor, specialized subject matter and, where children have been grouped into "manageable units," operated by standardized procedures and curricula. Children have been subjected to uniform examination in the earliest grades to assess their intelligence and/or achievement and, later, to nationwide tests that determined their suitability for college.[133]

As presently organized, the inescapable truth is that our schools seldom promote and frequently deny the objectives we, as a nation espouse. Rather than being assisted and encouraged to develop their own individuality, our children are locked into a regimented system that attempts to stamp them into the same mold. The student is filled with facts and figures which may accidentally and infrequently have anything whatsoever to do with the problem and conflicts of modern life or his own inner concerns.[134]

Events in this last decade emphasized that educational critics were not alone in their disenchantment with the "impersonal machines" into which many schools had evolved. Students themselves were suspicious of those conceptions that portrayed schools as the preparation essential if they were to live meaningfully in society. Schools had become the systems to "beat" in order to survive.[135]

Cultural pluralism and its attendant conflicts in America are increasing under the impact of industry; pluralism plus conflict appear to be part of the new quality of industrial, social, and cultural life. Thus, a condition which in eras only recently past was viewed as a strain in the social system now appears to be the system. The new adaptation is not a matter of choosing one of many cultures, it is to succeed with many cultures.[136]

In most simpler societies, the rites of passage from childhood to adulthood were a function of social need. The need, that is, for the kind of adult who would be responsible and who knew what role to assume. The tacit assumption and expectation of learning as an ongoing continuum as a result of close interaction between children and adults who need them to become contributing members of the society was clear. In the highly technological society, education has seen its responsibility as producing "marketable skills" and paid little attention to helping children become "human."[137] Robert Hutchins's plea was to change the educational system from a working to a learning society.

> What education can and should do is help people to become human. The object of education is not manpower, but manhood . . . We can now make the transition from a working to a learning society.[138]

He saw education as the way to remedy the cultural problems that have been created by a society bent on production.

> Almost every "fact" I was taught from first grade through law school is no longer a fact. Almost every tendency that was proclaimed has failed to materialize . . . I am especially embarrassed by the facts and tendencies I proclaimed myself. I can only hope the students in the Yale law school have forgotten what I taught them. The courts have overruled and the legislatures repealed most of what I knew.[139]

The study of an entire class, such as low-income groups, has been extremely difficult. Even though groups under this classification had diversity between members and among social groups, social scientists had merged certain traits for the purpose of study. Thus, common characteristics were thought to determine an entire social class. The Coleman Report sparked such a controversy on how schools could respond to racial exclusion.[140] Although other issues were raised in the report, the emphasis was that black children's home environment was directly correlated to school underachievement.[141] Questions had also been raised as to whether schools should insist on whether children of the poor should adapt to the school's frame of reference.[142]

State-of-the-Art Survey

A preliminary phase to study the multicultural education state of the art was carried out from October 3, 1977, to January 31, 1978. In that time, over fifty personal contacts were made with federal officials, educators, sociologists, museum program staff, special project staff, and selected leaders from fields such as international education, multicultural education, bilingual-bicultural research, and so on. Communication was carried out through telephone, personal interview, and written means. (See tables 1 and 2.) The content of the contacts was divided into two parts, one asking personal opinions on culture and education, in the current scene, culture in education, multi-cultural education, as it now exists, and suggestions for further written and people resources. In addition, extensive searches were made through clearinghouses and other data banks using the multicultural education terminology. (See table 3.) Two conferences were attended for understanding present issues. First, the Ethnic Heritage: A Conference for Developing Successful Programs, held in New York City, November 11-12, 1978, and, second, a conference sponsored by the American Association of Colleges for Teacher Education and the National Institute of Education, National Institutes on Multicultural Teacher Education Standards, December 14–16, 1978, in Washington, D.C.

Summary of the State of the Art

It soon became apparent that a variety of terms were used to convey and to cover similar and subtly divergent concepts

TABLE 1

**FEDERAL OFFICIALS CONTACTED IN
BUREAUS AND DIVISIONS**

Federal Agency	Bureau and/or Division
Commerce Department	Central Office
Commission on Civil Rights	Central Office
Federal Committee on Education	
Inter-Agency on Children	
Department of Agriculture	Child Development
Office of Education	Adult Education
	Bilingual Education (elementary)
	Bilingual/English As a Second Language
	Citizenship
	Education Technology
	Education Statistics
	Emergency Assistance Schools
	Elementary and Secondary Education Act
	Ethnic Heritage
	Planning and Evaluation
	Teacher Corps
Office of Human Development/Administration For Children, Youth, and Families	Head Start
	Bilingual Specialist
	Education Specialists
	Children's Bureau
	Welfare
	Research and Demonstration
National Institute of Education	Multicultural/Bilingual
	National Laboratories and Resource Centers
Public Health Services	National Institute for Mental Health Child Development and Family Minority Studies
Smithsonian Institute	Institute on Immigration and Ethnic Studies
State Department	Educational and Cultural Affairs

TABLE 2

PROFESSIONAL CONTACTS (NONFEDERAL AND ACADEMIC)

(Directors and key staff)

Institution	Division
University of Connecticut	Human Development and Family Relations
Georgetown University	International/Intercultural Family Impact Study
California State University	National Network of Centers for Bilingual Education (Title VII) Assessment and Dissemination
National Council on Family Relations	
International Linkages in Higher Education	African-American Institute
Howard University	International Studies
Catholic University	Pennsylvania Ethnic Heritage Studies Center
Bloomsburg State College	

Educational Research and Development Supported by National Institute of Education (NIE)

Name of Institution	State Located
CEMREL, Inc.	St. Louis, Missouri
Far West Laboratory for Educational Research and Development	San Francisco, California
Appalachia Educational Laboratory, Inc.	Charleston, West Virginia
Mid-Continent Regional Educational Laboratory	Kansas City, Missouri
Southwest Educational Development Lab	Austin, Texas

PROFESSIONAL AND RELATED GROUPS

(Directors and key staff contacted)
Anti-Defamation League of B'Nai Brith
American Association of State Colleges and Universities
Italian-American Foundation

Association for World Education
National Education Association
  Civil Rights Division
  Educational Products
  Bilingual Bicultural Dissemination Project (NIE)
  Task Force on Multicultural Education
  Teacher Rights Task Force
InterAmerican Association
National Council for Social Studies
Center for Pluralism and Group Identity
National Ethnic Studies Assembly
Urban Ethnic Affairs

PROFESSIONAL AND RELATED GROUPS

Creative Learning
District of Columbia Board of Education, Audio Technical Division
  (Multiethnic materials)
American Association of Colleges of Teacher Education (AACTE) Ethnic
  Heritage Center for Teacher Education
Institute on Pluralism and Ethnic Identity
National Center for Urban Ethnic Affairs

TABLE 3

DOCUMENT SEARCH SYSTEMS (Multicultural Education and Theory)

System	Descriptors	Yield (abstracts)	Useful for Research
ERIC		206	72
	Over 100 descriptors covering education from pre-school to teacher training, educational trends, multicultural education, parenthood, parent-child relations, cultural awareness, nondiscriminatory, child rearing, equal		

	educational, culture, cultural pluralism, etc.		
Inter-Agency Panel on Early Childhood Education (Social Research Group, Georgetown University. Data from thirty-five federal agencies)	Bilingual, bicultural, multicultural education	502	0
National Technical Information Service	Bilingual, bicultural, multicultural education	0	0
Project Share (Federal National Clearinghouse for Improving Management of Human Services)	Bilingual, bicultural	51	0
Smithsonian Science Information Exchange	Bilingual, bicultural	61	0
Xerox Corporation (Comprehensive Dissertation Abstracts)	Multicultural education, intercultural, cultural, cultural pluralism child, children, childhood, sociology, race relations, international, cross-cultural, etc.	74	13
National Education Association Educational Products	In-service, social science studies, history of minority groups, black experience, skill building, equal educational opportunity education	9	2

Administration for
Children, Youth and
Families/Head Start
(November 1978)

Four performance
standards relating to
ethnic/race/culture

From quarterly validation reports of eleven regional offices (including Indian and Migrant Division): 210 grantees had in-depth validation of 248 performance standards out of compliance in those identified as direct to descriptors, and total of 575 performance standards identified as indirect to descriptors were out of compliance.

United States Government Printing Office Subject Bibliography and Government Administrative Offices (Congress).

(March '77)	Minorities	108	2
(May '77)	Social Welfare	113	1
(April '77)	Children and Youth	312	0
(June '77)	Day Care	31	0
(September '77)	Educational Statistics	45	3
(May '77)	Secondary Education	94	4
(March '77)	Anthropology	22	0
(February '77)	Teachers and Teach-Methods	60	3

and goals. Consequently, multicultural education, cultural pluralism, polyculture, ethnicity, racial equity, equal educational opportunity, cross-cultural, inter-, intra-, infra-, and trans-cultural education were expressions embracing a myriad of ideas with many different connotations and foci. This "state of the art" task was necessary in order to grasp the range of concepts and goals in order to decipher the relevant elements of this research.

Meanings apparently depended on who used a particular term and from what political vantage point. Various meanings and intent were outgrowths of different political factions. There seems to have been very little energy spent at arriving at some agreement as to the implications of various concepts and proposed programs. Definitions had been attempted by groups and individuals interested in cultural pluralism, equity, minority rights, humanistic and future education. In surveying the literature and in speaking to experts from the field, several themes emerged. One pervasive political issue was the role of government and the courts related to desegration problems and the education of "minority children." Another major problem related to the piecemeal and scattered broad areas for funded projects. For example, the short-term projects of the Ethnic Heritage Programs had been funded for one year. When contracts and grants were terminated, projects ceased. In unusual circumstances, some "special projects" were picked up locally or by a foundation. In most cases, funds for the dissemination of developed materials did not exist. They were unavailable at the project's termination.

In some situations, selected materials were picked up by commercial businesses. During this survey, most of the National Institute for Education's Laboratories and Development Centers had been terminated. Very few had found other funds for continuity. The majority of Resource, Research and Development Laboratories tended to change focus depending on the funding priorities of the particular federal agency.

EMPAC, the newsletter of the Ethnic Millions Political Action Committee, in its June 1977 issue, represents the precariousness of national interest in ethnic cultural concerns.

> President Carter's administration is threatening to abolish the National Advisory Council on Ethnic Heritage Studies, along with other advisory councils. Such advisory councils are ordinary citizens whose task is to criticize, evaluate, and advise government bureaucrats in their work. This is a strong form of citizen participation with direct statutory clout. The abolishment of this advisory council would set back the Ethnic Heritage Studies Program decisively. All who care about ethnic heritage studies should communicate their concerns immediately to Mr. Joseph Califano . . .[143]

One effort to keep up the sparse multicultural attempts to filter into the public schools may have been through the teacher education colleges. In order to be accredited, those colleges must now meet multicultural education standards at the master's level. The major goal of the standards was to have multicultural elements permeate all phases of teacher education. The section on multicultural education later expands on this and related issues. There have been a number of definitions for "equal educational opportunity," depending on the particular American group's orientation. Another driving force perpetually connected to education has been the compulsion with "achievement," "gains," or academic skills in the "basics." These interests, framed around a backdrop of the strong inclination of the American public, the federal government, and Congress, to hold tenaciously to traditional dominant standards to try to "mold" each child into the existing system, caused problems for some groups. Individualizing the curriculum, for example, continues to be based on a deficit model, the key value and standard being conformity. And the question of "language" in bilingual programs continues to serve to cloud the more pervasive accepted dominant ethnocentric issue, more fully discussed later. Other acceptable concepts such as minority rights, compensatory education, intervention techniques, mainstream culture, and parity remained complex and unsolved, comprehensively addressed in the problem components in the first chapter of this study. Specialists interested in educational reform have been struggling with ethnic studies, bilingual, bicultural, multiethnic, and multicultural education, and have advocated cultural pluralism in the classroom. Selected programs attempted to take on a superficial and narrow approach, primarily concentrating on *minority* ethnic groups for "equal opportunities," as a means to gain power. The most important conclusion arrived at from examining the current thinking and efforts in this field is the lack of a theory that embraces "culture" as a dynamic force for learning in educational approaches.

Research

The status of research in areas subsumed under multicultural education and/or multiethnic education had narrow foci. One direction had been on bias in teaching and its effect on student learning.[144] Another area examined teaching skills.[145] A third tack was curriculum and material development and teacher training.[146] Most research had been on language acquisition, which had been related to bilingual programming.[147] Cross-cultural research cut across areas such as anthropology, sociology, psychology, linguistics, and nonverbal communication.[148] Very little research had been carried out directed toward classroom learning and teaching.[149] Research connected with desegregation issues was beginning to expand.[150] And finally, in educational circles, values clarification and "affective education," plus "moral development," had attained some recognition for working with children in the classroom setting. The proponents suggested that in modern society it was very hard to "choose those values" as meaningful criteria for effective living.[151] As a result, "value confusion" produced symptoms such as apathy, feelings of insecurity, extreme discordance, and so on. Programs designed to defeat these kinds of turmoil assisted people in gaining confidence and developing enthusiasm and a sense of usefulness. Research in values naturally fell into the domains of cultural anthropology. The application of "values education" was beset with numerous problems. The first had to do with definition. Several competing ideas and theories had significant divergent goals, approaches, and subject matter.[152] Also, they carried a wide variety of assumptions and implications which ranged from social and political criticism, the teaching of specifically selected values, to keeping away from any kind of values in education. Some attempt had been made to assist education personnel and curriculum developers in applying cultural anthropology to values clarification in education.[153] However, consistent and systematic analysis and study remains to be done.[154]

Compensatory Education: Is It
Educational Reform?

Brief Background

American educational reform, which followed Russia's
1957 launching of Sputnik, was directed toward increasing
courses such as physics and mathematics. It was thought that
teaching highly precise subject matter gave promise to the
production of a steady steam of scientists. The process of eliminating "frill" subjects in the arts and also in the humanities
while saving tax dollars, was applauded by public opinion and
school boards alike. Against this background, however, was
the sudden realization that education, the "key to success," did
not effect social mobility for everyone. Instead, society was
faced with illiteracy, urban blight, rural poverty, and ethnic-
racial tensions. It became more obvious that certain Americans
could not get an education at all unless particular ethnic cultural habits were to be annihilated.[155] The differences between
those who succeeded and those who did not was not in what
could be learned but rather what, in one's background, must
be thrown out. The gap between the school culture and the
different social styles grew progressively larger. There had
been and still are a handful of concerned educators who recognized and spoke out against the school's priorities and inequities. They were critical of the mechanistic, the efficiency-
oriented, uniform teaching methods and subject matter.[156]
However, administrators plagued by public opinion were not
interested. The public has yet to be convinced that it is the
responsibility of the public schools to be responsive to the diverse cultural groups differing in interests and expression.[157]

To be sure, the educational system was not producing sufficient numbers of scientifically and technologically proficient products, but a lack of academic orientation could
hardly be blamed for the school's failure to cultivate the
human resources of the country; rather this rigidly academic

orientation itself was forcing growing numbers of children to fall behind or to drop out altogether, and a good many of those who succeeded, even through college, were severely lacking in conceptual skills. Therefore, by advocating that the purpose of the schools be "changed" to put even greater stress on academic mastery, these school critics merely helped to further entrench the rigid and outdated system.[158]

America, as the great melting pot, began to erode, and social economic class became identified with selected ethnic groups. Class difference had made the achievement difference in schools.[159] Grace Graham's examination of social-class groups cut across religious, ethnic, and political lines. She concluded that middle-class children had the benefit of status with peers and teachers because they were academically successful. In general, they had better material possessions and "more opportunity to develop their personalities." Also, the locality influenced the "advantage" such as social class and status that seemed more important in the northeast and south than in the far west. The advantage also seemed to have been valid in older towns rather than in newer developments, and in schools with larger upper-middle class enrollments, etc. Finally, "schools usually tend to follow socio-economic lines, deviations can and do occur."[160] The type and form of social distinction depended on the culture of the school and the region, as well as staff quality. Segregation in large city schools deprived the "disadvantaged of equal opportunity."

Compensatory Education as Cultural Conditioning

Compensatory education, accepted by professional and lay people, was in keeping with the idea that learning disability could be produced by one's social background. This "environmental deprivation" concept, therefore, assumed that it (background) could be "corrected" through special "treatment."

Compensatory education appeared on the public education scene almost a decade after the Supreme Court desegregation cases. In accord with the ideological sociopolitical conditions, academic failure and retardation was/is seen as a function of early socialization, perhaps due to poverty and discrimination. Aspects of these phenomena were described in other parts of this study. The children, it was felt, enter school ill equipped for the academic work required. Special programs "should" be developed, whose purpose it was/is to assist them in "catching up" for their "handicaps" were/are socially determined. The "origins" of those handicaps that were/are articulated are sociological and not biological. However, it has been necessary to be reminded continually that the inherent racial and social class biases have been deeply rooted in American culture. The bias and discriminatory practices were challenged that had the effect of raising doubts about the compensatory hypothesis. The behavioral scientist Arthur Jensen, for example, argued that, indeed, it was the genetic influence that made the difference in poor school performance, especially in black children.[161] This theory affected the validity of compensatory education since its goals *could not* be accomplished because of the hereditary intellectual potential of low-income classes. The low-income classes "happened" to be the minority groups. This "scientific debate" was given a renewed level of respectability. Despite prompt rejection of the unsubstantiated claims made by Jensen, its impact served to eschew societal ideology. Repudiation of the "heredity" factor included geneticists such as Ashley Montagu. This study raised this issue in the problem component "Common Prejudices, Abuses, and the Great American Dream." The section systematically pointed to interrelationships throughout other related and/or interconnected concepts. Most poor children who have not "performed" according to schooling expectations gave school administrators and teachers the rationalizations for expecting and accepting the "problems" that these children brought with them to public education. This concept, also, had been elaborated on in the "Education, Schooling, Purpose, and American Tradition" section of the problem and permeated other components pointing toward contingency concepts. That is, when an hypothesis was formulated, the interaction between the individual and the behavior was explained consistently with the identified responses. The consequences shaped and reinforced the original hypothesis.

The research on the negative attitudes, low expectations, instructional approaches, and materials used currently in public schooling has been seen as a threat to traditional schooling—its methods and its curricula. And since it has not been customary to question the "system" or its ideology, traditional social scientists tended to ask questions such as, Why do disadvantaged children perform so inadequately in school? Consequently, the families and their children were studied with varying hypotheses that assumed the deficit model. Debates now fluctuate regarding the extent to which the "wrong" developmental patterns can be redirected toward academic "competence." This concept of potential reversibility has been at the core of compensatory education. And the issue of "reversibility" in education reinforced the debate on the educability of certain groups. The statistical methods used in the Coleman Report cast suspicion on the restoration of educational handicaps of the poor.

> . . . analyses of data from this study have raised serious technical questions . . . The appropriateness of the statistical techniques involved . . . when indices for two such closely correlated "independent" variables as socio-economic status and school service are subjected to regression analysis, the one entered first into the regression equation seems to show the greater explanatory power, since it tends to exhaust the major portion of the total variance carried by the two sets of indices together . . . Had the school-service variables been entered first, the results would have shown the school to be the major influence on pupil performance, thus contrary to widespread beliefs, the "Coleman Study" has not established that schooling makes but little difference

in the academic development of children. It affords no confirmation of the thesis that educational handicaps of disadvantaged children are irreversible.[162]

One of the first intervention techniques came from the recommendation of the New York City Board of Education's Commission on Integration in the late fifties. The Demonstration Guidance Project was designed to identify and stimulate "able" poor children. This six-year junior and senior high school project selected students from "culturally disadvantaged" neighborhoods.[163] Improvement in I.Q. test scores in the majority of students were reported. Also, more students completed high school, with some of them excelling and obtaining Regents scholarships, medals, or certificates for academic achievement. In addition were those intangible outcomes which contribute toward self-confidence. This 1959 project was extended to include all children in selected schools. The "results," however, did not match those of the previous experiment, with the arithmetic scores even less than were expected. Behavior and attendance, however, improved. Since "academic achievement" was thought to be the primary goal, "behavior and attendance" was not considered a worthy outcome; therefore, its causes were linked to social class and "ethnic" problems. Schools continue to be tormented by "discipline" problems that society still views as problems of desegregation issues, as noted in parts of the problem components of this study.

Private philanthropic groups such as the Ford Foundation supported the spread of compensatory education. A variety of approaches were used. In the early sixties, San Francisco developed a five-year project in black communities, which included elementary schools. Soon after, Cleveland, Detroit, Philadelphia, South Bend, and Grand Rapids had implemented compensatory education programs with New York, California, Maine, Rhode Island, and Pennsylvania financing statewide programs.[164]

The climate for the legitimacy of compensatory programs continues, although there has been some concern with the "separate but equal" settings. The apprehensiveness expressed by civil rights proponents apparently had been justified because the response to desegregation of many school systems was to "provide" compensatory education instead.[165]

Analysis of Deficits as Cause for
Poor Performance

The Client (Child) as Patient in the Medical Model

Compensatory education, as has been repeatedly stated, attempted to change the "disadvantaged" (diseased) child. This pattern for changing the child, as a fabrication of society, the product of an environment, gave credence to the idea that the purpose of "equal opportunity" has been to rehabilitate the individual to *fit* the existing (public school) system. The form of the rehabilitation, then, logically, has been remedial instruction in the "basic skills": reading, mathematics, writing. The failing student was to be "brought up" to his or her "grade level" through supplementary subjects, "enrichment," and other "special" experiences. These attempts were directly related to identified "weaknesses." The federal government, in 1978, allocated 12.3 billion for "Special Programs for Educationally Deprived Children" and $59 million in 1977 for Follow-Through.[166]

Programs are designed to give special educational assistance to children whose level of educational achievement is below normal for their age and to help overcome barriers to learning. Projects may provide such services as suplementary and remedial instruction in reading and mathematics, pupil and family counseling, cultural enrichment, and preschool activities. Project design and content are determined by the *imagination and discretion of local school leaders* who are developing programs to meet the varied and special needs of their disadvantaged children [emphasis added].[167]

Head Start, the largest federal program for young children, funded originally by the United States Office of Economic Opportunity, shifted the idea of "educational deficits" to an economic, political, and social orientation.* "Operation Head Start" was developed on the assumption that early education, parental involvement, and the provision of medical and social services will enable children of the poor to achieve cognitive parity with their middle-class peers. Then they will be able to leave the ranks of poverty.[168] Another example of the "medical model," Upward Bound, was established to assist the "disadvantaged" high school student for college. Here again is an illustration in which the colleges were not expected to change their traditional standards for admission (and even curriculum), but "disadvantaged" were to be upgraded.

The underlying philosophy in compensatory education continues to perpetuate the notion that the system itself is beyond reproach. It maintains the status quo in concepts in which efforts in supplementing activities with prescriptive content, when applied, will "cure" or "repair" or improve the child. When the "treatment" had been accomplished, the child would be ready for reentry into the "normal" learner's world. The "normal" learners were already involved in the "regular" standard educational process.†

Cynical Cyclical Trends

When old truths are challenged, the problems become even more complicated and masked. One dimension of the education dilemma surfaced when "disadvantaged groups" began to feel a psychological investment in rising expectations. The "War on Poverty" years stimulated the challenges of accepted prej-

*Authorization for Head Start came under Title II of the Economic Opportunity Act (EOA) of 1964, which provided for education of poor children within the framework of comprehensive services to the child and family.

†For more detailed examination of the concept of disadvantaged background, in addition to the problem component section on pp. 1–29 in this study, see the Metaphor: Expletive Recap, p. 121–122.

udices and "inferiority" by "minority" groups. Patriotism lost some of its fervor in the midst of the Vietnamese war. Compensatory education was/is thought to be the panacea for uplifting the poor. Social victims tended to emulate their dominant models unwittingly and perpetuate their own victimization. This notion is recapitulated in the metaphor developed for this research, which, in effect, introduces the theoretical model. Most compensatory education programs "labeled" and categorized children for the "purpose of" identifying their "weaknesses." They also tended to provide "guidance," "parental and community participation," and modified curricula. Retraining teachers in remediation skills became an integral part of the system. The National Institute of Education Report on Compensatory Education stated, "Remedial reading, mathematics, and language arts are three subjects most often provided to compensatory education students."[169] In a close look at these programs, one wondered how they differed from the "regular" program. And, according to the traditional criteria, one thought, *Shouldn't any "good educational program" include elements of this special program?* Programs tended to offer "more of" a particular subject matter or the watering down of subject areas. Usually, fewer children were in classrooms or had been taken out of "regular" classrooms. Some attempts were made at modifying teaching techniques. Where has there been educational reform? The system for allocating funds and mandated criteria further confused educational issues as they related to the concepts of the "disadvantaged."

The compensatory literature has been quite substantial and generally pointed out all the benefits to the child. Such goals as self-confidence, positive attitude toward school, increased motivation, and stimulation in academic achievement were outcomes. However, as the cost of living rose, there seemed to be less justification for such expensive and comprehensive programs.[170] The "patient" was left without the curing prescriptions. Society must continue to carry the unavoidable burden of "inferior poor" (which has been created by the environment). It seemed apparent that the schools will always have to face "the problem" of "poor learners," as defined by the system, if the criteria remain unchanged. This ongoing demand to furnish an education to the "disadvantaged" who need to receive "treatment," while ignoring that they are the victims of the dominant group criteria, continues to feed patterns that emerge from the hypothesis of self-fulfilling prophecies. It seems inevitable. Robert Marton's definition of self-fulfilling prophecy is pertinent: ". . . in the beginning a *false* definition of the situation evoking a new behavior which makes the originally false conception come true."[171] The difficulty in recognizing all the contingencies and their implications, as Merton pointed out, has been the oversight in comprehending how the concept of the self-fulfilling prophecy works. The case in point may be explained by the experiences of compensatory education programs in that they have not yielded overwhelming gains. The National Institute of Education evaluation of compensatory education reported that 53 percent of the instructional budget went to reading, 19 percent to mathematics, and 10 percent to language arts.[172] An average of 25 percent, or about five and a half hours a week of instruction, was provided to "a significantly higher concentration of minority group children." The report estimated that 85 percent of the compensatory education students were in reading, 66 percent in mathematics, and 63 percent in language arts as supplementary to regular classroom instruction. In 1977, the reasons for key changes in the way funds were allocated would have been interesting to examine.

Of the changes currently proposed for the allocation of Federal compensatory education funds, a shift from poverty measures to achievement scores is potentially the most far-reaching . . . the appropriate way to distribute education funds is on the basis of children's educational performance. Since the ultimate aim . . . to increase children's achievement.[173]

Also of interest has been the lack of reliable data. National evaluations of compensatory education were attempted by the Office of Education from 1968 to 1971, and data on "achievement" were not forthcoming from school districts; less than 10 percent of usable data was received.[174] As a result, the analysis of the first survey was not reported until 1970. The 1969 survey analysis was never released. The 1970 results, consisting of 1,200 tables, were never interpreted, and the 1971 data were never analyzed at all.[175] This report included examples of "failures" in providing national data. Although there had been vast sums of money spent for the vast amount of research in subject areas, instruction, environments, instructional time, teacher training, and so on, it seemed clear that many myths and the rhetoric of the disadvantaged have been fostered. It will continue as long as the concept "culturally deprived" is thought to be the basis of a viable theory.[176] Similarly, the "achievement concept" is still thought to be a valid approach in judging schooling matters and its "self-fulfilling" results remain a serious problem for the public schools, to say nothing of the aspirations of the "poor" minority groups. The quantitative-measurement approach to *tracking* continues also, while the complex interrelated elements related to the quality of *learning* have been generally ignored (in practice) as maintained throughout this study.

The Emergence of Valuing Diversity

Compensatory education may be a fraud perpetuated upon a poor and unsuspecting citizenry which has traditionally looked to education to lead it out of bondage. Compensatory education may be a hoax by which the politicians and educators of middle-class America salve their conscience and maintain the status quo. Or compensatory education may be simply the best efforts of a politico-educational complex blinded in one eye by prejudice and in the other by do-goodness—both equally detrimental to the welfare of children and society.[177]

The educational and sociological literature have been replete with descriptions of people in poverty, their low achievement, delinquency, and feelings of alienation. No doubt, there has been some validity, in varying degrees and scope, in any one of these individual characteristics; however, apparently missing from studies has been the acknowledgment of the severe restriction of freedom of choice and of those who responded from those "disadvantaged" groups.[178] The exhortations, especially in compensatory education, obscured the need to examine the total context, the elements of which could not be fairly separated from other cultural manifestations. Somehow, in the scheme of things, the schools had neglected the differences in human values and the acknowledgment as transcending all human activity. Rather, it persisted further in the singular search for increasing "cognitive skills." At least its major emphasis covered the importance of other competencies. In the midst of the "intervention era," Mario Fantini and Gerald Weinstein suggested that "most of us" are disadvantaged, indicating that schools had failed the middle-class child as well as the poor urban and rural child since, "All groups of people have a culture of some sort."[179]

The research on the "hidden curriculum," nonverbal, indirect communication, or double messages that helped shape individual personalities brought the variety of influences in social settings into professional consciousness. Ronald Lippitt's study showed that all established interests impinge on molding the child during the socialization maze.

> In our studies of community functionings, we have identified a number of clusters of personnel that have a vested interest in influencing the behavior and values of children and youth. Each of these clusters has a program of socialization.[180]

The issue, here again, has been one of values and specific criteria used for judging outcomes. Also, Marshall McLuhan's theory that the content communicated through television, for example, is abstruse when compared with the effects on the

perceptual orientation of viewers. It resulted from the interaction with the very nature of the medium (the television set
itself). "The young student today grows up in an electronically
configured world . . . not of wheels but of circuits, not of frag-
ments but of integral patterns."[181] Thus, the hidden curriculum" may be more pervasive, insidious, and obscure than
presently recognized.

Various aspects of the "hidden curriculum" had been in-
vestigated. It was raised earlier in this study in discussions on
its effects on "minority groups" through the economic and political structure in the United States.[182] It had also been im-
plicated in the cultural pluralism sections and the problem
components dealing with scientific conditioning. Fantini and
Weinstein described how the hidden curriculum affected learning style. Elements such as language acquisition, cultural
transmission, the effect of one's neighborhood (whether in city
slums, rural settings or suburbs), the family, the extended
family, family forms ("broken" or "single parent"), family rituals—all of these characteristics lead to their central thesis
for the need to develop a diversified curriculum.

In whatever direction the new educational system may go,
it must be founded on the existing facts . . . A most important fact to be considered is that this is a nation built from
a variety of cultures; it is historically and currently, a culturally diverse nation.[183]

The political issues involved in American society and in
education cannot be overstated. Saul Alinsky's critical concerns with the War on Poverty, expressed during the height
of its activities, in retrospect, could be validly reexamined since
most of the "community participation" ideas have been generally accepted as parts of "special programs."[184] He suggested
that the basis for meaningful and "real" participation occurred
when trust and power is given to people" . . . and that the development of power among our poor will be welcomed instead
of feared."[185] The idea of input and community consensus, how-

ever, can be misleading during the process of implementation. Ronald Lippitt describes vague and inconsistent responses when parents, teachers, and other socialization agents were interviewed on ". . . what they believe is expected of them in the way of products of their socialization efforts."[186] He maintained that professionals and parents can talk easily about methods and activities, but they are confused as to "end products," that is, the goals of these activities and their resultant values. Also, they are disconcerted about the conflicting messages (hidden curriculum?); for example, one message may be that teachers and parents' primary concern ought to be that of expecting high academic achievement and another message being self-motivation, while learning how to learn is mixed up with subject matter mastery.[187]

Another important political issue that influenced the way education was perceived resulted from opposing views of the compensatory education forces and the integration advocates.[188] Those who favor compensatory education based it on a deficit model, while the integration proponents were concerned with the problems of alienation of the "minority groups" from the larger society. Each segment studied the highly limited and precise "problems" consistent with the quasi-experimental, highly specified scientific methodology, ignoring the holistic outlook. It has not been surprising that studies in either case failed to find significant and long-term improvement. The Civil Rights Commission admitted that compensatory education in itself could not handle self-esteem and social class isolation.[189] The debate may continue ad infinitum if the concept of "human needs" are seen in the either-or configuration, that is, either social or biological, either individual or group, that human nature is either malleable or inflexible, and so on. Each era had its special idiosyncrasies. The sixties were guided by the hope of necessary changes to provide justice, decency, and a society whose values benefit all.

Consciousness: Multiethnic Style

It had been said that "society gets what it pays for." This kind of statement could only be validated as an afterthought. Thus, the past "racial" riots, disorders, and violence had shocked American leaders into attention.[190] A second shock wave resulted from the violence of the middle class at universities such as the Berkeley campus in California, Columbia University in New York, and the Kent State and Jackson State murders.[191] Part of those shocks may have been exacerbated by the violence and disorders of those who had sought social reform while, simultaneously, violence was sanctioned by the "law and order" institutions of society. It surely added to the confusion in the struggle for understanding. This was the time when "consciousness raising" in "minority ethnicity" and for educational relevance permeated the atmosphere.

Regardless of the quantity of studies or even the depth of analyses of investigations during this period, the tone and sense of dissatisfaction could not be "scientifically" intellectualized. Feelings, the consequences of values, have been powerful forces behind the desire for social change.[192] Amitai Etzione discussed alienation as a result of society's unresponsiveness to human basic needs.[193] He especially pointed out society's sources of unresponsiveness, the role of "inauthenticity," and resultant psychological factors that are involved in "the fear to challenge the existing social structure or its rhetoric . . . ."[194] In the beginning, the statement "Black is beautiful" became the symbol for new positions taken. "Negroes" no longer allowed the idea of an inherent intellectual inferiority to go uncontested or that educational failure attributed to social role would be espoused without a challenge. Terms like "disadvantaged," "culturally deprived," and "culturally deficient" were disputed regardless of the studies, which found the statistical data and correlations that showed low minority performance on standardized tests.

Just as "Black is beautiful," so is "red" and other Third World consciousness. American personalities began to take on a polychromatic appearance in the wake of the fizzling ideology of the melting pot.[195] A series of significant events led to education as the means for multicultural change and it seemed there was no way back.*

Ethnic Studies

The ethnic studies movement led by Afro-Americans demanded rights.

Blacks were keenly aware of the extent to which written history influences how a group views itself and how other groups view it. Consequently, they also demanded that versions of history be written that were more consistent with a Black liberation ideology and that textbooks which they considered racist be banned from the public schools.[196]

The black revolt served as an incentive to other ethnic groups to demand education reflective of actual American experiences.

Native Americans argued that their 30,000 year history in this land prior to 1492 should be highlighted in the curriculum. Puerto-Rican American scholars argued that the Treaty of Paris (1898) which ended the Spanish-American War needs to be interpreted from a Puerto-Rican perspective.[197]

*Some of the major developments were: in 1957, Congress established the Civil Rights Commission; between 1961 and 1962, litigation challenging discriminatory school practices; Voting Rights Act of 1963; Civil Rights of 1964; the Coleman Report of 1966; in 1971, school busing for equal quality in education; 1972, the proposed amendment of equal rights for women (1978, extension of ratification); 1972, Supreme Court orders bilingual programs (Spanish); municipal schools; 1972, *Board of Regents* v. *Perry* covered instructor's rights when colleges refuse to rehire without explanation or hearing; Native American litigation for compensation for lands taken away; students rights to due process in 1973; from 1968 to 1974, study of educational practices affecting Mexican-Americans in southwest; and 1974, when job discrimination in employment was challenged.

At first, courses classified as black studies, Chicano studies, and so on, were developed in school districts and communities in which the minority population dominated. The premise was that only the specific ethnic group needed to learn about its own heritage. This narrow conception contributed to the piecemeal, disjointed approach in which goals were vague and plans were devoid of clarity.[198]

James Banks made one of the earliest attempts at a theoretical base. He argued for an expanded definition of ethnicity in which knowledge, materials, and techniques would include teaching about white ethnic groups in addition to the ethnic minority.

> To conceptualize ethnic studies more narrowly will result in curricular programs which are too narrow in scope, and which will fail to help students fully understand both the important similarities and differences in the experiences of the groups that constitute America . . . A vital ethnic studies program should enable students to derive valid generalizations about the characteristics of all America's ethnic groups and to learn how they are alike and different, in both their past and present experiences.[199]

Banks further argued that ethnic content alone, the learning of facts, were insufficient goals for "lessons." The focus should be on higher orders of knowledge and analysis of values for the purpose of decision-making. The major emphasis should be on the "core" values within the various cultural groups.[200] His charge was for an educational reform through complete curriculum change.

The ethnic studies movement was a response to expand education for college students and teacher education. It was seen as the process as well as the product of individual motivation, as interacting with different ethnic groups and political gains.

Bilingual-Bicultural Education

"Language minority" children have been faced with un-usual kinds of discriminatory practices.[201] These stemmed not only from a lack of understanding of the English language but their resultant segregation. In addition, there has been the unsympathetic and cultural mismatch with the predominant curricula. Also, the low expectations and neglect from teachers contributed to isolation. The historic 1974 decision of the Supreme Court required that schools, under Title VI of the Civil Rights Act of 1964, must provide special language programs for children who are not proficient in English.[202] The controversy has been in how the children were taught and in the scope for maintaining the original language and not whether learning English is essential. There have been differences among the bilingual professionals in defining, the extent to which bilingual programs ought to emphasize the English as a Second Language approach. However, they generally tended to agree that the child's primary language and culture ought to be the foundation upon which other subject matter are learned to the point that English has been sufficiently mastered.

The bilingual-bicultural movement has been part of the "equal educational opportunity" movement. And, as such, the debates about the various bilingual models and the English as a second-language approach still remain a heated issue.[203] There are those who define bilingual-bicultural education in its widest sense advocating bilingualism for all American children. There are also those who believe ultimately in the monolingual approach.[204]

English as a Second Language, of course, is part of the bilingual-bicultural programs and has been used to describe the way instruction occurred in the regular curriculum. In the average program, children were taken out of the classroom for specialized work in English. Methods varied according to different language theories. Because the major efforts were directed toward the acquisition of the second language, problems in other subject matter were encountered. The language minority child, then, was not provided with similar educational experiences as were the other children. They, thereby, did not derive the full benefits from subjects other than the basic three R's. "Ideally, ESL replaces such courses in art, music, or physical education in the elementary grades."[205] In this sense, the children were deprived of the scope of education that other children had. This, no doubt, added to the furthering of disadvantagement.

The bilingual-bicultural methodology, although variations exist, viewed education in a more comprehensive manner than English as a second language. Self-concept was an integral component, and the curriculum usually included elements of history, literature, and cultural traditions. The use of language minority bilingual teachers and other bilingual staff (it was believed) provided positive role models and reinforcement often lacking in the monolingual classrooms.

> By giving the language and culture of the language minority child recognition within the curriculum, bilingual-bicultural education allows the child to feel acceptable as a language minority individual and thus to develop positive attitudes toward learning English and the dominant cultural group.[206]

Funds appropriated under the Bilingual Education Act of 1968 sponsored demonstration programs rather than supported research in identification and development of effective approaches to meet differing needs.[207] The federal policy included monies for planning, developing, and operating programs from early childhood education to adult education, preservice training, dropout vocational projects and courses in the culture and history of the language minority groups served.

The National Task Force on Bilingual Bicultural Education was formed in 1975.[208] It was requested by the Commissioner of Education, as required, in response to the poor performance in English and mathematics of many bilingual children. Almost ten years after legislation, there had not been a philosophical approach, systematic concepts, or clear goals. Nor had major attempts been made to analyze techniques, curriculum, and so on. The Task Force was charged with developing "a working philosophy for future endeavors in bilingual-bicultural education."[209] The twenty-one recommendations covered improving methods, identifying appropriate strategies in content areas, research efforts, teacher training, career ladders for community people and staff. It was not until the National Advisory Council on Bilingual Education, mandated in the 1974 legislation, that the concept was expanded and modified to emphasize the positive values of diversity in education.[210] It also challenged the remedial nature of the bilingual programs.

A national awareness of bilingual/multicultural education as an asset should be further encouraged. A first step would be the creation of a 1977 White House Conference on Bilingual/Multicultural Education to reflect the commitment of the Executive Branch of the Federal Government. The Council requests that the President initiate this program of national awareness as a positive example to the people of this country of the benefits of a bilingual/multicultural education system. . . the Legislative Branch redefine and amend Title VII to reflect the pluralistic, social and economic values which are representative of the Nation and are inherent achievements of quality bilingual/multicultural education.[211]

When the American Institutes for Research released the findings of the first national impact study, it created some controversy.[212] The report claimed that Title VII children, on the average, were doing worse than the comparison children of Hispanic descent in regular classes. While they seemed to do better in mathematics, both groups were below the national norm. Although an important goal of Title VII had been to improve school attitudes, the report stated that children's attitudes toward school were scarcely different from those in the regular classes.

The legislation has been so broad that the definition of eligible children could include many children who are proficient in English. They could be admitted into the bilingual programs based on their surnames, Census Bureau, and other conditions which do not necessarily know how well the children understood, read, or wrote English. The legislation provided for bicultural programs, it gave only minor emphasis to instructional designs. Is the answer devising and bestowing of language proficiency tests, as many have suggested? Or is it possible that the deep resistance to systemic change from valuing conformity to diversity is the major deterrent?

In an attempt to assist policy makers in decision making, Noel Epstein examined the legislation, regulations, and legal history of bilingual bicultural education.

> After nearly nine years and more than half a billion dollars in federal funds, however, the government has not demonstrated whether such instruction makes much difference in the student's achievement, in their acquisition of English, or their attitudes toward school.[213]

The dichotomy of the direction that the federal government had taken can be separated. First, it could be related to serving children with limited or no ability in English. Both the legislation and the courts mandated special services to these children. Second, program design for bilingual programs tended to segregate the children from the mainstream schooling process. Other issues remain unsolved. The "maintenance" advocates have been opposed to using the child's native language as only a bridge to English. They wanted equal value to be given to both languages and cultures. Children could learn partly in the native tongue and partly in English. Schools should bear the responsibility for teaching about the respective ethnic groups even if children can function in English. The debate here had been whether the federal government ought to carry maintenance programs. Most of the programs remained segregated. The irony, as Epstein brought out, was that maintenance programs were more likely to "erode" the native language and culture rather than "nourish" them. Another issue was the lack of effective research into the methodology of bilingual programs. The "political" factors far outweigh the need for evidence about the approaches now in use. Have these programs led to better or worse relations? Distressing to all concerned were the educational consequences and possible bitter linguistic "politics" that resulted from lack of agreement. The diversity among and within the ethnic groups raised questions about respect for the varieties of language styles within a language and cultural pluralism in general.

When certain factors were isolated, such as standard English or Castilian Spanish for the purpose of an efficient and uniform "acceptance" mechanism, the biases of either researcher or teacher ought not to have been ignored. The language factor alone became a poor criterion for focusing on educational difficulties of children who did not do "well" in school. These issues parallel those raised in deficit models.

The findings from the American Institutes for Research study and the concerns raised in Epstein's "alternatives" were consistent with acceptable quantitative research methodology. This being the case, again, one cannot help but focus on the cyclical criticism because of the political issues involved. José Cardenas's response pointed out that this study was poorly conceived and even more poorly implemented.[214]

It is inconceivable that USOE would conduct a study to determine the effects of reading rather than a study of a specific methodology used in the teaching of reading. It is rather obvious that the difference in treatment is indicative of the USOE commitment to reading as a desirable social value and lack of similar USOE commitment in bilingual education.[215]

As is well known, conclusions on the "workability" or the "desirability" of a program have been dependent upon *how* a problem is framed. In philosophical questions and scientific findings, the problem, metaphorically, could be compared to a glass being half full or half empty. One of the crucial issues raised by this research has been how "reality" is perceived by different groups. Taking the problem components and the theoretical bases together, "reality" is culturally determined and is a variable.

I am convinced that the value-free, value-neutral, value-avoiding model of science that we inherited from physics, chemistry, and astronomy where it was necessary and desirable to keep the data clean and also to keep the church out of scientific affairs, is quite unsuitable for the scientific study of life.[216]

Multicultural Education

In the United States, the multicultural education phenomena were propelled by both minority group pressure (under-employed and unemployed) for equal educational opportunity and by the reactions of the white ethnics (low-income middle class) who felt neglected.[217] The repudiation by minority groups of the genetic and cultural deficiency theories was paralleled by the "new ethnicity" in communities euphemistically labeled "hardhats" or "superpatriots."[218] The legislation for the 1968 Bilingual Education Act and the passage of the Ethnic Heritage Act in 1972 provided some support for programs to take into consideration cultural elements from various ethnic groups for educational purposes.[219]

In 1964, the American Association of Colleges for Teacher Education was instrumental in providing leadership to the profession for desirable changes. The National Institute for Advanced Study in Teaching Disadvantaged Youth was established to clarify and address teacher education issues. *Teachers for the Real World*, the publication, resulted from those efforts

and called for alternatives in teacher education, developed
guidelines for projects, supervised conferences and studies, and
developed publications. The Steering Committee reviewed
teacher education, social settings for children, racism, relevancy of teacher education of the "disadvantaged," and so on.*
In 1970, a subcommittee of the Board of Directors of the
American Association of Colleges for Teacher Education
(AACTE) established a Commission on Human Rights in
Teacher Education. Its report recommended the establishment
of a Commission on Multicultural Education. It was formed in
1971. An important statement, "No One Model American," was
one of the outcomes after the Kent State and Jackson State
tragedies, reemphasizing that it was education's task to value
cultural pluralism.[220] Other professional organizations shared
a commitment to cultural pluralism in education, for example,
the National Council of Social Studies, the Association of
Childhood Education International, and the Association for
Supervision and Curriculum Development.[221] The above organizations still provide the major written material for multicultural education.[222] A few publications developed as a result
of particular projects funded by the Ethnic Heritage Program
and National Institute of Education's Resource Bilingual Network.

Federal and State Legislation

Federal legislation concerned with ethnicity in America
can be divided into two categories. First, for schools that are
located in culturally diverse neighborhoods in which special
needs for nonwhite and language minority peoples live and,
second, for meeting the educational needs of a multicultural

*The AACTE is a professional nonprofit organization. It works closely
with the National Council for Accreditation of Teacher Education. Recently,
the final version of the standards for accreditation included a standard for
multicultural education for the postbaccalaureate programs, effective January
1, 1979. See Standards for the Accreditation of Teacher Education, 1750 Pennsylvania Ave., N.W., Washington, D.C. 20036, p. 13.

society. Laws either promote U.S. foreign policy, or they enable school desegregation, integration, or racial balance.[223] State legislation tended to cover specific cultural, bilingual, or women's issues. According to the 1975 American Association of Colleges for Teacher Education's survey, at least thirty-two states had laws covering multicultural curricula, nineteen states made specific reference to multicultural or multiethnic education, twenty-one required curricula for bilingual education, three states for American-Indian Studies, and one state required activities in Spanish-American and Italian-American studies.[224]

Philosophical Premises of Multicultural Education

Basic philosophical questions had been brought to the forefront that endorsed ideas consistent with the pluralism that characterizes American society. Concepts of multicultural education differed.[225] The cultural pluralist ideology supported ethnic identification as essential while recognizing that competing ethnic groups have a stake in political and economic interests. The pluralist argued that it is very important for an individual to develop a sense of his or her ethnic group, especially if that ethnic group is oppressed by more powerful ethnic groups within the American structure. It was assumed that an ethnic group could be included and fully participate when it bargained from a more powerful position. Pluralists believed that schooling had to be dramatically changed to reflect cognitive styles, cultures, and aspirations of ethnic groups, especially those considered to be from the "minority." They maintained that learning materials be culture specific to enable the child to be effective within his or her own ethnic group. This would serve as a basis for gaining power for survival in the larger national culture.[226]

Multiculturalism is coming to be seen as more in keeping with those principles of democracy which suggest that all people should have equal opportunity for involvement in the continuing reformation of an open society while main-streaming their own sense of identity.[227]

James Banks was representative of the "Pluralist-Assimilationist" ideology, "... which is more consistent with the realities of American society."[228] The assumption was made that ethnic groups had developed unique cultural characteristics but that all groups shared many cultural traits. The pluralist-assimilationist felt that the curriculum should reflect various ethnic groups' particular heritages and the common culture. While children were receiving the respect of the ethnic heritage in positive ways, they would also be given options regarding their political choices and actions in regard to their ethnicity. The major goal, then, was to assist the individual to function competently within the national culture, one's own ethnic culture, and other ethnic cultures. Pluralist-assimilationists just felt that this ideology should reflect the development of curriculum, and they argued that it was more appropriate for sound teaching in multicultural education.

The educational literature in multicultural education covered bilingual, bicultural, ethnic studies, education for cultural pluralism, and multiethnic studies. Banks delineated three separate classifications: multicultural education, multiethnic education, and ethnic studies.[229] In multicultural education, the focus was on groups that had experienced discrimination and prejudices. The objectives were to reduce the discrimination and provide equal educational opportunities, while providing all students with cultural options. Multiethnic education directed attention to all ethnic groups for the similar purpose in reducing discrimination against groups that had been victimized. The objectives were equal educational opportunity and a reduction of isolation. The ethnic studies approach was for all ethnic groups to help children clarify attitudes and develop valid generalizations about ethnic groups. Proponents discussed ethnic literacy and wanted to help students learn how to be active in eliminating racial problems.[230]

Modes of Multicultural Education

Several designs were currently in use that attempted to manage multicultural education in a functional way. These programmatic modes of operating strived to render intelligible underlying assumptions and make the aims explicit. To distinguish among them, they have been categorized for identification.

The Culturally Different Multicultural Education Mode

Originating from the idea of school achievement failures and retardation, the purpose of this mode was to provide minority ethnic groups with "equalization" opportunities. The compensatory-deficit hypotheses were rejected. The underlying assumption was that minority group children are handicapped because of dominant values. In order to counteract this, programs should close the school and home gap. The culturally different child, in this mode, has been seen as being only on the edge of mainstream society. There are differences between the dominant and minority groups. Since public education is ruled by the mainstream culture, the discrepancies between the home and school have been large. It has been this variance between home and school that caused learning problems for the culturally different child.[231] The school, not the home, has to change. With an increase in home and school compatibility will come more academic success. The target for this multicultural education was from the minority groups who are farthest behind in national school performance norms. The attempt was to legitimize the cultural differences in child rearing and to lay the burden of "failure" on the homogeneity standards in society. The school should adopt the special needs of the culturally different.[232]

Learning Cultural Differences Multicultural Education Mode

In this model, it was expected that all students learn about cultural differences.[233] The idea was to have children learn to value differences and respect that right. Schools shape attitudes and, therefore, were expected to enrich all children. This has been seen as resulting in a decrease in discrimination. Strategies differed from the ethnic studies methods in that cultural teaching could occur in all subjects.[234] This approach not only assisted the child in feelings of ethnic pride but provided a vehicle for a fairer share to minority groups, particularly in academic realms. Most people agreed with "hoped for outcomes"; however, translating the objectives into a curriculum carried with it the danger of stereotyping and classifying an ethnic group as a monolithic unit.[235]

Education for Cultural Pluralism Mode

Proponents of this approach affirmed the cultural pluralist nature of American society. The assimilationist theory was rejected both as philosophy and in practice. It was an activist position in the social organization in the United States. The term "cultural pluralism" had been used in numerous ways. It has been seen as an ideal goal to which the democratic structure ought to address itself. Anthropologists have used it to describe societies and as an analytical tool. Also, cultural pluralism has been seen as a social theory for intergroup relationships.[236] In the broad sense, the maintenance of cultural pluralism has been thought to be crucial for group identification.[237] The target population is each group with the intent to diminish the power of any one group. Separatism or assimilation were not desirable. The melting pot notion has not been possible. Schools ought to assist in maintaining diversity. Methods proposed for programs augment the pitfalls of assimilation and pay close attention to the role of minority decision making. Decision making was seen as both a learning tool and a motivation for "academic success." The "majority" or dominant group was viewed as the prime target for change to value cultural pluralism.[238]

Bicultural Education Mode

These options were usually linked to bilingual education previously described. The major goal was to develop persons capable of effective functioning in two different cultures. Educational justice and opportunities were seen as an outcome in the understanding of one's heritage, for self-identity while lessening prejudice. The variations were numerous, as already indicated, although there was general agreement as to the benefits for functioning in two cultures.

Margaret Gibson's analysis of multicultural education approaches showed confusing concepts, ". . . and bound with untested and sometimes unsupportable assumptions regarding goals, strategies, and outcomes."[239] She suggested that the different multicultural education models confused schooling with educational processes. Education mostly occurs outside the classroom. All modes were concerned with social justice; however, except for the education for cultural pluralism, the tendency had been to ignore the larger society and political environment of conventional institutions. Gibson introduced an approach she called "Multicultural Education as the Normal Human Experience."[240] It was based on Ward H. Goodenough's work.[241] Goodenough showed how individuals in all societies each have multicultural experiences. Gibson used this basis and concepts from education and anthropology.

> We may now define multi-cultural education as the process whereby a person develops competencies in multiple systems of standards for perceiving, evaluating, believing and doing.[242]

Here the educator was not expected to assist the child in gaining "cultural competence" but needed to take into account the relationship between what goes on in school in the formal and informal sense and be cognizant of learning that occurred in the community. Culture, in this approach, was not equated with an ethnic group because individuals interacted in many settings where cross-cultural activities occurred. Some of those activities resulted from common interests and others related to different standards, but not of one particular ethnic group. This would result in promoting the understanding of similarities and differences of different ethnic groups. These objectives would facilitate constant interaction rather than separatism. "Which culture an individual will draw upon on any given occasion will be determined by the particular situation."[243] The probabilities were greater for decreasing the dichotomies between the mainstream and that of ethnic cultures.

... breakthroughs in biology have accelerated the prospects of genetic engineering and modern techniques of communication and persuasion leave one unaware of the erosion of free choice. Operant conditioning is hailed as a sometime saviour, and the vision of a salivating dog is but a distant memory. Technology is placing in the impersonal hands of monolithic government and its increasingly beholden servant, public education, such potential for the destruction of individuality that new forms of education and new protections for the rights of man must be developed without delay.[244]

Three-Pronged Components in the Theoretical Base

Introduction

The theoretical basis of this research was drawn from concepts within anthropology, particularly cultural relativity, social and political theory as conceptualized in cultural pluralism, and humanistic education. Cultural relativism postulated about the role of culture in the lives of human beings, the limitations, and characteristics of cultural change. Cultural pluralism dealt with the type of society in terms of structure and organization and the effects, expectations, and aspirations of differing ethnic cultural groups. And humanistic education provided the means through which education can be appropriate to divergent ethnic groups that make up a complex society. The theoretical model, which has as its foundation acceptance, was derived from the above components.

Cultural Relativity

Cultural relativity assumed that each culture is unique, and any element in a culture can only be interpreted within that given culture's context. Furthermore, that it is not possible to articulate any simple law regarding a "cultural human nature." Each culture had been characterized by relationships of a complex nature of interdependencies and relationships that were contingency referents and context dependent between the individual personality and varying cultural aspects. Even in the physical sciences, such as physics, scientists like Thomas Kuhn conceptualized that basic changes in the assumptions made about phenomena under investigation were either natural (objective) or arbitrary.[245] "In short, consciously or not the decision to employ a particular piece of apparatus and to use it in a particular way carried the assumption that only certain sorts of circumstances would arise."[246] He stated further that even if a tool existed, innovation evolved only for the individual who had precise knowledge of *what to expect.* "Anomaly appears only against the background provided by the paradigm."[247] His notion of "scientific paradigms" and the presuppositions made by scientists were culture-bound, a type of "cultural relativism of historical periods within the history of science."[248] Albert Einstein's "theory of relativity" advanced scientific thinking in the physical sciences, namely, that the universe was basically a matter-energy system. His theory challenged the traditional thought of the physical sciences, that there was an absolute space and an absolute time in which natural events moved. Instead, the hypothesis stated that space and time are attributed to particular events and that, in fact, they were forms of relationships between happenings.[249]

Cultural relativism drew attention to the bias of social scientists (and any other professional) whose ideas, values, and beliefs were an outgrowth of the culture into which that individual had been born. Therefore, the scientist could not be exempted by reason of objectivity. Among the world cultures, the fact remains that there are widely different belief systems coherent within their own particular contexts. The individual "culturally" inherited a pattern of covert assumptions as well as overt learnings about the world. The notions of classifications, categories, and meanings, in effect, influenced daily life interactions, thoughts, and world view. There has been a difference (variations) however, from how an individual may act within a specific culture and what is expected from the whole culture itself (sometimes called "deep culture").

> Cultural relativism, in all cases, must be sharply distinguished from concepts of the relativity of individual behavior, which would negate all social controls over conduct . . . The very core of cultural relativism is the social discipline that comes of respect of differences—mutual respect. Emphasis on the worth of many ways of life, not one, is an affirmation of the values in each culture. Such emphasis seeks to understand and to harmonize goals, not to judge and destroy those that do not dovetail with our own.[250]

This concept was equally applicable to any scientist or science and this dynamic understanding penetrated concepts when studying and interrelating with other cultures. In short, every individual is biased.

> But we certainly possess one of the most powerful ethnocentrisms in the experience of mankind . . . Even today, it

is difficult for us not to, what I term, "thinking colonially" by applying to peoples whose ways of life differ from our own dreary vocabulary of inferiority . . . Unless we realize that perhaps we do not have the only answers to questions of common concern, and that our own biases, though they seem natural enough to us, cannot be universally accepted, we will be in for some very difficult times.[251]

The ethnocentric biases can be articulated according to cultural relativism, when cultural manifestations were identified and descriptions were made so that judgments and conclusions were *always* within a comparative (whole culture) frame of reference. The ethnocentrism of scientists (and others) could be mediated through its recognition. For example, categories, labels, and "truths" are ideas that come from or are sparked by the enculturation process of a particular culture or society. That they are not universal or any more "natural" than any other invented cultural genus needs to be recognized and articulated. One culture did not make "mistakes" in conceptualization but reached its particular conclusions in terms of divergent referents.

The theory of cultural relativity clarified and brought attention to the critical nature of values, developed by a given group, for its members to live by. Anthropologists have not held that any one culture is superior to any other. The belief (on an unconscious and conscious level) that one's own culture is "better than" another culture had been recognized by theorists in the study of "other" cultures.

Ethnocentrism is salient and occurs universally. In short, no human being is so "objective" as to be exempt from these biases. The concept of ethnocentrism (bias being a part of it) serves a function related to self-identity that is culturally determined.

The implications of all the above characteristics in the theory of cultural relativity brought into focus the need to redefine "objectivity," which influences the scope and nature of decisions that are thought to be based on "external truths" as well as in the concept of the absolute. The controversy on projective, achievement, and I.Q. tests had been on this very issue. This writer also questioned the validity of *measurement* outcomes from educational endeavors as representative of either indicators of *capacity* or learnings. Redefinitions did not imply any less interest intended in the goals of seeking "scientific objectivity" as currently aimed. Nor did it imply any less interest in scientific progress. It did assume that the scientific foundations, especially in the human sciences (science of culture), needed to be reexamined for the delusional aspects of absolutism and "irrational" biased explanations. In the methodology of cultural relativity, the assumption was made that it is possible, under particular circumstances, to transcend one's own cultural conditioning and values to empathize the "subjective" ethnocentric frame of mind as an advocate and/or participant in a culture other than one's own. This of course required that the observer was open to the world view of the group being observed, while simultaneously collecting the data that was reflective of the specific ideological context.[252]

Cultural relativity was a means to examine the characteristics and the roles of values in a given society. In the consideration of cultural relativity as a theoretical construct for promoting pluralism, it was critical to distinguish the concept of "absolute" from the concept of "universal." Absolute implied that identified phenomena were constant, having an existence outside the realm of custom and thought whether natural (consisting outside of human perception) or social (human invention). This thought conveyed that variation did not exist. The most obvious example was in the concept of "God," that is, "He" existed in a particular time and space regardless of how it ("she," "they") may be conceived by different cultures. Morality or any set of norms believed to be fixed, constant, in time and space was another common example of an "absolute" value. Universals were those common phenomena drawn from the extent of variables found in all cultures or in the natural environment. For example, aesthetic standards, morality, and the concept of family and kinship were universal factors; however, each factor continues to be differentiated in form and is influenced by the particular experiences and inventions of a society.[253]

Major components in the theory of cultural relativism were: values (judgments derived from the enculteration process and are not fixed), reality (understood through the particular culture's symbolism, and, therefore, its ideology sets the stage for all behavior), ethnocentrism (the myths, linguistic expressions, and social norms in which people center their views, that is, to judge according to one's own cultural standards and conditioned perceptions; two forms of ethnocentrism are "bias" and "colonialism"), communication (to impart common meanings that are framed by and within the limitations of the group's sanctioned beliefs and behavior), manipulation and control (dependent on the scope of variability in the natural and social behavior patterns in which a given culture is engaged), and the dynamics of change (related to the degree of variability, flexibility, and diffision characteristic of a culture).

Cultural Pluralism

The myth of a "national character," based on assimilationist criteria, began to explode with the events that led up to and included the rise of the civil rights movement and the "Great Society Programs."* Part of this awakening included the demand for a different perception of the concept of "cultural pluralism."[254] Especially influential and giving impetus to this shift was the pervasive racism in America acknowledged by the Report of the National Advisory Commission on Civil Disorders.[255] Heated debates accompanied issues such as desegregation, housing, unemployment, low achievement and I.Q.

*"The War on Poverty," the vernacular for the strategies that were developed stemming from the Economic Opportunity Act of 1964 legislation, which established the Office of Economic Opportunity to implement a variety of programs to attack "poverty."

scores, "culturally disadvantaged," and the concomitant "intervention strategies" for remediation in education of the poor (usually "minority groups").[256] These events were followed by confrontations with public educational institutions about their responsibility to face up to the rhetoric of representing a "democratic" institution. The Supreme Court decision in the *Brown v. Board of Education* case brought attention to the inequality of education of black children. The courts required that school desegregation be instituted based on the assumption that the dual educational system was damaging to the achievement of black children.[257]

William Newman, in his book about group conflicts, stressed the opposing conclusion in the United States on the nature of intergroup relationships and urged social scientists to reshape theories within the total sociological context. He wanted them to deemphasize the concentration on an individual ethnic group.[258] The problem of definition also became conspicuous when social problems were explained without reference to specific relationships to all the events in time and place. Definition is a variable in the historical sense. The term "minority group," for example, two decades ago referred to the Jews, Poles, Irish, and other immigrants. "Equality" was another term in which there had been little agreement in definition, especially when terms such as social class, political power, prejudice, discrimination, and other relational conceptualizations were raised within limited boundaries.[259] Frequently, there have not been distinctions made among the different social phenomena such as when living in a pluralistic society "minority groups" were continually confronted and wedged between identification as members of the larger society and their allegiance and identification as members of a unique group. This ongoing coping with "many realities" accounted for different group interpretations of what it meant to be a member of a given group, especially when "majority," "minority" perceptions conflict.

Although not carved in concrete, and recognizing that further explorations were necessary, a working definition for "cultural pluralism" came out of the Conference on Education and Teacher Education for Cultural Pluralism.

> A state of equal co-existence in a mutually supportive relationship within the boundaries or framework of one nation of people of diverse cultures with significantly different patterns of belief, behavior, color, and in many cases different languages. To achieve cultural pluralism, there must be unity with diversity. Each person must be aware of and secure in his own identity and be willing to extend to others the same respect and rights that he expects to enjoy himself.[260]

Basically, the dilemma of living in a multicultural society in which there are contiguous relationships with different values, behaviors, and beliefs from divergent ethnic groups either directly or indirectly has led to intergroup conflict, as had been previously pointed out, especially when those groups that were considered the "minority" became aware of the institutional inequities. However, diversity of cultures within a society could also be thought of as an asset.[261] Reexamining the "melting pot" version of assimilationist ideology provided the challenge for reform.[262]

The disparity between the democratic ideology and democratic practice in which selected ethnic groups were economically and politically exploited, rejected, and neglected served as the setting to establish indigenous social institutions within community enclaves. With varying degrees of success, power bases for certain services developed in regions, colloquially referred to as Little Italy, Greektown, Germantown, Little Lithuania, Little Warsaw, Jewtown, and many other national groups in a "we take care of our own" attitude. This resulted in a specialized meaning of the word "nationality." The terms were adapted to the subculture of the immigrants and their subnationalities within the larger society of the United States. In a sense, the de facto cultural pluralism had been in reaction to exclusionism practiced by the dominant group. The revival of the concept and renewed conceptualization of cultural pluralism,

> ... would include different cultural groups existing in the same society while maintaining their cultural identity; having mechanisms for easy interaction with one another and equal opportunity of access to the institutions of that society; as well as equal opportunity for participation in the formation of the values which regulate that society.[263]

It was the sociopolitical theory that encompassed redefining American democratic ideologies such as "cultural democracy," "equality," "opportunity," and society's attempt to redress the unequal practices of the "current minority" groups (through federal and state legislation and litigation).[264] Cultural pluralism as a concept, provided the means to understand ethnocentric attitudes and perceptions of ethnic groups and to relate positively to different groups, social race, and social-class groups. The theory maintained that ethnic identification was essential for the individual's self-identity, commitment to the group in which one has been reared, and especially for those groups that have experienced oppression.[265] This sociological theory was consistent with the anthropological postulate instrumental to this study.

James Banks delineated three ideologies related to pluralistic and assimilationistic ideas in ethnic relations; the cultural pluralist, the pluralist-assimilationist, and the assimilation ideology. He promoted the pluralist-assimilationist view.[266]

> The pluralist-assimilationist assumes that while the ethnic group and the ethnic community are very important in the socialization of individuals, individuals are strongly influenced by the common culture during their early socialization, even if they never leave the ethnic community ... while ethnic groups have some unique cultural characteristics, all groups in America share many cultural traits.[267]

The dichotomy, yet to be resolved within the contemporary thinking of cultural pluralism, was the schism between the so-called "minority groups" of today (black-American, Hispanic-American, Native American) and the other "blue collar" ethnic Americans. The polarization during the early black struggle focused on black-white emotionally laden confrontations. The tendency to stereotype groups, while ignoring the wide range of differences among the black population and nonwhite groups, was not only confusing but perpetuated hostilities. It further clouded understanding that touched on intercultural relations and economic class issues. The fragmentation and power struggle over ethnic issues would continue until the question of ethnic diversity was valued and the means found for acceptance and respect for every cultural group, coupled with letting go of the desire of some groups to dominate others. John Hodge, Donald Struckmann, and Lynn Trost's poignant book carefully traced the historical origins of the basic assumptions in the ideologies and social institutions in "Western culture."[268] The point was made that certain kinds of oppression, through their tacit features, values, and beliefs, were actively promoted.

That the people of a culture should view themselves as culturally superior is certainly common. But not so common is the feature contained in Western cultural thinking that the superior should control the inferior. It is this kind of thinking, which emphasizes the value placed on control, that produces a missionary imperialism. The notion of "white man's burden" is also derived from this type of thinking. Western control over non-western peoples is thereby often considered morally defensible. Although racism and sexism are examples of oppression which exist in many other countries, these kinds of oppression are not universal, and are not necessarily features of human life.[269]

The uniform unvaried structure which produced the dichotomy was an implied dualism. The notion of ethnocentrism, as was shown in cultural relativity theory, is universal. The idea of superiority came out of the belief that the uneducated "primitive" thinking is a stage of development moving toward a stage of "civilization" and reflected ethnocentrism. This attitude provided the rationale to "control" those who were considered to be "inferior" (primitive or disadvantaged). One dominating group (either missionaries or compensatory programs) manipulated (controlled) the other group because it was thought to benefit "them" in some way. This thinking had been thought to be "reasonable" since it had been thought to be in the "nature" of the individual (all human beings) to want the "best" (from those who have "it"). The dualistic properties in the above examples are described as an "either/or mentality"—either "civilized" or "primitive," good or bad to be educated in a specific way, and so forth. Institutions in this society have been structured around values of good or bad, realistic or unrealistic, black or white, in the way that its institutions are structured.

"Either/or" thinking occurred throughout Western thinking such as evil *or* good, inferior *or* superior, right *or* wrong—the value placed on a hierarchial scale. However, it is also possible to perceive in terms of equal value *but different* in nature (culture). What was needed, then, was a society that advocated and valued this concept. The point about "human nature" could be put to rest since behavior of human beings could not be isolated from culture, as was pointed out in the discussion earlier on the difference between universal phenomena and the concept of the absolute.

Thus, it was held that the validity of theories that began with an either-or ethnocentric assumption was both empirically and "logically" fallacious. Recent studies had shown how these opposing views were acted out through "double messages," "hidden curricula," or covert and biased attitudes that influenced schooling outcomes.[270] These were important data regarding the dualistic views that permeated the American (national) society. In short, cultural pluralistic theory postulated that different but equal roles and diversity within unity would lead to harmonious infra-, inter-, intra-group relations.

Humanistic Education

Education in a modern complex society created social institutions which formalized the transmission of cultural patterns. Education and schooling had been used as synonymous terms, but they differed in meaning. While education, in its broadest function, is a part of the individual's enculturation, the means through which it is carried out needs to be distinguished. Education is that learning process in the enculturation of an individual to become a participating member of a given society. It continues throughout one's life. Schooling refers to both the teaching and learning experiences that take place outside the home for a designated time by people who are specifically trained for particular tasks.[271] Education borrows and uses concepts from the variety of disciplines in the human sciences, but especially from philosophy, biology, sociology, psychology, and anthropology.

As philosophy, contemporary humanism is multidimensional, representing the view of humankind's relation to the universe. Nature has been seen as the all-embracing, constantly changing structure of matter and energy that existed independent of any other "mind," "being," or consciousness extracted from scientific laws. *Naturalistic* humanism postulated that the unearthing of any phenomena was the result of natural laws and not due to "supernatural" occurrences. Humanism maintained that the human potential for problem solving occurred through reason, scientific understanding, and creative choice in concert with the individual's capacity for imagination. This process occurred through synthesizing elements in personal development toward the goals of personal satisfactions while contributing to the well-being of the social group. These two critical aspects were particularly emphasized; the one, involved in the dynamics of personal growth, and the other, in the role that social consciousness played in the life of a person to the group. To appreciate humanistic thought, it was necessary to understand the essential place that human values have and how they are carried out through ethical systems developed within democratic procedures.[272] They were applicable to all cultural groups.

For the purpose of this study, a distinction was made between the different philosophical attempts to synthesize an integrated understanding of the universe, of human nature, of society, and the particular values that were promoted for humankind and that of "naturalistic" humanism.

> . . . in its most accurate philosophical sense, implies a worldview in which there is no supernatural and in which man is an integral part of Nature and not separated from it by any sharp cleavage or discontinuity. This philosophy, of course, recognizes that vast stretches of reality yet remain beyond the range of human knowledge, but it takes for granted that all future discoveries of truth will reveal an extension of the *natural* and not altogether different realm of being commonly referred to as *the* supernatural.[273]

The social psychologist Eric Fromm, in his disagreement with Sigmund Freud, represented the thinking of the humanistic psychoanalytical school. In Fromm's view, there was a fundamental dynamic relationship of the individual with society that was separate and distinct from instinctual satisfaction or frustration.

> The most beautiful as well as the most ugly inclinations of man are not part of a fixed and biologically given human nature, but result from the social process which creates man.[274]

Fromm further hypothesized that the individual also developed a "social character" that was derived from a given group's common experiences. The individual's "character" is developed as a result of the contact with his or her culture in accord with such factors as physical constitution and temperament.

The parents and their methods of child training in turn are determined by the social structure of their culture. The average family is the "psychic agency" of society, and by adjusting himself to his family the child acquires the character which later makes him adjusted to the tasks he has to perform in social life . . . The fact that most members of a social class or culture share significant elements of character and that one can speak of a "social character" representing the core of a character common to most people of a given culture shows the degree to which character is formed by social and cultural patterns.[275]

Humanistic psychology dramatized the concept of the "basic needs" of the organism. These needs emanated from the drive for survival. As part of the notion of "existence," the human being had the need for a sense of relatedness (through the concept of "love"), transcendence including creativity, a sense of causation or origin including comradeship, a feeling of identity and individuality, and the need for a context, that is, for a way to express allegiance.[276] Humanist psychological theory viewed the person from a holistic view, which differed from both the psychoanalytic and behavioral approaches. As a whole, the individual is seen as having choices formulating purposes and goals for which one strives to attain. This notion was in contrast to the structural approach, which studied the human organism by categorical parts seeking homeostatic mechanisms.[277] Thus, behaviorism saw the organism as building and reducing tension, which drives toward gratification, throwing out all elements related to consciousness and mental state. The human being attempts to maintain homeostasis, that is, an inner balance. The person, according to the humanistic psychology, was much more than a balance machine. The series of actions in the search for goals themselves created tension, which, in turn, promoted consequences on processes such as planning, organizing, and testing choices. All aspects influenced the accomplishment of desirable goals.

The concentration on process and not on structure provided the approach to comprehend the dynamic nature of humanity in all its complexity—as an aspiring individual and as a social being. The humanist's approach to the nature of the human being as proactive (as well as reactive) postulated that the person's identity was formed *by all* of the cumulative experiences of a given culture. It recognized the embeddedness of alternatives, goal formulation, creativity, and the attempts for potential fulfillment as basic in the development of the human beings.[278]

Humanistic education assumed that teaching/learning events were primarily a relationship between the teacher and the learner. It assumed that human behavior, human meanings, and human understandings developed from variables unparalleled in human experience. Thus, feelings and perceptions were equal in importance to thinking and attaining knowledge.[279] It assumed that "realness" and "authenticity" were basic concepts to education. This view goes beyond the thought that attitudes "influenced" the facilitation of learning. The "teacher" as person as well as in the role must also be "real" to enable meaningful learnings, "being what he is, entering into a relationship with the learner without presenting a front or facade . . ."[280] In humanistic education theory, factors inherent in the "being real" aspect related to the teacher's attitude which, in turn, included concepts of acceptance, trust, empathy, and valuing the learner's own experience congruent with those actions resulting in the affirmation of alternatives. Abraham Maslow's self-actualization concept placed the human organism in relation to the setting in an active role by making choices within the boundaries that were understood by the individual.[281] This proactive determinant of human development allowed the individual to understand the environment to be governed by that understanding and communicated this to other members.

Schooling, as was shown earlier, is the formalized mechanism for transmitting the meanings of a "national culture" in the United States. For at least half a century, the increasing division among opposing forces in both education theory and practice had been developing and influenced the current trends in schooling customs. The steps taken in the 1920s when business values were applied to education, euphemistically referred to as "scientific education," emphasizing economy, efficiency, productivity, and management.[282] These are still considered the basic criteria for a "good" educational system.[283] The "scientific education movement" focused on specific content areas, basic minimums, and the dependence on normative testing. This approach was diametrically in opposition to humanistic education that was advanced during the short-lived "progressive era" that came into much criticism after Russia launched Sputnik.[284] The successful space venture resulted in the reaction and reawakening of the competitive temper of Americans in the race for superiority in the technology of outer space. This event was seen as a threat to national security. Public schools reflected the shift to the concentration on subjects such as mathematics and science, while devaluing the "arts" and humanities in cost effective budgets.[285] The limited definition of "education" as an intense subject-content interest plus the narrow view of behavioral educational objectives thrust of the 1960s, inspired by poor and "minority groups" school "failures," came into ideological contention with the ethical humanistic education views and the need for relevance for all ethnic groups in the United States.

A discrepancy exists between subject matter and behavior because the behavioral objectives of education have become submerged, if not obliterated, by narrow subject-matter objectives, which include nothing about the student's behavior and his relations with others . . . In most schools today, curriculum is based more on the requirement of the various subject disciplines than on their needs.[286]

Humanistic education theory supported the total spectrum, the process as well as content in learning. It was particularly concerned with the quality of the "environment," that is, experiences and interactions between the learner, the learning events, and those in control of them. Humanistic education recognized the critical power exerted by the interrelated, interacting aspects of ideas, people, and things as "emergent" recriprocal phenomena and processes. All of these determined the definition of the "environment," thus the holistic view. This epistemological principle prohibited predescribed, premeditated, predesigned experiences. The implications for practical application in humanistic education were in the organization of the multifaceted and diverse preferences for options that supported the humanistic-existential dimension displayed by the variables in humankind.

Modern education must produce far more than persons with cognitive skills. It must produce humane individuals, persons who can be relied upon to pull their own weight in our society . . . to behave responsibly and cooperatively. We need good citizens, free of prejudice, concerned, loving, caring fathers and mothers, persons of good will whose values and purposes are positive, feeling persons with wants and desires likely to motivate them toward positive interactions. These are the things that make us human . . . We can live with a bad reader; a bigot is a danger to everyone.[287]

Summary

The literature review raised concepts and identified some of the universal phenomena that occur in all human beings and in all cultures as a basis for developing the means to value diversity in education in the United States. It took into account particular circumstances and beliefs on which American values are based. Stimulated at first by demands from minority groups for educational equity, then later from the "new pluralists," federal, and state laws were passed that cover a myriad of concepts, views, goals, and expected outcomes. It was evident from a review of the literature that there has been little coherent recognition or comprehensive insight into the complex issues raised by this research. Formal education has been much too narrow in scope for the changing perceptions of these times. Also, emerging from the literature was the dearth of systematic attempts in multicultural education, the lack of a demarcation of issues and concepts, ideological views, a solid philosophical cultural foundation, the ambiguity of program goals, and a tendency to predetermine outcomes. The disposition of educational systems to standardize goals and objectives, often unrelated to many of the ethnic groups, pointed out the inflexible dimension of educational institutions. Schools still tend to base their programs on limited knowledge and do not have viable mechanisms to internalize the scientific information accepted in cultural anthropology today. It further suggested that public institutions were either unable or unwilling to abstract cultural implications and assumptions inferred by the theory of cultural relativism. That there is little agreement as to methods and goals in multicultural education was predictable, even understandable, due to political ramifications and a general resistance to change. Furthermore, enigmatic points appeared to stem from the perplexing issues that confused formalized schooling with the broad concept of education and with that of "culture" that derived from ethnic identification. Other serious concerns became evident related to discrepancies among educational policy, pressures for change, and the general public's ignorance about the anthropological conceptualizations of "culture," thus affecting formal schooling. The ambiguities that also surfaced when examining structural mechanisms (schools), cultural ideologies (democracy), and practices (the either-or mentality of the inferiority syndrome), denoted an absence of a systematic cultural referent to permeate educational foundations and developmental theory.

The major task indicated was to work out a *new* "discipline" that encompassed the art of, science of, and the philosophy of ... the process and the content for an education for cultural pluralism within the multicultural framework of the

United States. This study offered the theoretical model that could assist in developing "culture sense" while providing the criteria to combine knowledge with tonal feeling in such a way as to make it possible to impart the suggested ideology through simple means. What seemed imperative was that the common person on the street be able to carry the values and attitudes that accepted and respected differences without negative judgments, that is, moralizing about the inferiority of ethnic groups other than one's own. The role and knowledge of the "specialist" had to be translated simply so that the individual citizen could be comfortable with the advocated generic concepts. Culture is inevitable; therefore, it could be judged to be "good." Acquisition of cultural traits had not been seen as a smooth, painless process. Neither had any change, whether limited or radical. Safeguards could be built into a system through rearing and educational alternatives. When tension, conflict, and struggle existed during the socialization processes in childhood, they could be understood; they could be facilitated through positive methods by appreciating those elements consistent with individual cultural styles. Likewise, it was also seen as possible to change the dominant ideology and schooling system to one that valued diversity. This study suggested that it was not necessary to denigrate the customs of cultures that are different from one's individual personal experiences. Choices have to be made, to be sure, but processes could be developed to meet these needs. Culture has been satisfying, so why continue to ignore it? All cultures have had something to contribute to the knowledge of humanity. Each could be recognized for its unique intrinsic worth, especially in an environment in which each could contribute to the total acceptance scheme. The past had been ever present in current events and belief systems contributed to the future events. Cultures adapted, adjusted, and integrated their members, so why not utilize this information for educational purposes? In every culture, humans behaved in a variety of ways. Education for everyone (through schooling) would offer those alternatives and value them rather than produce "guilt" for not conforming to one dominant mode or to act (and react) in the limited ways to events and feelings about others. In the dynamics of culture, anthropologists agreed, for example, that latent beliefs and covert behavior exist. This was considered to be useful information. The variety of experiences could be a delight.

Culture communicates through a variety of symbols. Symbols needed to be placed in relationship to the goals of a particular culture as well as to the larger group. We have acquired knowledge about the role of the individual in a culture. A person's mental health has been at stake when "education" devalued the cultural aspects of a given group, so why continue to do that through existing perceptions, ideology, and structures? Potentially, Americans are educable! Despite the discomfort, interruptions, or embarrassment, the need for massive changes to accommodate the diversity of peoples ought to be made. Human beings are thought to be capable of defining a variety of states and conditions as "real"; thus, the consequences of those situations were also "real." The response to others, as Jean-Paul Sartre observed, is subtle and highly complex and at the heart of humankind's existential puzzle.

If it is agreed that man may be defined as a being having freedom within the limits of a situation, then it is easy to see that the exercise of this freedom may be considered as *authentic* or *inauthentic* according to the choice, made in the situation. Authenticity, it is almost needless to say, consists in having a true and lucid consciousness of the situation, in assuming the responsibilities and risks that it involves, in accepting it in pride or humiliation, sometimes in horror and hate.

There is no doubt that authenticity demands much courage. Thus, it is not surprising that one finds it so rarely.[288]

Chapter IV

The Theoretical Model

Prelude

Metaphor: Expletive Recap

No educational process is without bias, unprejudiced, indiffer-
ent, or without qualification. Education is either a means used
to socialize children in a selected system of values or to indoctrinate people to conform to a particular rationale. It becomes
a means for self-discovery and a rehearsal for how to deal with
the world. The central concern, the core issue for humankind,
is "humanization."[289] That process is carried out only by the
individual who is allowed to transform the environment, and
by this process alone, the individual moves on to other possi-
bilities. This occurs on an individual and on a collective level.
It creates a satisfying life. The world is dynamic within a given
"reality" in which the problems of life need to be solved. While
it is within the possibility for technology to provide solutions,
technology does not exist alone, absolute, or outside the value
systems of a culture.

Politics is, inherently, only an accessory after the fact of the
design-science revolution. Despite this historically demon-
strable fact, world society as yet persists in looking exclu-

121

sively to its politicians and their ideologies for world problem solving.[290]

Buckminster Fuller maintained that it was possible to be liberated from inequities by concentrating on the environment and leaving human beings to be who they are—energy should go into the science of the physical environment and not into "changing people." The Club of Rome "Project on the Predicament of Mankind" had concluded, also, that it was possible to establish favorable conditions to meet the needs of every individual on earth if the world decided to strive for it.[291]

Victimization

For the sake of emphasis and further conceptual clarity within the synergistic context, the education problem components raised in this research could be analyzed through a paradigm of the concept "victimization." The victim being someone who is not only the target for change but is seen as the cause of the "problem." The metaphor utilizes Paulo Freire's and William Ryan's works on oppressed peoples and victimization, respectively.

Ryan described the ideological setting and the necessary elements for "blaming the victim."

In the sense that Karl Mannheim used the term, an ideology develops from the "collective unconscious" of a group or class and is rooted in a class-based interest in maintaining the *status quo* (as contrasted with what he calls *utopia*, a set of ideas rooted in a class-based interest in changing the *status quo*). An ideology, then has several components: First there is the Belief system itself, the way of looking at the world, the set of ideas and concepts. Second, there is the systematic distortion of reality reflected in those ideas. Third is the condition that the distortion must not be a conscious intentional process. Finally, though they are not intentional, the ideas must serve a specific function, the *status quo* in the interest of a specific group. *Blaming the Victim* fits this definition on all counts . . .[292]

To recognize the concept of humanization was to realize that "dehumanization" is not only an ontological possibility, but also a historical reality.[293] These related concepts presupposed that there are those who act and that there are those that are acted upon. In political terms, there are the oppressors and those who are oppressed. In educational terms, the metaphor could be sketched thus: the dominant group sets the tone, criteria, and performance standards and develops the pattern for judging the criteria and performance of the nondominant groups' behaviors. Dominant ways equal success (as judged by performance, accomplishments, kinds of goals, that is, test scores, speaking standard English, "good" self-image, nuclear families, holds onto jobs, and so on), and the nondominant equals failure (as judged by dominant standards), discipline problems, nondominant behavior patterns, lack of accomplishments and goals, low I.Q. scores, nonstandard English (or a language other than English being spoken), "poor" self-image, "disorganized" nonnuclear families, unemployed, uneducated, and so on.

Both Freire and Ryan provided a paradigm that paralleled actions and consequences. Freire postulated that "dehumanization" was the process by which the oppressor takes away the "humanity" from the oppressed. However, it was seen as a two-way street. It (dehumanization) became a historical distortion, but the oppressor cannot admit to stealing from the "vocation of becoming more fully human." To admit to being responsible for dehumanization would lead to "cynicism or total despair." The struggle for humanization is meaningless; therefore, the struggle took on a more practical air—"an unjust order." The oppressed eventually struggled against those who had "stolen" their "humanization" because it would be a distortion of being fully human.[294] Those who had the power are incapable of freeing themselves or the oppressed from oppressing acts and must continue to be unjust. Freire believed that only the oppressed had the power to free both.[295] The process or the struggle of the oppressed, however, goes through certain stages. At first, instead of attempting to become free of that oppression, they themselves fall prey to becoming oppressors or "sub-oppressors." In a sense, they follow the mode of the oppressor. The ideals of the oppressors become the valued goals to prove their worth. Their perception of what is happening had been "impaired" by their submersion in the reality of oppression. At this initial stage, there would be no confrontation with the contradiction.[296] They "fear freedom."

> One of the basic elements of the relationship between oppressor and oppressed is prescription. Every prescription represents the imposition of one man's choice upon another, transforming the consciousness of the man prescribed to into one that conforms with the prescriber's consciousness. Thus, the behavior of the oppressed is a prescribed behavior, following as it does the guidelines of the oppressor.
>
> As the oppressed, having *internalized* the image of the oppressor and adopted his guidelines, are fearful of freedom . . . Freedom acquired by conquest, not by gift [emphasis added].[297]

When the oppressed, who had become resigned, realized they wanted to be free, they were afflicted with the "duality" of not being authentic and fearing freedom. The principles spelled out in *Pedagogy of the Oppressed* as a model for "liberation" were contingent upon the oppressed realizing that they played an active role in participating in the oppressor's goals.

> As long as they live in the duality in which *to be* is *to be like* and *to be like* is *to be like the oppressor*, this contribution is impossible. The pedagogy of the oppressed is an instrument of the critical discovery that both they and their oppressors are manifestations of dehumanization.[298]

Ryan's paradigm appeared to be more directly related to some of the specific issues of this study because of his involvement in the civil rights and War on Poverty activities. He provided important insights and observations too hard to ignore.

Victim blaming is oblique and "is cloaked in kindness and concern and bears all the trappings and statistical furbelows of scientism; it is obscured by a perfumed haze of humanitarianism."[299] The causes of social problems were still to be found within the people themselves, only the explanation became the environment in which certain communities lived rather than genetics, although "inferior" or "defective" hereditary theories still persisted. While this ideology ascribed the deficits to the inheritable characteristics of poverty, ghettoes, social injustice, prejudice, and racial discrimination, the defects could still be found within the victim and not in the structure of society.[300] In Freire's terms, the oppressor would denounce the social and economic living conditions but *ignore* social influences and concentrate on changing, not those forces but the oppressor. Ryan was less harsh in terminology, emphasizing the subtlety of the concept. The rationality of the victimization was seen as a reasonable premise to the liberals, especially if solutions were attempted in a sympathetic, philanthropic, and intellectual manner.

> First identify a social problem. Second study those affected by the problem and discover in what ways they are different from the rest of us as a consequence of deprivation and injustice. Third define the difference as the *causes* of the social problem itself. Finally, of course, assign a government bureaucrat to *invent* a humanitarian action program to correct the difference [emphasis added].[301]

In other words, to focus on the individual who was affected by poverty (or race or some other "problematic attribute") shifted the responsibility away from the "in-group" (those in control). Ryan's views were based on a concept of "universalism." He offered his "exceptionalism-universalism" concepts and two approaches for analysis and the means for solving social problems.[302] The exceptionalist saw social problems in conditions that were "private, voluntary, remedial, special, local, and exclusive," the implication being that certain categories of people had certain problems and those problems were seen as special and thought of as the exception to the rule. A number of explanations and remedies were provided, tailored to the group (prescriptions). Implied in the universalistic outlook was the assumption that special problems were a *function* of community conditions (or society) and that these conditions could be understood, were predictable, and solvable. The particular circumstances through which they occurred were through "public" legislated, promotive or preventive, general, national, and inclusive means. Ryan did not go into the individual role in which the victim assumed the "dominant" model in the same way that Freire posed; however, he did relate to how "being poor" is *learned,* and he implied that the various effects of poverty on the poor, their perceptions, and aspirations, as victims, influenced their role on the way out of poverty. Perhaps the differences in this area were due to cultural differences of each author's style and historical circumstances. Both suggested that the *power* of freedom of the *oppressed* or *victim* was central to the issues of liberation.

The Universal Culture Affective Theoretical Model

Communication is culture, and culture is communication. Learning is culture, and culture is learning. Communication as mediated through the cultural process is a complex uninterrupted continuity comprising numerous verbal and nonverbal contingencies. It is implicit in the Universal Culture Affective Theoretical Model (UCAM). The UCAM is based on the premise that the foundation of education is to transmit knowledge, values (material, rights, privileges, status), and recognized methods for access to them. It is, thus, deemed proper that such institutionalized structures, the schools, approve and take advantage of multicultural repertoires. Also, because the schools represent the core priorities and values of the society, it is charged with familiarizing learners with acceptable and appropriate behaviors and relationships of the society. It provides the systematic means for enculturation.

Four major components or classifications have been delineated to make up the model solely for the purpose of description for articulation and understanding. None of the components can ever be entirely isolated from the others.

Each leads, interrelates, and overlaps into each other, to further subcomponents in reciprocal eventualities, resulting in holistic channels. Human beings have the tendency to categorize things whether material or abstract; accordingly, the components render the UCAM comprehensible. However, the reader is advised that it is that whole, the complete synthesis, that permeates all the processes, events, values, and actions portrayed in life, which cannot be separated. It is that quality symbolizing the values, beliefs, and acts that the members of a given culture can be conditioned to fulfill.

UCAM is a theory for integrating culture knowledge, sensitivity to, and the recognition of different social realities and for authentically valuing diversity. It combines culture-context, sets the tone and mood for devaluing the superiority-inferiority dichotomy through a humanistic relativistic approach.

The UCAM theory maintains that culture determines the individual and individuals determine culture through intimate relationships with the natural and invented phenomena. From these relationships, diversity is generated originating from environmental and historical variables without qualitative differentiation among sociocultural groups. In short, one ethnic group is no better than another. It must be emphasized that the primary axiomatic concept in UCAM is universalism. All cultures have certain features that are categorically in common no matter how simple or complex a culture's structure may be.

The blends, flows, and interrelatedness of the conceptual data represented in UCAM is crucial to the theory for application to any formal and informal educational process or content. To leave out or prioritize the components is to realize that desired effects have been violated. The UCAM maxims, principles, and postulates can also be used as criteria for educational methods and content. The components cover process and content focusing on valuation. The diagram that follows illustrates the theoretical model.

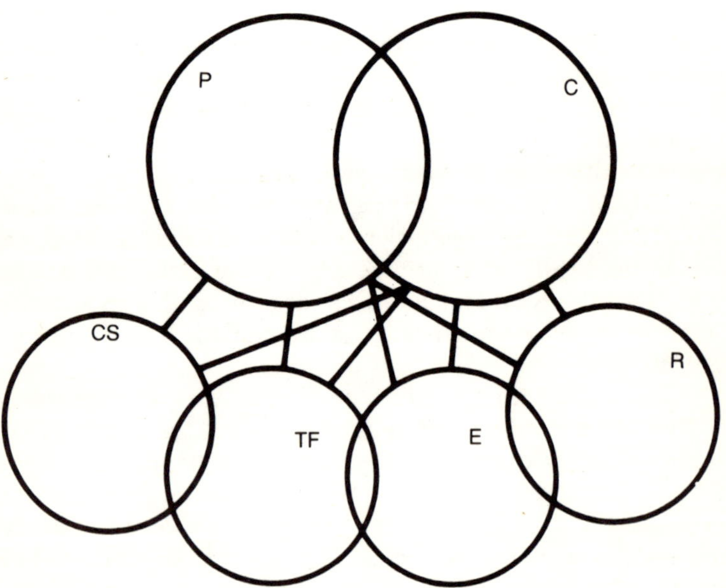

Figure 1. UCAM components (theoretical model). Key to abbreviations: P = Process, C = Content, CS = Culture Sense, TF = Tonal Feeling, E = Environment, and R = Relativity.

Basic Components Defined

Culture Sense

Culture sense is the knowledge and cognitive internalization of culture dynamics, cultural process, and cultural content as both taxonomy in the universals and variables. The categories that exist in all cultures are the universals. How cultures adapt to those universals, the natural and political environment, how a given culture creates its own perceptions, symbols, formulates its own world view, its practices, are the variables. Culture sense also encompasses classifications and theories about learning itself, the nature and relationships of facts, concepts, generalizations, theory, and decision-making processes and the like.

Tonal Feeling

Tonal feeling is the state of mind or mood that involves a mental attitude, posture, outlook, and caring emotions. The allegiance to a concept is demonstrated through an affection for, or a predisposition to, or being passionately involved with, or having the sensibility to, an ideal or standard. These various emotional states cover tonal feeling. It is a psychological imperative.

Environment

Environment is manifested through cultural pluralism as the cultural reality of complex industrial societies. Cultural pluralism both orders the universe and determines its interactions for all its members. The attainment of social competence to move comfortably in many cultural worlds is seen as both spontaneous within a given culture and essential for effective membership in the larger society. The culturally pluralistic context imposes the recognition and valuing of diversity as the negotiating factor for a harmonious (whole) society. In short, multiplicity is the norm.

Relativity

Relativity is the utilization of the impelling force of humanistic principles as the penetrating theory within a comparative system that influences equitable and impartial behavior. The dynamics of personal growth and development, plus the role that social consciousness has to the group within a given cultural milieu, are central to relativity. The practice of acceptance and respect without moral judgment serves as the axiom to parallel acceptance and respect for different ethnic and other social groups. The concept of comparative or relativistic determinism is viewed as a social imperative in education. It includes early socialization, formal schooling, and later adult encounters.

To summarize, culture sense symbolizes the knowledge-base or content but cannot be separated from the tonal feelings, the environment in which an activity occurs, or the way in which one practices a belief based on a value system. These undulating interrelationships are equally applicable to conditional humanistic approaches described in the relativity component. It is not possible to take an amiable, considerate stance without cognizance of culture content, specific processes, the environment, the context, or the tonal feelings of a given culture. Inferred in all the UCAM components is the concept of "human values" and its place for individual self-esteem as well as for cultural identification. It is crucial to realize *and* accept the value concept as the nexus of all behavior patterns and belief systems regardless of origin. All cultures develop values and value systems. The concept "value" (what a group holds to be true), more than any other concept, is the intervening variable that unites and integrates diverse interests in the behaviors of human beings in a culture. Although cultures are defined as being constant and persistent, the human capacity for fancy, imagination, and playfulness is a function of viewing unique rearrangements and novel solutions to old problems.

Organization and Relationships:
Maxims in the Universal Culture Affective Model*

Maxim 1

The nature of a sociocultural system can be understood by its structure and by its particular orientation to the world through knowing the conditions under which it operates, the kind of relationship between it and the particular environment, the characteristics of the environment, and the people in it.

Maxim 2

Cultural traits and traditions represent the communication among people, about the general nature of things, under what conditions, and what can be done about them.

Maxim 3

The need for order is strong in human beings, and the attempts to organize ideas are accomplished through classifying natural and cultural phenomena.

Maxim 4

Culture is a continuum (process) with parts (categories of

*Maxims serve as organization and analytical factors of the system.

content) merging into each other without definite breaks. The universal classifications within a culture give structure to human functioning in all environments.*

Maxim 5

Cultural content is a reserve of beliefs, knowledge, and behavior shared by members of a sociocultural group. They are the traits and traditions in each of the classificatory activities and behaviors in a given group.

Maxim 6

As changes in conditions and time occur, new issues and conditions cause other content to modify cultural traditions without doing violence to the cohesiveness of the culture.

Maxim 7

The disposition or the ways that phenomena are defined and the sanctioned implications are characterized as the ethos or the style of a sociocultural group.

Maxim 8

As solutions are found to problems, innovative processes, regulations, and controls occur. Diffusion results in producing changes in behavior and the rules. The complexities may be diagrammed.

*The structure determines the function.

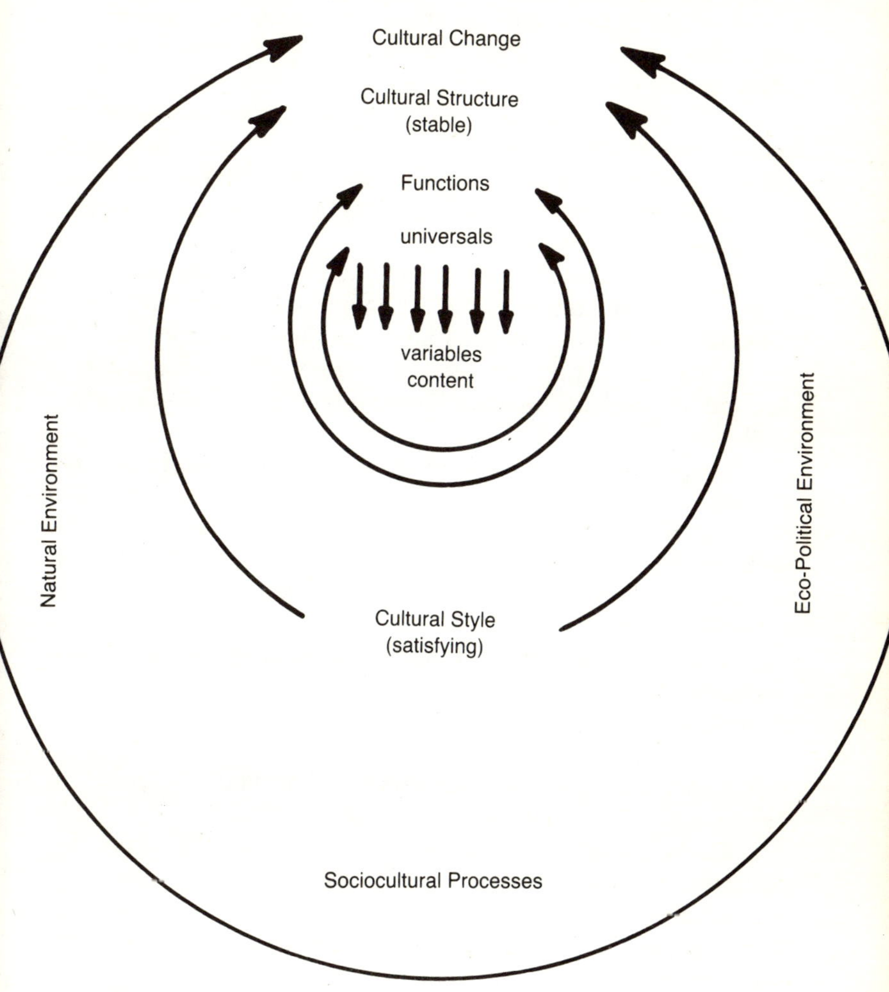
Cultural Change
Cultural Structure
(stable)
Functions
universals
variables
content
Natural Environment
Eco-Political Environment
Cultural Style
(satisfying)
Sociocultural Processes

Postulates by Components

I. Culture Sense

    A. Sociocultural systems are independent entities because particular members come together to make decisions for the whole group. Culture organizes human experiences.

    B. Cultural features are classified by process and content, and it is that whole that includes tradition, world view, and values to which members are conditioned to perform.

    C. Categories are reflective of assumptions, expectations, and beliefs.

    D. Cultural traditions that are transmitted to its members imply the particular patterns of thoughts, feelings, and practices. All beliefs are generally based on the same premise.

    E. Cultural traits, beliefs, and values follow in logical order and are rational when all available data have been gathered.

    F. Understanding comes from the human capacity to generalize.

    G. All cultures use the same methods for classifying objects and people, although the classifications vary widely. Each category carries with it interpretive means for identifying relevancy.

    H. Important parts of study in a cultural system are those features of the environment that influence activity among members.

    I. Much of knowledge is tacit.

    J. The degree of overt and verbal strengthening of cultural values varies enormously from culture to culture.

    K. All cultures form methods for controlling behavior. No culture is totally shared by all its members.

    L. The individual members in a cultural group conform to traditions in a variety of ways. Members assume the existence of order and patterns and commonality.

    M. Human activities carry with them significant economic, sociological, and political aspects and relationships. These have cognitive and affective ingredients.

N. All cultural systems maintain a balance of power and a system of privileges for men and women.

O. In socialization processes, children appear to benefit most when the same norms of action and thinking occur through many routes and interactions.

P. Socialization techniques in the ways children and youth are treated at culturally determined stages vary greatly from group to group. Continuities and discontinuities occur, and all educational processes serve to enable appropriate behavior as adults.

Q. Incentives for culture change develop in a variety of ways.

R. The degree and nature of culture change depends on the type of culture, how flexible or inflexible it is (open or tightly knit, cooperative or competitive, etc.). Synthesis in change is a variable.

S. All cultures have many subsystems that can be identified (family patterns, education, health, etc.); it is, however, a single ongoing system.

T. Sociocultural systems develop patterns for determining status and decreed roles resulting in a prestige hierarchy. The cultural view and behavior are promoted by the leadership.

U. Cognition, perception, and learning are mediated processes to be understood only cross-culturally through the cultural style of the group (ethos). All knowledge transmission is learning.

V. Cultural cognitive styles, or the cultural preference, in the method of abstraction differs from group to group. For example, analytic, inferential, or relational may be the preferred method of organizing knowledge in a particular culture.

II. Tonal Feeling

A. Cultural reality consists of the conclusions reached by members of a particular cultural system. Certain members are regarded as leaders.

B. What people tell other people is a major part in understanding what is believed.

C. Cultural traditions have official standard rationales and perceptions about things and their appropriate affects.

D. All cultural systems classify their members as part of their traditions, and it defines reality. It includes what kinds of people do what, the appropriate relationship among them, and the rules for the ways people treat each other.

E. Ceremonies are normative descriptions of a sociocultural system. People involved in executing a ceremony usually have an obscure understanding of meanings they represent.

F. Ritualistic performances function as announcements, reinforcers, and facilitate status change. Generally, ceremonies cause changes in behavior.

G. All human cultures tend to include magic, religion, moral values, recreation, regulation of marriage, and education.

H. Emotional attitudes and feelings are culturally transmitted and lie dormant in economic, sociological, religious, and educational behavior.

I. As relevant behavior and standards break down in traditional patterns due to culture changes, personality characteristics take on more significance.

J. Most participants in a culture learn how to act in certain roles rather than "learn the cultural system."

K. Culture content is felt as a coherent and integrating principle.

L. When studying other cultures, an individual experiences confusing and frightening realities until the world of the other cultural system is understood and develops feelings of empathy.

M. Feelings of a member adapt to requirements on the prestige scale of values. They are experienced in many ways in various roles. How a person feels is dependent upon what is done.

N. The carrying out of a status role corresponds to viewpoint, attitude, and feelings.

O. Sociocultural systems vary in spatial and temporal conceptualization and have a forceful affective component. They are expressed in innumerable ways in daily living and transactions.

P. Attitudes relate to the type of work that people do in a culture and the positions in the value scale. Behavior patterns are determined by the context, level of technology, and status.

Q. The norms of the larger society influence behavior, attitudes, and feelings of self-worth of its various members.

R. Learning style of the individual is conditioned by cultural style. The way knowledge is transmitted determines the frame of reference for other learnings.

S. Education is embodied within the cultural orientation. Knowledge transference of the larger society influences the relationship, nature, scope, and degree of knowledge transmission to subcultures.

T. Status of particular subcultures in a larger society is a variable.

U. Ethnocentrism in a given culture sets the standard for judgments, assumptions, motivations, and behaviors about other cultural groups.

V. Nonverbal language and covert behavior are universals.

W. Cultural systems develop many ways of communicating. Communication is context referenced.

III. Environment

A. Sociocultural groups solve the problems of survival. These solutions vary enormously.

B. The elements of the sociocultural system are so intertwined and flowing that change in any one component influences changes in the others.

C. Outside forces have an impact on cultural systems, and the ecological relationships are the connectors between it and external conditions.

D. Sociocultural systems are orderly in such a way that a succession of interwoven occurrences, initiated under specific settings, also ends under specific settings.

E. Cultural heritage is a variable representing accommodational patterns and standards handed down by one generation to the next and is part of every distinct social group.

F. All cultures get involved in moving people within their own cultural system and outside the cultural system. This usually requires a modification in behaviors matched to the circumstances.

G. When members of a given cultural group divert from one status to another, those concerned accept it and look forward to the new behavior.

H. The nature, scope, and degree of independence permitted in a society are important variables.

I. Every culture allows for some experiences in discontinuities as its members grow up. The abruptness and timing differ widely from culture to culture.

J. In societies in which there is a significant inconsistency or incompatibility between the standards and actual experiences, between the goals and behavior, conflicts occur and are transmitted, and this bears heavily on confidence, trust, and self-esteem of individuals.

K. The acceptance of different cultural styles will have an important presence on dispelling stereotypic myths held and on the behavior of members in the larger society.

L. Dualism, as a concept, penetrates Western thinking and governmental practice and is expressed in attitude, social life, economic relationships, and institutional structures.

M. Traditional Western culture promotes the belief and practice of a culturally dominant elite sex-engendered governing structure. Its basic premise is to have rulers who believe they are superior and should rule over others thought to be less capable for one reason or another.

N. Cultural diversity through thought, behavior, and activity is a natural part of human experience.

O. The in-group, out-group ideology is a failure in understanding the values through the relativity of cultural traits, belief systems, and actions of unique social groups.

P. Conflicts occur when people of a given group suspect that their world or that "forbidden territory" has been invaded.

Q. Cultural groups in societies in which they are not thought to be equally capable and are discriminated against form renewal and cultural loyalty organizations as a reaction to stress and disappointment.

R. Cultural systems are influenced by external conditions and environmental forces and affect the internal states of mind of their members.

S. Cultural tradition includes impressions of and attitudes toward the outside world.

T. Contradictions occur in all societies. Since regulations can neither cover every act, nor can it be expected that every member understand conduct completely, efforts for social control usually restore the function of the system.

U. The methods through which the organization of knowledge is conducted affirm its values and beliefs.

V. Transcultural tonal feelings, culture sense, direct, and vicarious experiences with diverse cultural groups will influence attitude and behavior and necessary changes.

IV. Relativity

A. The comparative study of different cultural systems provides for understanding the conventions and values that elucidate differences and commonalities.

B. The inductive method frames any issues or questions that may arise from observations.

C. Observations guide the individual along many paths that lead to more observations. They become the basis for criteria and standards for understanding and empathy.

D. In any given group, social classifications enumerate the types of people and what they are required to do for others and the requirements for personal interactions.

E. All cultures develop the reality for their members by a "right" and a "wrong" system. Diffusion modifies the system under specific conditions.

F. All cultural groups have some form of hierarchy. Differentiation causes the beliefs in certain people to differ for some reason, and for their having certain qualities consistent with those roles.

G. The primary family, relatives, neighbors, and the entire community know the "right ways" to rear children in cultural groups that are relatively unchanging.

H. Behaviors in a cultural group follow a systematic pattern based on the way the culture defines itself and how it views the world around it.

I. All cultural groups have kinship classifications and a kinship network for the purpose of potential relatives and to earmark those that need to be avoided.

J. All cultural systems have complicated processes for the regulation and distribution of labor. Methods are devised for who goes where and does what. These methods vary from culture to culture.

K. All cultures develop procedures for control over their membership through social institutions such as birth, marriage, death, stress, and so on.

L. Processes and content are conducive to comparative analysis of cultural systems for identifying the universals.

M. The study of a variety of cultural systems and the study of the movement of a single cultural system through time, taking cognizance of space and conditions, maximize the valuing of diversity.

N. Every culture has members who may be considered as nonconformists.

O. Cultural systems are created when interrelated patterns of human beings develop and use a set of traditions and establish predictable relationships with an environment.

P. Every culture provides its membership with basic ideas about the nature of things, how they should operate, and what happens to influence the operations.

Q. Human beings tend to believe in the meaning and importance of their actions.

R. Where rapid change is the norm, in a complex society, there is no "average" community. In all cultures, there are many different kinds of people who live many different kinds of lives.

S. The transmission and acquiring of culture occurs in many ways. During the process of change, some things remain the same, while other things change.

T. Individual members participate in varying degrees and at various levels in a society, thus experiencing subcultures.

U. In any culture, the participants move in and out of several subcultures as part of daily living.

V. In highly complex industrial societies, through diffusion, the various subcultures tend to share many common traits and goals.

W. Procedures that initiate individuals for role change are usually striking gestures. These activities occur throughout varying phases of growth and development defined by a given culture. Passage into the next role frees the individual to develop and have other experiences. These vary from group to group.

X. Members of a given society tend not to experience other cultures, in relation to their own; thus, they perceive their own as inevitable and the best way to live.

Y. Change produces feelings of anxiety and resistance until the new cohesiveness integrates as a social orientation.

Z. Social consciousness respecting diversity is learnable within the framework of self-identification and self-perception.

Principal Concepts by Components

Universal Culture Affective Model

I. Culture sense (cognitive unfoldments and discoveries)
  A. Knowledge of cultural systems
    1. Culture process
    2. Culture content
    3. Role of values
    4. Dynamics of culture change
    5. Effects of culture change
  B. Knowlege of cultural forms and features
    1. Methods
    2. Structures
    3. Functions

4. Organizational arrangements
5. Mediational elements
6. Historic evolution (of culture)
7. Classifications (of nature and cultural elements)
  C. Knowledge of major cultural influences
1. Natural environments (in relation to culture)
2. Geographical environments
3. Political environments
4. Universal categories (family, kinship, child rearing, etc.)
5. Range of variables within universals

II. Tonal feelings (sociocultural consequences expressed through overt and covert means)
  A. Tonal feeling in a culture
1. Individual personality in culture
2. Self-esteem
3. Ethnocentrism
4. Group loyalty
5. World view
6. Role of absolutes
7. Cultural style
  B. In-group (in a given culture)
1. Primary family
2. Extended family
3. Kinship systems
4. Friends
5. Community
6. Hierarchies
7. Absolutes
  C. Tonal feeling out-group (other ethnic cultures)
1. Neutrality in differences
2. Neutrality in commonalities
3. Impartiality in diversity
4. Devaluing superiority-inferiority models
5. Universalism and comparative absolutes
6. Devaluing control and those who "should be" controlled (by ethnic group)

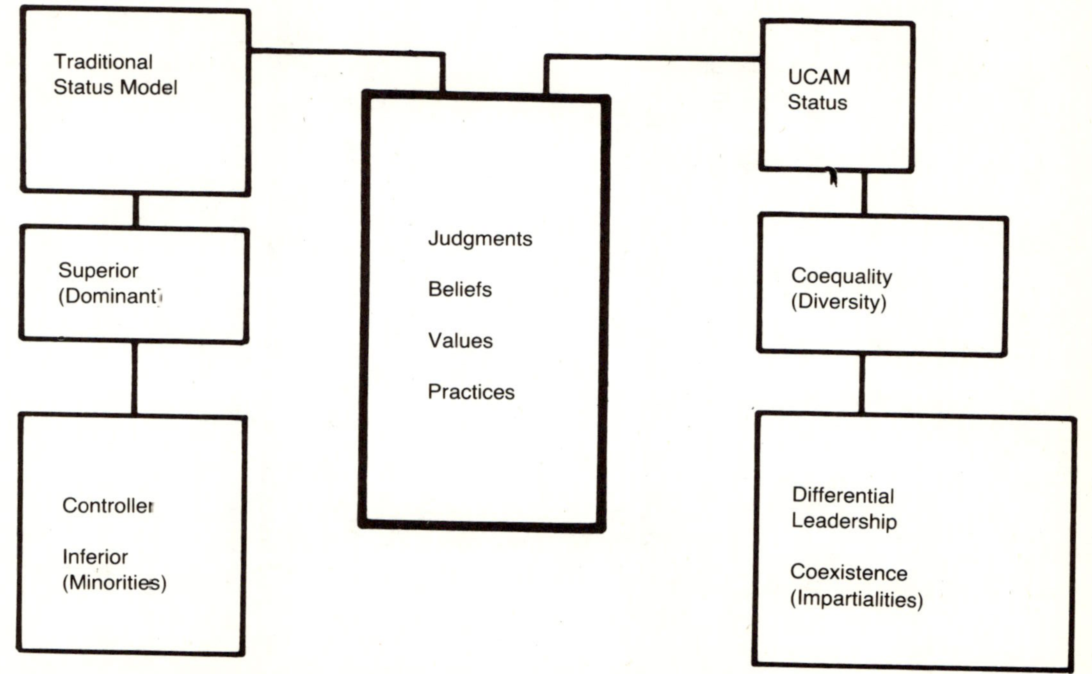

Figure 3. Difference between the traditional and UCAM sphere of influence.

III. Environment (cultural pluralism of complex societies)
  A. Cultural pluralistic modes
  B. Cultural relativity (ethnic cultural group differentiation and larger society through systems operations)
     1. Historical conditions
     2. Political conditions (governing orientation)
     3. Economic conditions
     4. Social conditions (status and position)
  C. Cultural reality as multiplicities and in relation to the larger society
  D. Viewpoints of history, literature, lifeways from the individual ethnic cultural perspective
  E. Cultural competence (attaining social adeptness in many cultural worlds and to function effectively in each)
  F. Futuristic projections (cultural global view)
IV. Relativity (humanistic principles permeate and are merged in holistic approach)
  A. Knowledge, attitudes, feelings in the internalization of UCAM
     1. Personal development
     2. Social consciousness
     3. In-group
     4. Out-group
     5. Support network
  B. Ethic of diversity
     1. Goals embodied in facilitating alternatives and their variations
     2. Objectives facilitating the art-science (UCAM)
     3. Art-science proficiency (practice)
     4. Correlations of commonalities and differences
  C. Paradigms using holistic theories (such as field theory, gestalt theory, phenomenological wholes, and cultural anthropology)

Assumption

Sociocultural attributes shape intellectual functioning. Conceptualization, perception, memory, cognition, and thoughts are intricately confined to culturally patterned activity, culturally patterned interactions, and culturally patterned communication during the socialization process. The differences in transmission processes and content are culturally determined resolving in cultural learning styles.

Universal Culture Affective Model Construct

In its most broad sense, education is an art-science that incorporates processes and subject matter that influences the mind and character of the individual. The type of personality that is developed and the physical potential are influenced by education. It is a lifelong process. There has not been a viable means nor the interest, by the dominant society, to internalize the current scientific data from cultural anthropology, let alone affect education practice. Also, there has not been the ideology for valuing diverse life styles stemming from the variety of ethnic and other cultural groups in the United States. Furthermore, public educational institutions have not taken it upon themselves to abstract crucial implications and make relevant assumptions inferred from ethnic group conflicts, "poor academic performance," especially by certain ethnic groups, and the democratic principles for "equal opportunity" in a relativistic mode.

On the contrary, schools tend to perpetuate the "smart-dumb" syndrome in the midst of genetic-environment debates. Competitive means such as ranking, grade systems, tracking, and deficit approaches to teaching are common. There is no systematic or consistent theoretical foundation on which to build programs for meeting the educational needs and capacities in an "equal but different" mentality that respects diverse cultural characteristics. The current dominant style is competitive and is primarily concerned with subject matter in ever-increasing efficiency techniques. It attempts to shape the children to fit the "matter" in "advantaged-disadvantaged" theories.

Education, through schooling, among other institutions, on every level, historically has been suspicious of ideas that enhance pluralistic images. Conforming to dominant "norms" is comfortable, rings true, and is "natural" to the group that has control over its direction. The political implications of the "ethnic minorities" and the emerging "white ethnics" can only be properly comprehended through the politico-eco-historical viewpoints from each cultural group's perspective. Although civil rights proponents work toward more equity in the hiring of ethnic minorities in schools as role models, it has its limitations. From a practical standpoint, it is not possible to hire qualified adults to be available at the appropriate levels and times for each linguistically and culturally different learner in every school at every level.

A more serious concern, however, is that professionals have almost no way to respect nondominant cultures through the bureaucratic maze other than through vague rhetoric. Courses in social studies, ethnic studies, or minority legislative mandates cannot possibly be effective by themselves. It will take fundamental changes in what is valued, believed, and practiced. The multicultural and multiethnic movement, in effect, as the metaphor illustrates, emulates the existing dominant model. Only, this time, the dominant criteria would be replaced by certain "ethnic minority" criteria under specialized conditions. The writer has witnessed frequent conversations in which are heard statements such as "The majority of the minorities should set the standards." This point of view does not take into account that it represents the same superiority-inferiority standards of the dominant model. It represents the first step in the victims becoming the victimizers, the difference being only in that the "actors" change. More to the point is the need for a complete understanding of the impact of culture on the lives of all human beings, the function of ethnocentrism, and the "naturalness" of diversity as it happens in natural and cultural environments.

The educational priorities, during this period, seem skewed. The "Back to Basics" movement has meant teaching reading, writing, and computational skills. Seen in this narrow sense, it separates the subject matter from the context and from the individual personality. It is a mirage. What is basic to humankind? Is it not "matter" arranged in interactive relationship with the energies of the people who organize around their relationship to the environment that makes the difference? Are these relationships not responsible for motivating people to act and learn in creative ways? What is culture? What are its features and drives and aspirations? How does it affect knowledge transmission, behavior, learning styles, self-worth and cooperation? Why are there differences in cultural style? Why are concepts like "good and bad" or "superior and inferior" in use? What functions do they serve? What kinds of behavior are predictable from such understandings? What is common to all groups? Should every individual feel successful through schooling experiences? Many other questions need to be raised.

The dominant Western ethnocentric view, reinforced by the missionary spirit, has been responsible for the frustrations of many Americans. They have suffered from feelings of isolation, low status, lack of success, and also for their not appreciating cultural variation. Most of these groups experience poverty. Values, as echoed throughout this study, emphasize and interpenetrate all human activity. Every culture provides the "should be" and "should not be" for its human interpersonal relationships. Stress, anxiety, and frustration in subcultures are manifest aspects of cultural adaptation. These occur in reaction to misunderstanding, misinterpretation, and dissatisfactions brought about by the dominant group.

Every culture has a recognizable structure, an interdependent system of behaviors, beliefs, and activities arranged in ways that its members "feel them" as well as "know them." Even though the current accepted scientific methodology prizes the precise measurable domains, in both overt and covert means, the reality still remains that cultural phenomena can be "sensed" and "felt." They have "style." The ethos of a culture of an ethnic group is recognizable and comes from comprehension of the whole system and not by studying its parts in isolation.

Scientific reality is the belief that every sociocultural system creates its own set of plausible judgments and inferences. The most salient parts of an environment are the perceived images and values of the membership of the cultural system. Experimental design, for example, is but one part of the context of a cultural system, and it reflects hierarchies, specified procedures, rules of the game, and so on.

Should education institutions be preparing the members of this complex society for mutual understandings, collaborative mechanisms that ease its members into the culturally pluralistic world? Should they prepare their members to be competent to move in and out of different cultural systems without stereotyping and denegrating subcultures? This research addresses the emphatic "yes" by the creation of a theoretical base to assist in system change.

The "basics" in UCAM integrate elements into a holistic frame of reference. It establishes the art-science, the stability-change of culture itself with the idea of educating people to view humanity in a relative rather than an absolute right-wrong mode.

For innovations to occur, it must be understood by the members of a society not only as a nonthreatening mental phenomena but also as a desirable goal, something to be valued enough to make the effort. American democratic philosophy encompasses numerous guidelines from which conscious choices and "fair play" can be made. High priority must be given to respect differences, recognize universal commonalities, while also being responsive to the multicultural needs of the population. Culture-context understanding is just as plausible an idea as is the dominant culture's idea for controlling its "minority groups." The difference between the animal kingdom and the human kingdom is that for humans, ideas and feelings can be rendered comprehensible. It is reasonable to assume that it is possible for educational institutions to initiate thought and lead activities. All it takes is the willingness to accomplish such a change and then take steps in that direction.

The first task, it seems, would be to change the role that educational institutions have from caretaker of past tradition to that of change agent. Another task would be to openly and explicitly articulate scientific, philosophical, and ethical knowledge about human behavior in its commonalities and variations in cultural approaches in meeting life's problems. Another task would be to examine sociocultural systems through comparative similarities and differences by the universal classifications. Examples of universal categories are that culture:

1. Designates to certain members the role of transmitting beliefs, customs, habits, and attitudes to its members.

2. Has specific concepts that explain the person's relationship to the universe.

3. Has standards and rules that are considered "ideal" while also permitting a range of acceptable behavior.

4. Has members who deviate from the standards and rules. These are influenced by the individual's own drives, needs, and experiences for performance in relationship to the patterns.

5. Adjusts to new and changing situations coping with problems and creating other cultural patterns.

Another task for education would be to understand mental health and socialization processes through relativistic arrangements. Another vital task would be to develop ways to integrate schooling issues with adult activities such as reinforcing means to enhance diversity. There are, of course, many other tasks to be considered that are psychologically humanistic in a comparative approach.

A lot is known about human beings, how they grow and develop, the natural environment, the implications of culture on the individual, and how attitudes develop and change. Studies in human values point to evidence in possible "natural value systems," that is, values apparently follow similar structural patterns and even content. Massive changes are necessary; a metaphor for change needs to be formulated. Alternatives for administering programs can be developed to enhance cultural diversity without scapegoating selected groups. The UCAM is an attempt at providing the theoretical principles for policy decisions and for designing such programs.

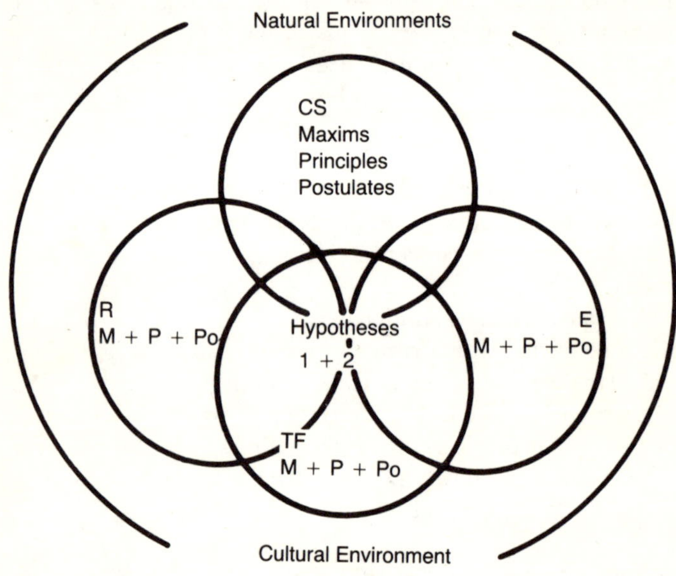

Figure 4. UCAM construct, Key: C = culture sense; TF = tonal feeling; E = environment; R = relativity; M = maxims; P = principles; Po = postulates.

Hypotheses

Two hypotheses have emerged as a result of this research; one deals with belief and the other with approach.

Belief

Ethnocentrism, behavior variation, and world view are functions of a sociocultural group's structure to create individual and group identity. Change in orientation can be mediated through consciousness raising, motivation, and valuation through educational ideologies and designs.

Approach

When members of a society are deliberately informed, can observe, find verification causally or directly, are provided with ideological rewards, are corrected when appropriate, and are esteemed by both dramatic and indirect means, they cannot help but learn and/or relearn to value and behave in different ways.

Universal Culture Affective Model Paradigm

Paradigms are vehicles for looking at phenomena through a social perspective. UCAM is a meta-theory based on paradigms discussed in the three-pronged theoretical base of this research, namely, cultural relativity, cultural pluralism, and humanistic education. The metaphor provides the frame of reference to link historical realities to these transitional times for the purpose of considering radical change in education through the schooling system. Social situations are represented by beliefs, acts, and values. Controls lie in governmental leadership at the present time and the degree to which dissatisfactions of ethnic groups create the type of pressure for modifications as well as in possible other unforseen events that impact on culture change.

The critical variable lies in factors such as the role of technology, as leaders view it, and its relationship to the socioeconomic environment of society's members. Conditions described in the metaphor must be taken into consideration, and so is the notion of the "self-fulfilling prophecy." For social change to happen that benefits all subcultures, the dominant group must recognize the dehumanizing effects on nondominant groups. There are stages and intervening variables that need to be consciously identified in a synergistic configuration, one example being that the kind of advocated change is not seen as a threat to the dominant group's security or as a conflict in ideology. This group needs to understand and believe that there is a stake in changing, that one gains rather than loses in the change. There needs to be a "therapeutic" element built into the change-design. Change in attitude is a reciprocal affair, that is, the victims have to change as radically as the controlling group. Roles and responsibilities have to change consistent with the innovative values. There are phases that need to be considered. Complications result from the phase in which victimized people, in moving "up," have distorted perceptions about moving out of the role of victim of nonacceptance into acceptance. Generally, in transitional phases, the victims become victimizers, favoring the dominant model of those who have been in control. The current multicultural multiethnic approaches for schooling characterize the first phase, especially in competitive structures. In the attempt to be treated "respectfully" and to be "accepted," minority ethnic groups imitate the dominant group by becoming "sub-oppressors." Other ethnic groups retaliate in similar constructions. The results of the confrontation of the sixties produced meager "gains" for some minority groups. The condition of the seventies reveal the uphill battle to retain the gains, with little assurance for increasing advances. The "model" followed by ethnic groups has been to find other "victims," for example, "Whitey," "hardhats," or other ethnic groups considered to be lower on the status ladder in the social structure of this society. Following this course, in reality, is a smoke screen to their need to "get even" and the "revenge" in the perception about being the oppressors of others. This is part of the competitive system. In other words, that they were themselves oppressed "justifies" the oppression of others. It is cyclical. Fringe "victims" are caught between the two worlds. The new victimizers do not recognize that they are modeling the dominant group, nor can they have a broad lucidity concept of their actions. They "sense" the vulnerability of the "gains" as typified in statements such as, "It's our turn now to get a piece of the pie." They do not realize that changing the ethnic status without changing the structure and the fundamental relationships is perpetuating the superior-inferior paradigm. The shortsighted view outweighs the long-term eventuality of their own demise.

The duality of the precariousness of "gains" in the dominant mode needs to be realized and internalized. This analysis is recognized by few but certainly not by those who lobby for compromised issues with political leaders. The victim's role in perpetuating the dominant dualistic model must be recognized for real change. As long as there are victims, oppressors, disadvantaged, inferior, and minority groups to be "mainstreamed" theories, there will be frustration, anger, and conflict by whichever group is at the bottom.

Social institutions function best by a balanced correspondence between the needs of the larger society and those specialized needs of its members through its subcultures. To focus on and be satisfied with modifying only "parts" (for whatever reason) of society without involving basic structural transformations in the ongoing system is a fruitless endeavor. This "illusion" can only last for designated periods of time and is directly proportional to the socioeconomic conditions related to the technological wants of the few. The UCAM paradigm is a step toward seeking a means through which solutions that value the contributions of any sociocultural group can be maintained. It attempts to promote a relativistic democratic structure in which there are *no hierarchical arrangements based on particular perceptions of sociocultural groups*. That is, that the rulers possess special qualities such as being superior (for some reason or another), are genetically superior, and so on. The UCAM also attempts to divert attention from one *cultural group's* control over other *cultural groups*. It further advocates

for the conceptualizations in which values between and among
social phenomena, natural conditions, cultural behavior,
knowlege, etc., become the foundation on which culture change
can benefit all sociocultural groups. What is truth? An individual learns "truth" from how a culture defines it. One can
learn about one's own culture by relating the commonalities
and differences to other ways peoples of other groups define
themselves. The realization that there are different realities
originating from other views rather than an absolute standard
will enable persons to recognize that choices can be made, that
options are available, that one can have control over one's own
destiny. Realizing that no culture is inferior or bad is to move
away from dualistic thinking. The valuation of reciprocal values and relationships is to parallel and to be compatible with
the rest of the natural environment. The matter-energy continuum representing stability and change is diagrammed (Fig.
5).

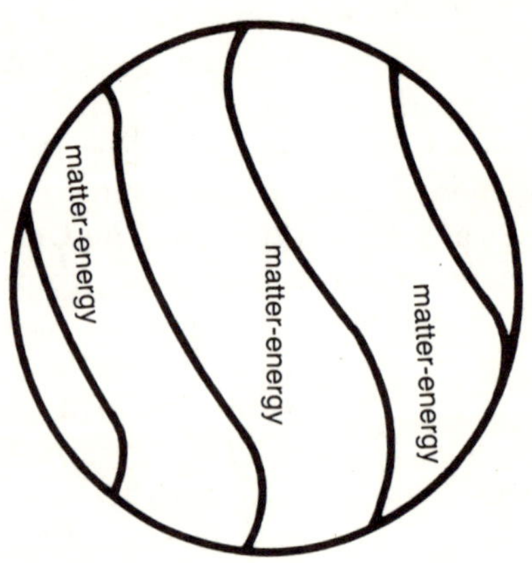

Figure 5. Culture (matter-energy continuum).

Conclusions and Recommendations

This research has shown that public schooling in the United States does not value or accept responsibility to transmit attitudes and cultural knowledge to prepare its citizens for living noncompetitively with different ethnic-cultural groups. It also pointed out the critical need to move away from deficit theories of education to a more authentically humanistic reality-based philosophy consistent with evident culturally pluralistic life styles of the nation's peoples. The outcome of this research is a theoretical base that provides the underlying principles and concepts, the "basics," to value culture knowledge, awareness of cultural dynamics, insight, and diversity for relevancy in relating to the life tasks of Americans.

Both administrative policies and educational implementation models, at all levels, need to be developed to validate and refine the Universal Culture Affective Theoretical Model. It must be stressed, however, that systemic changes must be made for a fair evaluation of its validity. Parts of the theory cannot be applied to incompatible philosophical underpinnings. To do so would be to undermine the results and approach. The Universal Culture Affective Model is a total theory that takes into account structure, functions, roles, responsibilities, process, and content valuing many alternatives in every facet of life. It is a theory that negates the idea that one social group is "better" than another. It provides the foundation for a future in which the larger society is united by accepting, respecting, and expecting cultural differences. Several recommendations flow from the research and model for application to educational realms. The need for:

1. The formulation of administrative and programmatic policies for the development of guidelines for educational options from early childhood years to college level.

2. The design of approaches for educating teachers who teach teachers and community workers.

3. The development of means for institutional change in view of culture-context variables.

4. Questions of scientific research to be raised in the light of culture boundness of "theory" and contingencies.

5. Designing curricula alternatives from early childhood years to college level.

6. A re-examination of criteria within the UCAN orientation to suggest that what is thought to be "health," what is considered to be "successful," or the standards of achievement and other desirable qualities need to be judged from a different world view.

7. The development of systems that redress inequities while including supportive mechanisms of all cultural groups.

8. Creating conditions and standards for communication among culturally different groups and opening paths of inquiry for cooperation and harmony.

9. Promoting an ethic of affirming multicultural social realities.

10. Reevaluating the technical, efficient, cost-effective mentality for social goals within the humanistic, relativistic frame of reference.

There are many other aspects of life to which the Universal Culture Affective Model can be applied. It is entirely possible that a "new discipline" will emerge that encircles the art of living, the science of reliability, and the ethics of concern for humankind through processes and content of living within a pluralistic universal world view. The task seems enormous, the complications numerous, but the effort must be made. Tuning in to the "news" almost any day reveals the struggle of divergent peoples for acceptance and recognition. The human rights issue cannot be selectively applied without building in conflict and eruptions.

Notes

1. Edward T. Hall, *Beyond Culture* (New York: Anchor Press/Doubleday, 1976), p. 6.

2. See Melford E. Spiro, "Religion: Problems of Definition and Explanation," in *Anthropological Approaches to the Study of Religion,* ed. Michael Bauton (London: Tamstoch Publication, 1966), p. 6. A group's cultural heritage was actually mediated through religion providing the beliefs and customs for the interaction between the living world and supernatural powers. Also, see Bronislaw Malinowski, *Magic, Science and Religion* (New York: Anchor Books, 1954), who maintained that there were no cultures at any level of complexity that did not have a "religion and magic."

3. See Melville J. Herskovitz, *Cultural Relativism: Perspectives in Cultural Pluralism* (New York: Vintage Books, 1973), Clyde Kluckhohn, *Mirror for Man: Anthropology and Modern Life* (New York: McGraw-Hill, 1971), Edward T. Hall, *Beyond Culture*, and John J. Honigmann, *Understanding Culture* (New York: Harper & Row, 1963).

4. James B. Starr and Suzanne F. Wilson, "Some Epistemological and Methodological Issues in the Design of Cross-Cultural Research," in *Topics in Cultural Learning*, vol. 5, Richard W. Brislin and Michael P. Hammett, eds. Honolulu, Hawaii: East-West Center, East-West Learning Institute, August 1977. 1777 East, West Road, Honolulu, Hawaii 96848, p. 128.

5. See Arthur R. Jensen, "How Much Can We Boost I.Q. and Scholastic Achievement?," *Harvard Educational Review* 29 (1969) 1-233; R. Herrnstein, "I.Q.," *Atlantic Monthly*, August 1971, pp. 43-64, and William Shockley, "Negro I.Q. Deficit: Failure of a 'Malicious Coincidence' Model Warrants New Research Proposals," *Review of Educational Research* 41, no. 3 (June 1971); 227–248.

6. See Melville J. Herskovitz, *Cultural Relativism: Perspectives in Cultural Pluralism* (New York: Vintage Books, 1973).

7. See Leslie A. White, *The Science of Culture: A Study of Man and Civilization* (New York: Farrar, Straus, and Giroux, 1973). White suggested that words like "science" and "art" could be used as verbs, that is, one sciences dealing with experiences that have underlying assumptions. Especially, see chapter 1, "Science Is Sciencing," pp. 3–21.

8. Wolfgang, Kohler, *The Place of Value in a World of Facts* (New York: Liveright, 1976), p. 64. Also, see chapters I, II, IV, "The Case Against Science," pp. 15–37; "Theories of Value," pp. 35–58, and "Beyond Phenomenology," pp.

87–115. Also, in H.L. Neiburg, *Culture Storm: Politics and the Ritual Order* (New York: St. Martin's Press, 1973), "Paradigms and Reality," pp. 9-16; A.H. Maslow, *The Farther Reaches of Human Nature* (New York: Penguin Book, 1977). See chapter 8, "Fusions of Facts and Values," pp. 101–120; Margaret Mead and Martha Wolfenstein, eds., *Childhood in Contemporary Cultures* (Chicago: University of Chicago Press, 1974), chapter I "Theoretical Setting," 1954, pp. 3-20; Ashley Montagu, ed., *Culture and Human Development: Insights Into Growing Human* (New Jersey: Prentice Hall, 1974), "Just What Is Equal Opportunity?," pp. 35–44.

9. Myth, according to *Webster's Seventh New Collegiate Dictionary,* 1967 (G. & C. Merriam Co., Springfield, MA), "traditional" story of ostensibly historical events that served to unfold part of the world view of a people or explained a practice, belief, or natural phenomenon. Also, see Bronislaw Malinowski, *Magic, Science and Religion* (New York: Anchor Books, 1954).

10. *Report to the President: White House Conference on Children*, Washington, D.C., U.S. Government Printing Office, 1970, pp. 123–124.

11. See Andrew T. Kopan, "Melting Pot: Myth or Reality," in *Cultural Pluralism*, Edgar G. Epps, ed. (Berkeley, Calif.: McCutchan Publishing Corp., 1974), pp. 37–55.

12. See Gerhard Hirschfeld, "Teachers Should Understand Mankind," *The Educator Speaks*, March 1969, pp. 541–548.

13. See Martin Carnoy, *Education as Cultural Imperialism* (New York: David McKay Co., 1974). See, especially, pp. 1–12.

14. See William A. Haviland, *Cultural Anthropology* (New York: Holt, Rinehart and Winston, 1975), p. 276.

15. See also Fred Plog, Clifford J. Jolly, and Daniel G. Bates, *Anthropology Decisions, Adaptation, and Evolution* (New York: Alfred A. Knopf, 1976), p. 436. Also, Donella H. Meadows, Dennis L. Meadows, Jorgen Randers, and William W. Behrens, III, *Limits of Growth*: A Report for the Club of Rome's Project on the Predicament of Mankind (New York: Signet Book, 1974).

16. For an extensive review of the history of education and public purpose, see Sheldon White et al., *Federal Programs for Young Children: Review and Recommendations*, vol. 1: *Goals and Standards of Public Programs for Children* (Washington, D.C.: The Huron Institute, 1973).

17. Edward P. Cubberly, a well-known educator in 1909, advocated that public schools assimilate immigrant children and teach them "Anglo-Saxon ideas." See *Centers, Hearings Before the General Subcommittee on Education*, referenced and quoted by Roman Pucinski in *Ethnic Studies and Urban Reality*, p. 78.

18. As quoted in Seymour Itzkoff, "Curriculum Pluralism in Urban Education," in *School and Society* 94, no. 2281 (November 12, 1966); 385.

19. Literature from multicultural education and the new pluralism movement addressed issues related to an "American" being many models. See James Banks, *Multiethnic Education: Practices and Promises* (Bloomington, Ind.: Phi Delta Kappa Educational Foundation, Fastback 87, 1977); John Carpenter and Judith V. Torney, "Beyond the Melting Pot: Overview, Beyond the Melting Pot to Cultural Pluralism," in *Overview and Research in Children and Intercultural Education* (Washington, D.C.: Association for Childhood Education International, 1974), pp. 14–23; Colin Greer, *The Great School Legend* (New

York: Viking Press, 1972); Michael Pap in a speech, "Why Title IX: Why Do We Need an Ethnic Heritage Studies Program?" Presented at the *First National Meeting of the Ethnic Heritage Program Directors,* October 22, 1974, in Washington, D.C.

20. Colin Greer, *The Great School Legend.*

21. Spearheaded by white ethnic groups, articles and books on the "new pluralism" began to appear in the literature, e.g., see Murry Friendman, ed., *Overcoming Middle-Class Rage* (Philadelphia, Penn.: Westminster Press, 1971).

22. Irvin M. Levine and Judith M. Herman, "The New Pluralism," in *Overcoming Middle-Class Rage*, reprinted by the Project on Ethnic America (Philadelphia: Westminster, 1971)..

23. For example, see Kathy A. Hecht, "Teacher Ratings of Potential Drop-Outs and Academically Gifted Children: Are They Related?" *Journal of Teacher Education*, 26, no. 2 (Summer 1975): 172–175; Robert Rosenthal and Lenore Jacobson, *Pygmalion in the Classroom* (New York: Holt, Rinehart and Winston, 1968); Ray Rist, "Student Social Class and Teachers' Expectations: The Self-Fulfilling Prophecy in Ghetto Education," *Harvard Educational Review* 40, no. 3 (August 1970): 411–451; Seaver W. Burleigh, "Effects of Naturally-Induced Teacher Expectancies," *Journal of Personality and Social Psychology*, 28, no. 3 (1973): 333–342.

24. See footnote 5.

25. Martin Carnoy, *Education as Cultural Imperialism*, p. 3.

26. See Neil Postman and Charles Weingartener, *Teaching as a Subversive Activity* (New York: Delta Books, 1969); see also Benson R. Snyder, *The Hidden Curriculum* (Cambridge: MIT Press, 1973).

27. See David T. Tyack, "Victims Without Crimes: Black Americans," pp. 217–229 and "Americanization: Match and Mismatch," pp. 229-255, in *The One Best System: A History of American Urban Education* (Cambridge, Mass.: Harvard University Press, 1974); Edsel Erickson, Clifford Bryan, and Lewis Walker, "Part C: Cultural Pluralism and Educational Problems," in *Social Change, Conflict and Education* (Columbia, Ohio: Charles E. Merrill, 1972) pp. 227-488; and William Ryan, *Blaming the Victim* (New York: Vintage Books, 1976).

28. See White et al., *Federal Programs*; see also Paul A. Olson, "Introduction," in *Badges and Indicia of Slavery: Cultural Pluralism Redefined*, Antonia Pantoja et al. eds., especially the section on "The Art of Empire: Some History," pp. xv-xvi. Also, Melvin Tumin, "Teaching in America," in *The School in the Social Order: A Sociological Introduction to Educational Understanding*, Francesco Cordasco, et al., ed. pp. 39-45, and Irving M. Levine, *Ethnicity and American Education*, Institute on Pluralism.

29. For further discussion, the following sources contain the etiology of "historical visions" related to the hopes of peoples who have emigrated to the United States and the conditions that result when their goals were unrealized and frustrated. See *The Desegregation Literature: A Critical Appraisal,* July 1976, Health, Education and Welfare, National Institute of Education, *School Desegregation and Cultural Pluralism: Perspectives on Progress, Selected Presentations of the 1974–1975 STRIDE Workshops*, Far West Laboratory for Educational Research and Development, San Franscisco, California 94103; B.

Othaniel Smith, Saul B. Cohen and Arthur Pearl, *Teachers for the Real World: For the Task Force of the NDEA National Institute for Advanced Study in Teaching Disadvantaged Youth*, the American Association of College for Teacher Education, One Dupont Circle, N.W., Washington, D.C. 20036, September 1969; *Violations of Human and Civil Rights: Tests and Use of Tests Report of the Tenth National Conference on Civil and Human Rights in Education*, February 18-20, 1972, NEA, National Education Association, 1201 16th Street, N.W., Washington, D.C.: *Instructional Strategies in Schools With High Concentration of Low-Income Pupils: A Report to the U.S.O.E., Welfare and Optimum Computer Systems, Inc., Education and Human Resources Development Division; A Better Chance to Learn: Bilingual Bicultural Education*, U.S. Commission on Civil Rights, Clearinghouse Publication #51 (May, 1975); Alfredo Casteneda, Richard L. Jones, and Webster Robbins, *The Educational Needs of Minority Groups*, Professional Educators Pub. Inc., Lincoln, Nebraska, 1974; Garlic A. Forehand and Marjorie Bagosta, *A Handbook for Integrated Schooling, Report to United States Health, Education and Welfare Office of Planning, Budgeting, and Evaluation, July 1976; Summary of Findings, Brown versus Califano for Office of Civil Rights in Health, Education and Welfare; The Condition of Bilingual Education in the Nation: First Report by the U.S. Commission of Education* to the president and the Congress, November 1976; Ashley Montagu, *Man's Most Dangerous Myth: The Fallacy of Race* (London: Oxford University Press, 1974); and Peter Watson, ed., *Psychology and Race* (Chicago: Aldine Publishing Co., 1973).

30. Lawsuit began in 1971; see "Blacks Challenge Placing of Retarded Based on I.Q. Tests," *Boston Globe*, 7 June 1978.

31. ERA supporters were engaged in lobbying efforts for the extension of deadline for ratification for seven more years. See "Extension Support Grows," *NOW Times*, 11, no. p.1. 5–6 (April/May 1978), official *Journal of the National Organization of Women*.

32. D. J. de S. Price, *Little Science, Big Science* (New York: Columbia University Press, 1963); M. Scriven, "The Methodology of Evaluation," in R. Tyler et al., *Perspectives of Curriculum Evaluation* (Chicago: Rand McNally AERA Monograph, #1, 1967), pp. 39–83; F. G. Caro, "Issues in the Evaluation of Social Programs," *Review of Educational Research* 41 (1971): 87–114.

33. James Barclay, *Controversial Issues in Testing* (Boston: Houghton Mifflin Co., 1968), pp. 1–37.

34. By 1972, twenty-three (23) states had enacted accountability legislation, while sixteen (16) additional states were pending in 1973. Legislation covered management methods such as cost effectiveness of educational programs, information systems, state testing and assessment programs and evaluation of professional staff. See Phyllis Hawthorne, *Legislation by States: Accountability and Assessment in Education*; revised April, 1973 for The Cooperative Accountability Project, Colorado Dept. of Education, 1362 Lincoln St., Denver, CO 80203.

35. Carol H. Weiss, *Evaluation Action Programs: Reading in Social Action and Education* (Boston: Allyn & Bacon, 1972), pp. 3–27.

36. See the following articles for discussion: Ernest G. Lake, "The Case Against External Standardized Tests: They Create an Elite and Slur Our Average Students!" *The Nation's Schools* 70, no. 2, (August 1962): 51–54;

Jonathan Kozol, "Free Schools: A Time for Candor," *Saturday Review*, 4 March 1972; Fred M. Hechinger, "Reappraising the Open Classroom," *Saturday Review*, 19 March 1977; in *Young Children*, see Helen Rand, "Experimental Learning Reevaluated," September 1970, pp. 363–366 and Robert Bentley, Ernest Washington, and James Young, "Judging the Educational Progress of Young Children: Some Cautions," November 1973, pp. 5–18. In *Childhood Education*, "Testing and Accountability," 49, no. 7 (April 1973): 338-372; Monroe D. Cohen and Lucy Prete Martin, eds., *Testing and Evaluation: New Views* (ACEI, 1975).

37. See Ashley Montagu, *Man's Most Dangerous Myth*, p. ix.

38. E. F. Schumacher, *Small Is Beautiful: Economics As If People Mattered* (New York: Harper & Row, 1973), p. 82.

39. Robert Dahn, *Pluralist, Democracy in the U.S.* (Chicago: Rand McNally, 1967); Milton M. Gordon, "Assimilation in America: Theory and Reality," *Daedalus, Journal of the American Academy of Arts and Sciences*, 90, no. 2 (Spring 1961): 263–285; John Higham, *Strangers in the Land: Patterns of American Nativism, 1860-1925* (New York: Atheneum, 1972); Horace M. Kallen, *Cultural Democracy in the United States* (New York: Boni & Liveright, 1924); Andrew T. Kopan, "Melting Pot: Myth or Reality," in *Cultural Pluralism*, Edgar G. Epps, ed. (Berkeley, Calif.: McCutchan Publishing, 1974), pp. 35–55; Mark M. Krug, "Cultural Pluralism: Its Origins and Aftermath," *Journal of Teacher Education*, 28, no. 3 (May-June 1977): 5–9; Michael Novak, *The Rise of the Unmeltable Ethnics* (New York: Macmillan, 1972).

40. John I. Goodlad, *Facing the Future: Issues in Education and Schooling*, Judith S. Golub, ed. (New York: McGraw-Hill, 1976), part II, pp. 73–164; Jules Henry, *On Education* (New York: Vintage Books, 1972); Alvin Toffler, ed., *Learning for Tomorrow: The Role of the Future* (New York: Vintage Books, 1974).

41. See the following in *Majority and Minority*, "The American Slave Plantation and Our Heritage of Communal Deprivation," pp. 167–177, Leon F. Litwack, "The Federal Government and the Free Negro, 1790–1860," pp. 178–192, Nancy Oestreich Lurie, "The American Indian: Historical Background," pp. 207–229. See also in *Cultural Pluralism*, Epps, Reed Ueda, ed., "The Americanization and Education of Japanese Americans: A Psychodramatic and Dramaturgical Perspective," pp. 71–90. Also, "You've Got To Be Realistic About Being a Nigger," by Malcolm X, in *Demystifying School: Writings and Experiences*, Miriam Wasserman, ed. (New York: Praeger Press, 1974) pp. 81–82.

42. "The largest Federal education effort provided $2 billion, most of which was used to improve educational programs for low achieving students in school districts serving children from low income families." See, U.S. Health, Education and Welfare. National Institute of Education, *Evaluating Compensatory Education Study: An Interim Report on the National Institute of Education Compensatory Education Study*, December 30, 1976, p. 101.

43. Social Research Group, George Washington University, prepared for the Interagency Panel on Early Childhood Research and Development, Washington, D.C., September, 1972. *Research Problems and Issues in the Areas of Socialization*. This report described about fifty-six studies held from 1935-1972 on educating poor minority children. Also, Sheldon White, et al., *Federal Pro-*

grams. This report covered 225 studies on ethnic racial group differences, criteria for disadvantaged and characteristics of disadvantaged home environments.

44. See Esther Hovey, *Ethnicity and Early Education* (Urbana: University of Illinois, Eric Clearinghouse on Early Childhood Education, 1975). Forty-six (46) studies from the compensatory fields are cited.

45. References on the desegregation issues, concepts of cultural pluralism, and ethnic identity discussed both historical and reactions to frustrations and disappointment. See Irving M. Levine, *Social Policy and Multi-Ethnicity in the 1970s* (New York: Institute on Pluralism and Group Identity, Working Paper Series 1, January 1975), Paper published by the Institute on Pluralism. Joseph Giordano and Grace Pineiro Giordano, *The Ethno-Cultural Factor in Mental Health: A Literature Review and Bibliography*.

46. See Martin Deutsch, "The Disadvantaged Child and the Learning Process," in A. H. Passow, ed., *Education in Depressed Areas* (New York: Teachers' College Press, 1963), pp. 163–180; J. McV. Hunt, *Intelligence and Experience* (New York: Ronald Press, 1961); Carl Bereiter, *Acceleration of Intellectual Development in Early Childhood* (Washington, D.C., USOE, 1966), Vera P. John, *Position on Preschool Programs: A Brief Survey of Research on the Characteristics of Children From Low Income Backgrounds*, Disadvantaged Document ED 00186, Eric, United States Department of Health, Education and Welfare; V. P. John and L. S. Goldstein, "The Social Context of Language Acquisition," *Merrill-Palmer Quarterly of Behavior and Development*, 10, no. 30 (1964): 265–276.

47. See legislation for compensatory programs such as Head Start, Title 1 of ESEA, Follow Through, and Title VII of ESEA.

48. Arthur Jensen, "Can We and Should We Study Race Differences?" in *Race and Intelligence*, pp. 10–31; Richard Herrnstein, "I.Q.," in *Atlantic Monthly*, September 1971, pp. 43–64; Samuel Bowels and Herbert Gintis, "I.Q. in the U.S. Class Structure, Social Policy," *Social Policy*. 3:4 3, no. 4, 5, (January–February, 1973); pp. 65-96 Christopher Jencks, et al., *Inequality: A Reassessment of the Effects of Family and Schooling in America* (New York: Basic Books, 1972).

49. U.S. Department of Labor, *The Negro Family: The Case for National Action* (Washington, D.C.: Government Printing Office, 1965; the Moynihan Report); James S. Coleman, *Equality of Educational Opportunity*, U.S.O.E.: William Ryan, "Mammy Observed: Fixing the Negro Family," in *Blaming the Victim*, pp. 63–88.

50. White, et al., *Federal Programs*.

51. Charles Laurencall, "The Bakke Case: Are Racial Quotas Defensible?" *Saturday Review*, 15 October 1977, pp. 11–16.

52. See Raymond Giles and Donna Gollnick, "Ethnic/Cultural Diversity as Reflected in Federal and State Educational Legislation and Policies," in *Pluralism and the American Teacher: Issues and Case Studies*, Frank Klassen and Donna Gollnick, eds. (Washington, D.C.: Ethnic Heritage Center for Teacher Education of AACTE, 1977), pp. 115–160.

53. For some examples, see Hovey's *Ethnicity and Early Education*, especially see the section, "Determinants of Intergroup and Intragroup Attitudes and Behaviors," pp. 44–162. See also *Research Problems and Issues in the Area*

of Socialization, Prepared for the Inter-Agency Panel on Early Childhood Research and Development. Washington, D.C., George Washington University, Sept. 1972.

54. Ibid.; also, for further insights, review Joseph Giordano, *Ethnicity and Mental Health Research and Recommendations*. Institute on Pluralism and Group Identity, 165 E. 56 St., N.Y.C. 10022.

55. Culture is a term frequently used in many ways. Over 160 definitions are cited in A. L. Kroeber and Clyde Kluckhohn's work, *Culture: A Critical Review of Concepts and Definitions* (New York: Vintage Books, 1972).

56. See James Banks, "The Implication for Multicultural Education for Teacher Education," in *Pluralism and the American Teacher*, pp. 1–30. Also, Maxine Dunfee, *Ethnic Modification of the Curriculum*. A Report on a Conference on Ethnic Modification of the Curriculum, 20–22 Nov. 1969. Washington, D.C.: Association for Supervision and Curriculum Development, NEA.

57. H. L. Neiburg, *Culture Storm: Politics and the Ritual Order* (New York: St. Martin's Press, 1973); "Beyond Pain and Pleasure," pp. 6–9.

58. Mary A. Golladay, *The Condition of Education: A Statistical Report on the Condition of Education in the U.S.*, vol. 3, part 1 (Washington, D.C. DHEW of National Center for Educational Statistics, 1977) U.S.H.E.W. 1977 edition. National Center for Education Statistics, p. 145.

59. Ibid., p. 147.

60. Ibid., p. 146.

61. Montagu, *Most Dangerous Myth*, p. XI.

62. See also C. Loring Brace and Frank B. Livingstone, "On Creeping Jensenism," in *Rape and Intelligence*, C. L. Brace, G. R. Gamble, and J. T. Bonds, eds. (Washington, D.C.: American Anthropology Association, 1971), pp. 64–75.

63. The term "ethnic group" popularized in the mid-1950s as a theoretical construct of behaviors and values that separate it from nationality, religion, class . . . see R. A. Schermerhorn's paper presented at the National Conference on Ethnicity, Cleveland State University, May 12, 1970, "Ethnicity in the Perspective of the Sociology of Knowledge," in *Ethnicity: A Conceptual Approach*, David E. Weinberg, ed. Cleveland Ethnic Heritage Studies (Cleveland: Cleveland State University, 1976), p. 5.

64. White, et al., *Federal Programs*.

65. See *The Condition of Education*, chapter 5, pp. 100–139.

66. See James A. Banks, ed., *Teaching Ethnic Studies: Concepts and Strategies*, National Council for Social Sciences, NEA, 43rd Yearbook 1973; Alfredo Castaneda, Richard L. James, and Webster Robbins, *The Educational Needs of Minority Groups* (Lincoln, Neb.: Professional Educators Publishing, 1974); Carl A. Grant, "Exploring the Relationship Between Teacher Corps and Multicultural Education," *Journal of Teacher Education*, 26, no. 2 (September 1975): 119-120; Harry N. Rivlin, "General Perspectives on Multiculturalism," Ibid., pp. 121–122; Alexander Frazier, *Learning More About Learning: Papers and Reports from the Third ASCD Research Institute*, 1959, NEA.

67. See Draper L. Kauffman, Jr., "Futurism: and Future Studies," NEA *Learning for Tomorrow: The Role of the Future*. Alvin Toffler, ed. (New York: Vintage, 1975) pp. 29–42; Howard Kirschenbaum and Sidney B. Simon, "Values and the Future Movement in Education," in *Learning for Tomorrow: The*

Role of the Future in Education, Alvin Toffler, ed. (New York: Vintage Books, 1974), pp. 257–270; idem, *Future Shock* (New York: Bantam Books, 1974), p. 1–44. Those who want to raise the consciousness of "world crises" in human and physical ecology urge that education needs to be changed to avoid destruction of the human species. See R. Buckminster Fuller, *Earth Inc.* (New York: Anchor Books, 1973), pp. 3–26; idem, *Utopia or Oblivion: The Prospects for Humanity* (New York: Bantam Books, 1972); Donella H. Meadows, et al., *The Limits of Growth* (New York: Signet Books, 1974).

68. Educational Policies Commission, "The Central Purpose of American Education," in *Curriculum Planning: A New Approach*, Glen Hass et al., ed. (Boston: Allyn and Bacon, 1974), pp. 211–216. The question is again raised here "What is Truth? Reality?"

69. See Giles and Gollnick, "Ethnic/Cultural Diversity," in *Pluralism and the American Teacher*, pp. 114–162. See also an outcome of the American Anthropological Association Symposium; "Toward a Definition of Multiculturalism in Education," *Anthropology and Education Quarterly*, 7, no. 4 (November 1976): 1–54.

70. Melville J. Herskovitz, *Cultural Relativism: Perspectives in Cultural Pluralism* (New York: Vintage Books, 1973), p. 21.

71. See Milton M. Gordon, *Assimilation in American Life* (New York: Oxford University Press, 1964), pp. 19–59.

72. See Children's Defense Fund reports, Title 1 of ESEA, *Is It Helping Poor Children?* (Washington, D.C., Washington Research Project, Inc., and the National Association for the Advancement of Colored People (NAACP) Legal Defense and Education Fund, Inc., December 1960); *The Emergency School Assistance Program: An Evaluation*, with five other organizations, November 1970; *The Status of School Desegregation in the South*, 1970 and five other organizations, December 1970; and *It's Not Over in the South*, written by the American Friends Service Committee with five other organizations' cooperation, May 1972 (Children's Defense Fund or the Washington Research Projects, Inc., 1746 Cambridge Street, Cambridge, Mass. 02138).

73. Review footnotes 10, 13, 15, 16, 18, 19, 26, 35, 37, 39, and 42. See also Andrew M. Greely, *Why Can't They Be Like Us?: Facts and Fallacies About Ethnic Differences and Group Conflicts in America* (New York: Institute of Human Relations Press, The American Jewish Committee, New York), pp. 38–55.

74. Children's Defense Fund, *Children Out of School in America* (1974), p. 2.

75. Following the Second World War, the social sciences (and resultant subsequent public policies) were going through intellectual changes much of which were based on the concept of a "lower-class culture." See Charles A. Valentine, *Culture and Poverty: Critique and Counter Proposals* (Chicago: The University of Chicago Press, 1972). See especially, "Building the Frazier Tradition into National Policy: Moynihan Again," pp. 29–42.

76. Lester R. Brown, *The Twenty-Ninth Day; Accommodating Human Needs and Numbers to the Earth's Resources* (New York: W. W. Norton and Co., 1978), especially pp. 45-70 and 208-219. Also, Ralph H. Faulkingham, "Where the Life Boat Ethic Breaks Down," *Human Nature*, October 1978, pp. 32–39.

77. See Jules Henry, *Culture Against Man* (New York: Random House, Inc., 1963); Robert L. Heilbroner, *The Future as History* (New York: Grove Press, 1939); Irving N. Berlin, "Education for What?" in *The Record-Teachers College*, 70, no. 6 (March 1969): 505-511.

78. The numbers of research studies, surveys, reports, evaluations have been reaching in the thousands including federal, state and private foundation sponsorship. For example, covering TRUANCY: see William Buss, "Procedural Due Process for School Discipline: Probing the Constitutional Outlines," *Pennsylvania Law Review*, vol. 19 (February 1971): 577; LANGUAGE: see Noel Epstein, *Language, Ethnicity, and the Schools: Policy Alternatives for Bilingual-Bicultural Education* (Institute for Educational Leadership, The George Washington University, 1001 Connecticut Avenue, N.W., Suite 310, Washington, D.C. 20036); Three Papers From the Child Rearing Study of Low-Income District; racial discrimination literature is rather large and covers tests, labeling, low reading scores, high drop-out rate, etc., see Michael Cole, et al., *The Cultural Context of Learning and Thinking* (New York: Basic Books, 1971), *Child Care: Data and Materials*, Committee on Finance, U.S. Senate, Russel B. Long, chairman, October 1, 1974.

79. Subscriptions can be ordered from the Department of Anthropology, University of South Florida, Tampa, Florida 33620. Also, for further discussion on contemporary issues in anthropology, see *Conformity and Conflict: Readings in Cultural Anthropology*, James P. Spradley and David W. McCurdy, eds. (Boston: Little, Brown and Company, 1974).

80. See Frederik L. Bates and Clyde C. Harvey, *The Structure of Social System* (New York: Gardner Press, 1975).

81. Cornelius L. Grove, *Communication Across Cultures: A Report on Cross Cultural Research* (Washington, D.C.: National Education Association, 1976) p. 6.

82. Examples are compensatory education programs: Title 1, IV; the Bilingual Education Act; Title VII; Child Development, Head Start; Follow-Through; Office of Education, "Right to Read;" "Reading Is Fundamental," etc. (Sheldon White et al., *Federal Programs* (Cambridge: The Huron Institute, 1973) three volumes of extensive data plus vol. 4, Review and Recommendations). See also National Association for the Education of Young Children (NAEYC), *Preparing Teachers of Disadvantaged Young Children: Summary of a Conference of DNEA*, Bernard Spodek, ed. Institute for Teachers of Disadvantaged Youth, July 1965 (Washington, D.C., NAEYC).

83. Jerome S. Brunner, "Culture, Politics, and Pedagogy," *Saturday Review*, 18 May 1968, pp. 69–72, 89, 90.

84. See Shelton White et al., "Family Intervention Projects," in *Federal Programs*, vol. 2 pp. 238–315. Also, D. P. Ausebel, "How Reversible are the Cognitive and Motivational Effects of Cultural Deprivation?": "Implications for Teaching the Culturally Deprived Child," *Urban Education*, (1964) 1:16-39; Frank Riesman, *The Culturally Deprived Child* (New York: Harper, 1962).

85. For examples, see the following studies covering relevant issues, I.Q. SCORES: D. P. Ausubel, "Teaching Strategy for Culturally Deprived Pupils: Cognitive and Motivational Considerations," *Scholastic Review* 71 (1963): 454-463; S. O. Roberts and J. M. Robinson, "Intercorrelations of Primary Mental Abilities Tests for Ten-Year-Olds by Socio-economic Status, Sex, and

Race," *American Psychology* 7 (1952): 304–305; Martin Deutsch, "Heredity and Intelligence." Paper developed at the Social Policy Conference on IQ, New York (May 1973); Gerald Lesser et al., "Mental Abilities of Children from Different Social Class and Cultural Groups," *Monographs of Society for Research in Child Development* 30, no. 102 (1965): pp. 1–115. ACADEMIC PERFORMANCE: E. Milner, "A Study of the Relationship Between Reading Readiness in Grade One Children and Patterns of Parent-Child Interactions," *Child Development* 22 (1951): 95–122; J. R. Havighurst and F. H. Breese, "Relation Between Ability and Social Class Status in Midwestern Community," *Journal of Educational Psychology* 38 (1947): 241–247; B. S. Bloom et al., *Compensatory Education for Cultural Deprivation* (New York: Holt, Rinehart and Winston, 1965).

86. For further information on studies of bias, see Harry N. Rivlin, "Research and Development in Multicultural Education," in *Pluralism and the American Teacher: Issues and Case Studies*, Frank H. Klassen and Donna Gollnick, eds. (Washington, D.C., Ethnic Heritage Center for Teacher Education of the NACTE, 1977), pp. 81–86; also, Jerome B. Dusek, "Do Teachers Bias Children's Learning?" *Review of Educational Research* (Fall 1975): 45, no. 4: 679–680; E. K. Wickman, *Children's Behavior and Teacher Attitudes* (New York: Commonwealth Fund, 1928); Diana Hikirk and Susan Goon, "Desegregation and the Cultural Deficit Model: An Examination of the Literature," *Review of Educational Research* 45, no. 3 (August 1970): 411–451, quoted in Jerome B. Dusek, Anita A. Summers and Barbara A. Wolf, *Equality of Opportunity Quantified: A Production Function Approach* (Philadelphia: Department of Research Federal Reserve, Bank of Philadelphia, 1975); R. G. Rist, "Students Social Class and Teacher Expectations: The Self-Fulfilling Prophecy in Ghetto Education," *Harvard Educational Review* 40, no. 3 (August 1, 1970): 411–451.

87. See problem component section of this study, "Jargonese and Terms That Confuse," pp. 22, and review footnotes 51, 52, and 56.

88. See Fred L. Polak, "Responsibility for the Future," pp. 14–16; Jacques Ellul, "Search for an Image," pp. 22–25; Lester R. Brown, "Issues of Human Welfare," pp. 17–21; Robert T. Francoeur, "Human Nature and Human Relations," pp. 32–34 in *The Humanist*, November-December 1973. Review footnote 66 of this study. Also, the writer's report, April 15, 1972, on the speech by Dr. Chester Pierce, Harvard, "Beyond the Horizon: Question for Meaning" (given at the Association for Childhood Education International, April 2–7, 1972), (April 25, 1972).

89. Joan C. Baratz and S. S. Baratz, "The Social Pathology Model: Historical Bases for Psychology's Denial of the Existence of Negro Culture" (paper presented at American Psychological Association, Washington, D.C., 1969); E.B. Leacock, ed., *The Culture of Poverty: A Critique* (New York: Simon and Schuster, 1971); C. A. Valentine, *Culture and Poverty* (Chicago: University of Chicago Press, 1968).

90. See Raymond Giles and Donna Gollnick, "Ethnic Cultural Diversity as Reflected in Federal and State Educational Legislation and Policies," in *Pluralism and the American Teacher*, pp. 115–160.

91. See U.S. Commission on Civil Rights, *A Better Chance to Learn: Bilingual-Bicultural Education*, Washington, D.C., U.S. Commission on Civil

Rights, Clearinghouse Publication no. 51 (1975).

92. See *Minority Students: A Research Appraisal*, National Institute of Education Report by Meyer Weinberg, pp. 17–36, 72–94, 95–128; see also Richard Rothstein, "How Tracking Works," pp. 61–73; August Hollinghead, "Caste and Class in Education," pp. 74–80; Joan Baratz, "Languages and Cognition Assessment of Negro Children," pp. 148–158, in Wasserman, *Demystifying School*. And Montagu, "Just What is Equal Opportunity," pp. 35–44, "Sociogenic Brain Damage," pp. 45–73, and "Cultural Deprivation," pp. 158–178 in Montagu, *Culture and Human Development*.

93. Fred Polak, "Responsibility for the Future," in *The Humanist*, p. 15.

94. See John W. Sutherland, *A General Systems Philosophy for the Social and Behavioral Sciences* (New York: George Braziller, 1973); Melvin H. Marx, *Systems and Theories in Psychology* (New York: McGraw-Hill Book Co., 1963); Walter Buckley, *Sociology and Modern Systems Theory* (New Jersey: Prentice-Hall, 1967).

95. See Fernando Cortes et al., *Systems Analysis for Social Scientists* (New York: John Wiley & Sons, 1974); also, Frederick L. Bates and Clyde C. Harvey, *The Structure of Social Systems* (New York: Gardner Press, 1975).

96. In F. E. Emery, ed., *Systems Thinking* (Middlesex, England: Penguin Books, 1972); see A. Angyal, "A Logic of Systems," pp. 17–29, and W. Koehler, "Closed and Open Systems," pp. 59–69.

97. Thomas S. Kuhn, *The Structure of Scientific Revolutions* (Chicago: The University of Chicago Press, 1970), p. 10.

98. Marx, *Systems and Theories in Psychology*, p. 48.

99. Ibid., p. 16–17.

100. Buckley, *Sociology and Modern Systems Theory*, pp. 8,9.

101. Clyde Kluckhohn, "Parts and Wholes in Cultural Analysis," in *Parts and Wholes*, Daniel Lerner, ed. (New York: The Free Press, 1963). This book was a compilation of lectures sponsored by the Massachusetts Institute of Technology, School of Humanities and Social Studies, on the "classic problems," i.e., parts and wholes, in the different disciplines and includes papers on physics, economics, systems, engineering, language, etc.

102. Angyal, "Logic of Systems," p. 22.

103. Fuller, *Earth Inc.*, p. 176.

104. See Howard Leventhal, "Attitudes: Their Nature, Growth, and Change," *Social Psychology: Classic and Contemporary Integrations*, Charlan Nemeth, ed. (Chicago: Rand McNally, 1974), pp. 52–126.

105. Matthew Wakatama's study revealed that English children's attitudes toward (black) Africans were changed from negative to favorable when educational experiences were provided toward this end and especially if a black African teacher modeled the attitude and behavior. For example, geography lessons on Africa stressed similarities of peoples while stereotypic representations were avoided. "An Experimental Study of the Teaching of the Geography of Africa With Special Reference to Its Effects Upon the Attitudes of English Children Toward Africans." Master of Arts thesis, University of London, 1957.

106. See Robert Rosenthal, "Self-Fulfilling Prophecy," in *Readings in Psychology Today* (DelMar, Calif: Communications/Research/Machines, Inc., 1969), pp. 467–471; also, W. Victor Beez, "Influence of Biased Psychological Reports

on Teacher Behavior and Pupil Performance," in *Proceedings of the 76th Annual Convention of the American Psychological Association*, vol. 3, pp. 605-606, 1968; also review footnote 23.

107. For example, see *No One Model American: A Statement on Multicultural Education.* The Commission on Multicultural Education established by the American Association of Colleges of Teacher Education, One Dupont Circle, N.W., Washington, D.C. 20036; "Statement by Steering Committee of the National Coalition for Cultural Pluralism," in appendix A, *Cultural Pluralism in Education: A Mandate for Change*, p. 150; Alfredo Casteneda, "Persisting Ideological Issues of Assimilation in America," in *Cultural Pluralism*, Edgar Epps, ed. (Berkeley: McCutchen, 1974) p. 65; "Introduction" by Paul A. Olson, which contains the statement on a definition for "cultural pluralism" and its application to "The School System," pp. vi-xiii; National Council for the Social Studies Task Force, *Curriculum Guidelines for Multi-Ethnic Education: Position Statement*, 1976. James A. Banks, Chairperson (National Council for the Social Studies, 1515 Wilson Boulevard, Arlington, VA 22209); and James B. Macdonald, Bernice J. Wolfson, Esther Zaret, *Reschooling Society: A Conceptual Model*, Association for Supervision and Curriculum Development, 1201 Sixteenth Street, Washington, D.C. 20036. 1973.

108. See Thomas F. Green, *Work, Leisure, and the American School* (New York: Random House, 1968), in which he suggested that formal education in America served three functions: (1) socialization, (2) cultural transmission, and (3) the development of self-identity. See p. 148.

109. For examples, see Arturo Pacheco, "Cultural Pluralism: A Philosophical Analysis," pp. 16–20, and F. Chris Garcia, "Politics and Multicultural Education Do Mix," pp. 21–25 in *Journal of Teacher Education* 27, no. 3 (May-June 1977).

110. For example, see James F. Downs, *Cultures in Crisis* (Beverly Hills, Calif.: Glencoe Press, 1971); Ina Corinne Brown, *Understanding Other Cultures* (New Jersey: Prentice-Hall, 1963); and Wilma S. Longstreet, *Aspects of Ethnicity: Understanding Differences in Pluralistic Classrooms* (New York: Teachers College Press, 1978).

111. Refinements and variations differentiated emphases among such anthropologists as E. Adamson Hoebel, A. L. Kroeber, Ruth Benedict, Clyde Kluckhohn, and others. See Ake Hultkrantz, *General Ethnological Concepts, International Dictionary of Regional European Ethnology and Folklore*, 1 (Copenhagen: Rosenkilde and Bagger, 1960); see sections on "Configuration," pp. 51–2, and "Cultural Pattern," pp. 82–84. For an example, see Dorothy Lee, "Equality of Opportunity As A Cultural Value," in *Freedom and Culture* (New Jersey: Prentice-Hall, 1959), pp. 39–52.

112. For one example of this dispute and concern for meeting human needs in a modern industrial society, see Edward Sapir, "Cultural—Genuine and Spurious," *American Journal of Sociology* 29 (1924): pp. 401–429. Sapir expressed that modern life had not satisfied important human needs.

113. See John L. Hodge et al., *Cultural Bases of Racism*, especially, "Western Metaphysical Dualism," pp. 50–89.

114. In Robert Dentan's study of the Semai of Maylaya, he pointed out that Semai thought in terms of "both-and" and not in "either-or" categories. Robert Knox Dentan, *The Semai: A Non-violent People of Malaya* (New York:

Holt, Rinehart, and Winston, 1968), p. 94; Dorothy Lee suggested that Wintu, Native-American philosophy has "no law of contradiction" but only has categories that are inclusive, that is, one object is included in another, and its opposite does not exist. See *Freedom and Culture*, pp. 131. And the Zuni, according to Ruth Benedict, did not involve a stronger force in their lives; rather, they have the attitude that human beings are one with the universe. "They do not see the seasons, nor man's life, as a race run by life and death. Life is always present, death is always present. Death is no denial of life. The seasons unroll themselves before us, and man's life also." Ruth Benedict, *Patterns of Culture* (Boston: Houghton Mifflin, 1934), p. 312.

115. Categories include: A. Enumeratively Descriptive (Emphasis on Enumeration of Content); B. Historical (Emphasis on Social Heritage or Tradition); C. Normative (Emphasis on Rule or Way and Emphasis on Ideals or Values plus Behavior); D. Psychological (Emphasis on Learning, Emphasis on Habit, Purely Psychological Definitions); E. Structural; F. Genetic (Emphasis on Culture as a Product or Artifact, Emphasis on Ideas, Emphasis on Symbols, Residual Category Definitions) and G. Incomplete Definitions. See A. L. Kroeber and Clyde Kluckhohn, *Culture: A Critical Review of Concepts and Definitions* (New York: Vintage Books, 1952), pp. 77–156.

116. Ibid., pp. 165–170.

117. A. L. Kroeber, *Anthropology: Culture Patterns and Processes* (New York: Harcourt, Brace, and World, 1963), p. 1–13.

118. Edward B. Tylor, *Primitive Culture: Researches Into The Development of Mythology, Philosophy, Religion, Art and Custom*, 2 vols.; *Origins of Culture*, vol. 1, and *Religion in Primitive Culture*, vol. 2 (Gloucester, Mass.: Smith, 1958); original published in 1871.

119. For example, see Franz Boas, *Race, Language, and Culture* (New York: Macmillan, 1955); originally published in 1896, Bronislaw Malinowski, *A Scientific Theory of Culture and Other Essays* (Chapel Hill: University of North Carolina Press, 1944).

120. Alfred Kroeber's works present the theory of cultural patterns; see *The Nature of Culture* (Chicago: University of Chicago Press, 1952). The works of A. B. Radcliffe-Brown illustrate the theory of social structure; see *Methods in Social Anthropology: Selected Essays and Addresses*, M. N. Scriven, ed. (Chicago: University of Chicago Press, 1958); published posthumously.

121. David Bidney, "Cultural Relativism," *International Encyclopedia of the Social Sciences*, David L. Sills, ed. (New York: Macmillan and Free Press, 1968), pp. 543–544.

122. Ibid., p. 547.

123. In carrying out responsibilities as the Child Development Specialist in the New England Regional Office of Administration for Children, Youth and Families, in evaluation, monitoring and providing training and technical assistance to local Head Start grantees and education consultants, since 1967, the writer has had ongoing experience in encountering confusion, misunderstanding, and mixed emotions related to issues in "ethnicity," "race," and "culture." Numerous reports, position papers, and guidance were written by her and communicated to agency officials and to local programs such as "A Case for Multi-Ethnic Intercultural Education: A Philosophical View and Approach to Work with Young Children," 1975; "Culture and Education: A Case

for Multi-cultural Education: A Philosophy and Self-Development Model,"
1976; "Diversity and Values: Implications for Education," 1976; "Cultural Imperatives for Education in Head Start: A Position Paper," 1977; "Cultural Pluralism in the Education of Children," 1978; and others.

In 1973, the Head Start Policy on Performance Standards for the education component listed four separate standards that directly related to designing methods for dealing with pluralistic communities (language, culture, race) and about eight standards that have had an indirect connection to cultural aspects. See *Transmittal Notice* N-30-364-1 on Head Start Program Performance Standards, 1/8-73 and OCD-HS, Head Start Program Performance Standards, OCD-HS Notice N-30-364-4, July 1975, United States Department of Health, Education, and Welfare, Office of Human Development, Office of Child Development, Box 1182, Washington, D.C. 20013.

124. See Thomas Weaver and Douglas White, "Anthropological Approaches to Urban and Complex Society," in *The Anthropology of Urban Environments*, Thomas Weaver and Douglas White, eds. (Washington, D. C.: The Society for Applied Anthropology Monograph Series, Monograph 11, 1972) pp. 109-125. See also R. A. Schmerhorn, "Ethnicity in the Perspective of the Sociology of Knowledge," *Ethnicity: A Conceptual Approach*, Daniel E. Weinberg, ed. Cleveland Ethnic Heritage Studies, Cleveland State University, 1976, pp. 5–17.

125. Carlton C. Qualey, "Ethnicity and History," in *Ethnicity*, pp. 27–37.

126. Ibid., pp. 28–29.

127. Israel Rubin, "Ethnicity and Cultural Pluralism," in *Ethnicity*, pp. 94–95.

128. Alexis de Tocqueville, *Democracy in America*, trans. Henry Reeve (New York: D. Appleton & Co., 1901), p. 285, as quoted in Jules Henry's *Culture Against Man*, p. 6.

129. Ronald J. Busch, "Ethnic Assimilation vs. Cultural Pluralism: Some Political Implications," in *Ethnicity*, pp. 175–189. Also, Joseph P. Fitzpatrick, "The Importance of 'Community' In the Process of Immigrant Assimilation," in *Ethnicity*, pp. 81–89.

130. Henry, *Culture Against Man*, p. 9.

131. Ibid.

132. Ibid., p. 11.

133. Harold Sobel, "The Anachronistic Practices of American Education As Perpetuated by an Unenlightened Citizenry and Misguided Pedagogues Against the Inmates of the Public Schools." In *Foundations of Education: A Social View*, pp. 26-31, edited by Albert W. Vogel, David L. Bachelor and John T. Zepper, (Albuquerque: University of New Mexico Press, 1970).

134. Kathryn Johnson Noyes and Gordon L. McAndrew, "Is This What Schools Are For?" *Saturday Review*, 21 December 1968, p. 65.

135. Ibid.

136. Thomas C. Hogg and Martin R. McComb, "Cultural Pluralism: Its Implications for Education," in *Foundations of Education: A Social View,* Albert W. Vogen, David L. Bachelor, and John T. Zepper, eds. (Albuquerque, N.M.: University of New Mexico, 1970), p. 35.

137. See Robert M. Hutchins, "Education As Cultural Therapy," in *Social Foundations of Education: A Book of Readings,* edited by Cole S. Brembeck

and Martin Grandstaff (New York: John Wiley & Sons, 1969).

138. Ibid., p. 29.

139. Ibid., p. 24. Also, see Mark Kellog, "Indian Rights: Fighting Back with White Man's Weapons," *Saturday Review,* 25 November 1978, pp. 24–27.

140. See footnote 51.

141. See James K. Kent, "Race Class and Education," in *Social Foundations*, pp. 150-168, for critiques of a year-long discussion of the Coleman Report at Harvard University.

142. Ibid.

143. EMPAC, 12 (June 1977), p. 14

144. In addition to previous references, see Hilda Taba and Deborah Elkins, *Teaching Strategies for the Culturally Disadvantaged* (Chicago: Rand McNally, 1966), and Herve Varenne, "Culture as Rhetoric: Patterning in the Verbal Interpretation of Interaction Between Teachers and Administrators in an American High School," *American Ethnologist* 5, no. 4 (November 1978): 635–649.

145. Meredith Damian Gall, "The Importance of Context Variables in Research on Teaching Skills," *Journal of Teacher Education* 23, no. 3 (May–June 1977): 43–54; B. Rosenshine and N. F. Furst, "Research on Teacher Performance Criteria," in *Research in Teacher Education: A Symposium,* B. O. Smith, ed. (Englewood Cliffs, N.J.: Prentice-Hall, 1971), pp. 37–72.

146. In addition to previous references, see Jacqueline W. Johnson, "Human Relation Preparation in Teacher Education: The Wisconsin Experience," in *Pluralism and the American Teacher*, pp. 185–203.

147. In addition to previous references, see "Conference Proceedings, Bilingual Bicultural Preschool Projects Conference: Research, Staff Training, Curriculum Development, Resource Network," Administration for Children, Youth and Families, November 15–18, San Antonio, Texas.

148. See the entire issue of *Theory into Practice (TIP), Journal of College of Education,* 16, no. 3 (June 1977): 129–219, Ohio State University, on nonverbal communication. Sixteen authors discussed the subject from the level of the educator, classroom behavior, environment, to teacher skills.

149. Cornelius Lee Grove, *Communications Across Cultures.*

150. See Joan Cassell, *A Fieldwork Manual for Studying Desegregated Schools* (Washington, D.C.: NIE, 1978) and the special issue on Ethnographic Perspectives on Desegregated Schools in *Anthropology and Education Quarterly* 9, no. 4 (winter 1978), pp. 246–292. Five authors covered subjects related to court orders, desegregation, effects on an urban school, on student groups, social relations, and racially stratified communities.

151. See Philip G. Smith, ed., *Theories of Value and Problems of Education* (Urbana: University of Illinois Press, 1970); Nicholas Rescher, *Introduction to Value Theory* (Englewood Cliffs, N.J.: Prentice-Hall, 1969); Stafford A. Clayton, "Education and Some Moves Toward a Value Methodology," *Educational Theory* 19, no. 2 (Spring 1969): 198–210.

152. Douglas Superka et al., *Values Education Sourcebook* (Boulder, Col.: Social Science Education Consortium, Inc., 1976).

153 See Alan L. Lockwood, *Values Education and The Study of Other Children* (Washington, D.C.: NEA, 1976).

154. Ibid.

155. See Irwin R. Steinberg, "Class and Educational Meaning," in *Social Foundations*, pp. 169–177.

156. Joseph Featherstone, "Experiments in Learning," *The New Republic* (14 December 1968), and *Schools Where Children Learn* (New York: Liveright, 1971); David Hawkins, "Square Two: Square Three," *Forum for the Discussion of New Trends in Education* 12, no. 1 (Autumn 1969) pp. 4–6; Herbert R. Kohl, *The Open Classroom* (New York: Vintage, 1970).

157. See John Holt, *How Children Fail* (New York: Pitman, 1964); Charles E. Silberman, *Crisis in the Classroom* (New York: Random House, 1970); Neil Postman and Charles Weingartener, *Teaching as a Subversive Activity*.

158. Mario D. Fantini and Gerald Weinstein, *The Disadvantaged: Challenges to Education* (New York: Harper and Row, 1968), pp. 221–222.

159. Grace Graham, "Influences of Social Class Differences in Schools," in *Foundation of Education*, pp. 127—147.

160. Ibid., p. 145.

161. Arthur Jensen, "Reducing the Hereditary Environment Uncertainty: A Reply," *Harvard Educational Review* 39 (Spring 1961): 273–356.

162. Doxey Wilkerson, "Compensatory Education: Defining the Issues," in *Disadvantaged Child: Compensatory Education, A National Debate*, Jerome Hellmuth, ed. (New York: Brunner/Mazel Publishers, 1970), p. 28.

163. William B. Levenson, "Compensatory Education Programs," *Foundations of Education*, p. 301.

164. Ibid., pp. 303–305.

165. Ibid., p. 304. See also Fantini and Weinstein, *The Disadvantaged*, pp. 236, 435.

166. Title 1 of the Elementary and Secondary School Act ESEA) of 1965, (P.L. 89-10, and amendments). See *Compensatory Educational Programs, March 1977, Title 1 ESEA, Title IV, Community Services Act: Program Descriptions and Status Reports*, Office of Compensatory Educational Programs, Office of Education in HEW.

167. Ibid., p. 2.

168. Irving Lazar et al., *The Persistence of Preschool Effects: A Long-Term Follow-up of Fourteen Infant and Preschool Experiments, Analysis and Final Report*, prepared for HEW, Administration for Children, Youth and Families, September 1977, p. 1.

169. *Evaluating Compensatory Education*, p. xx.

170. Two articles in *The Public Citizen*, no. 8 (Winter 1978): discussed taxes, tax cuts and implications. California's passage of proposition 13 promised relief for property owners, the tax base which supported school systems. Almost immediately after passage, twelve other states followed California's lead. See Robert S. McIntyre, "Federal Taxes," p. 3, 12, and Diane Fuch's, "State and Local Taxes," p. 3. Headline for the two articles, "Some Winners, Some Losers."

171. Robert K. Merton, "Self-Fulfilling Prophecy," in *Children and Poverty: Some Sociological and Psychological Perspectives*, Nona Y. Glazer and Carol F. Creedon, eds. (Chicago: Rand McNally, 1970), p. 18.

172. *Evaluating Compensatory Education*, pp. xvii–xx.

173. Ibid., p. 11–14.

174. Ibid., pp. 111–118.

175. Ibid., pp. 111–119.

176. The NIE Report lists many studies; see bibliography, pp. iv–18 to iv–20.

177. James F. Winschel, "In the Dark . . . Reflections on Compensatory Education 1960–1970," in *Disadvantaged Child*, p. 3.

178. Ibid., p. 8.

179. Fantini and Weinstein, *Disadvantaged*, p. 2; see also pp. 2–39.

180. Ronald Lippitt, "Improving the Socialization Process," in *Socialization and Society*, John A. Clauson, ed., p. 334. Lippitt discussed at least nine such institutions; formal education, churches, recreational leisure time and cultural programs, social control and protection agencies (police, courts, safety, etc.).

181. Marshall McLuhan, *Understanding Media: The Extension of Man* (New York: McGraw-Hill, 1966).

182. Ibid., "Toward A Relevant Curriculum," pp. 338–373.

183. Ibid., p. 421.

184. Saul Alinsky, "The War on Poverty—Political Pornography," *Journal of Social Issues* 21, no. 1 (January 1965): pp. 41–47.

185. Ibid., p. 47.

186. Ronald Lippitt, "Improving the Socialization Process," p. 336.

187. Ibid., pp. 336–337.

188. See Daniel U. Levine, "The Integration-Compensatory Education Controversy," in *Foundation of Education*, pp. 338–346.

189. *Racial Isolation in the Public Schools,* vol. 1 (Washington, D.C.: U.S. Government Printing Office, 1967), p. 138.

190. See Otto Kerner, *National Advisory Commission on Civil Disorders Report* (Washington, D.C.: U.S. Government Printing Office, 1968); D. Walker, *Rights in Conflict, Report Submitted to the National Commission on the Causes and Prevention of Violence* (New York: Bantam Books, 1968).

191. See "The Education Game," in *The Daily Californian*, reprinted in *Toward Social Change: A Handbook for Those Who Will*, Robert Buckhaut and 81 Concerned Berkeley Students, eds. (New York: Harper & Row, 1971), pp. 432–433. In the same volume, see also Carol Matzkin, "$6,000 Degree in Boredom," pp. 433–434, and Jerry Rubin, "Burn Down the Schools," pp. 434–436.

192. See Stokely Carmichael and Charles V. Hamilton, "White Power: The Colonial Situation," pp. 97–102, and the Black Students Organization's "Credo of Black Students," p. 108 in *Toward Social Change*.

193. See Amitai Etzione, "Man and Society: The Inauthentic Condition," reprinted in *Toward Social Change*, pp. 24–28. See also William Van Til, "The Key Word Is Relevance," *Today's Education* (January 1969), pp. 14–17.

194. Etzione, "Man and Society," p. 27.

195. "Tio Taco Is Dead," *Newsweek,* 29 June 1970, pp. 22–28; Alex Hing, "The Need for a United Asian-American Front," reprinted in *Toward Social Change*, pp. 115–116; William Hedgepeth, "America's Indians: Reawakening of a Conquered People," *Look Magazine*, 2 June 1970, p. 23.

196. James Banks, "Ethnic Modification of the Curriculum," *Illinois Schools Journal,* vol. 55 no. 4 (Winter 1975/1976): 24.

197. Ibid.

198. James Banks, *Teaching Strategies for Ethnic Studies*, p. 27.

199. Ibid., p. 11.

200. James Banks, "Ethnic Modification of the Curriculum," p. 29.

201. See U.S. Commission on Civil Rights, *A Better Chance to Learn: Bilingual-Bicultural Education*. As used in this report, the term refers to "persons in the United States who speak a non-English native language and who belong to an identifiable minority group of generally low socio-economic status," p. 1.

202. In January 1974, the Supreme Court in *Lau* v. *Nichols* provided for equal opportunity in education through assisting children who know little or no English. See 414 U.S. 563 (1974).

203. See José M. Gonzalez, "Growth Pains in Bilingual-Bicultural Education since '66," *Report of Bilingual-Bicultural Institute* (Washington, D.C.: National Education Association Conference, 28 November-December 1, 1973; *The NEA Task Force on Bilingual-Bicultural Education*, 53rd Representative Assembly of the NEA, Washington, D.C.: NEA July 2, 1974; P. L. Engle, "Language Medium in Early School Years for Minority Groups," *Review of Educational Research* 45, no. 2 (1975): 283–325.

204. Ibid.

205. *A Better Chance to Learn*, p. 22.

206. Ibid., p. 60.

207. PL 90-247. The 1968 Bilingual Act or Title VII of ESEA of 1965, as amended, made provision for school districts interested in establishing programs for low-income English limited children. In 1974, amendments to the Act changed the low-income restriction to include any language minority child. It also provided a definition of a bilingual education program. See PL 92-380, for definition see 20 U.S.C.A. 880b-1 (a)(4)(A)(6). It also established a National Advisory Council.

208. *Instructional Strategies in Schools With High Concentrations of Low-Income Pupils: National Task Forces, A Report to the USOE*.

209. Ibid., p. 105.

210. *National Advisory Council on Bilingual Education: Second Annual Report*, prepared by Inter-America Research Associates, 2001 Wisconsin Ave., N.W., Suite 260, Washington, D.C. 20007.

211. Ibid., p. 7.

212. American Institute for Research, *Interim Report, Evaluation of the Impact of ESEA Title VII Spanish/English Bilingual Education Programs*, Palo Alto, California, February 1977.

213. Noel Epstein, *Language, Ethnicity, and the Schools: Policy Alternatives for Bilingual Bicultural Education* (Washington, D.C.: Institute for Educational Leadership, George Washington University, 1977), p. 11.

214. José A. Cardenas, *An IDRA Response With A Summary By Dr. Jose A. Cardenas* (Intercultural Development Research Association: 5835 Callagham Rd., Suite 350/111, San Antonio, Texas 78228, June 1977).

215. Ibid., p. ii.

216. A. H. Maslow, *The Farther Reaches of Human Nature*, p. 5.

217. Novak, Michael, "Among Middle-Class Ethnics: A Great Deal of Bitterness." *Interview with Michael Novak, Philosopher and Social Critic. Special Report U.S. News and World Report.* Reprinted by EMPAC, Ethnic Millions Political Action Committee, 1974.

218. See John Gurdo, "The Born-Again Ethnic," in *EMPAC: Newsletter of the Ethnic Millions Political Action Committee* 12 (June 1977), pp. 11-14.

219. B. Othaniel Smith, et al., *Teachers for the Real World*. Also, see text of ESEA of 1965, Title IX, as amended by the Education Amendments of 1972 and 1974, Ethnic Studies Program in Appendix A of HEW *Application for Grants Under the Ethnic Heritage Studies Program*, December 20, 1977, pp. 319-320.

220. Write to AACTE for reprints.

221. See William A. Hunter, "Antecedents to Development of and Emphases on Multicultural Education," in *Multi-cultural Education: Through Competency-Based Teacher Education*, William A. Hunter, ed. (Washington, D.C.: American Association of Colleges for Teacher Education, 1974) pp. 11-31.

222. Ibid., see the text of the Multicultural Statement, pp. 21-33.

223. Renée Davis, "Cultural Pluralism in the Education of Children" (address presented at the Rhode Island Conference for Early Childhood Education, April 7-8, 1978). The chart developed for this presentation, "Federal-State Legislative Mandates Related to Ethnic Cultural Diversity," unpublished.

224. Donna Gollnick, *State Legislation, Provisions and Practices Related to Multicultural Education*. Report for the NIE, January 1978 (unpublished).

225. See "Multiculturalism," *Journal of Teacher Education* 26, no. 2 (Summer 1975): 119-132. James Banks, "Cultural Pluralism and Contemporary Schools," *Integrated Education* 14 (Jan/Feb 1976): 32-36, and David Washburn, "A Conceptual Framework for Multi-Cultural Education," *The Florida FL Reporter* (Spring/Fall, 1972): 27-28.

226. James Banks, "The Implications of Multicultural Education for Teacher Education," pp. 1-30.

227. David E. Washburn, *Multicultural Programs, Ethnic Studies, Curricula, and Ethnic Studies Materials in the U.S. Public Schools, Department of Educational Studies and Services* (Bloomsburg State College: Bloomsburg, PA 17815. 1974)

228. Banks, *"Implications of Multicultural Education,"* p. 13.

229. Ibid., p. 6.

230. See *Multicultural Education and Ethnic Studies in the United States: An Analysis and Annotated Bibliography of Selected Documents in ERIC*, Donna M. Gollnick, Frank H. Klassen, and Joost Yff, ed. (Washington, D.C.: AACTE, No. One Dupont Circle, N.W., and ERIC Clearinghouse on Teacher Education, February 1976).

231. See Jack D. Forbes, *Education of the Culturally Different: A Multicultural Approach* (Berkeley, Calif.: Far West Laboratory for Educational Research and Development, 1968), and F. M. Cordasco and H. A. Bullock, *The School in the Social Order* (Scranton, Penn.: International Textbook Co., 1970).

232. See P. R. Sanday, "The Relevance of Anthropology to U.S. Social Policy," *Council on Anthropology and Education Newsletter* 3, no. 1 (1972).

233. Nancy Seifer, "Education and the New Pluralism: A Preliminary Survey of Recent Progress in the Five States" (Paper presented at the Annual Meeting of the National Coordinating Assembly on Ethnic Studies).

234. See Richard James, "Multicultural Education From a Black Educator's Perspective," in Hunter, ed. *Multicultural Education*, pp. 35-39.

235. See Ernest Garcia, "Chicano Cultural Diversity: Implications for

Competency-Based Teacher-Education," in Hunter, ed., *Multicultural Education*, pp. 146–157.

236. R. A. Schermerhorn, *Comparative Ethnic Relations: A Framework for Theory and Research* (New York: Random House, 1970).

237. See "No One Model American: A Statement on Multicultural Education," American Association of Colleges for Teacher Education.

238. William H. Newman, *American Pluralism* (New York: Harper & Row, 1972).

239. Margaret Alison Gibson, "Approaches to Multicultural Education in the U.S.: Some Concepts and Assumptions," *Anthropology and Education Quarterly* 7, no. 4 (November 1976): p. 14.

240. Ibid., pp. 15–16.

241. Ward H. Goodenough, "Multiculturalism As the Normal Human Experiences," *Anthropology and Education Quarterly*, pp. 4–6.

242. Gibson, p. 5.

243. Ibid., p. 16.

244. James Winschel, "In the Dark . . . Reflections in Compensatory Education," p. 9.

245. Thomas Kuhn, *Scientific Revolutions,* p. 59. See also "Anomaly and the Emergence of Scientific Discoveries," pp. 52–65.

246. Ibid., p. 65.

247. Ibid.

248. Donald T. Campbell, "Introduction," Herskovitz, *Cultural Relativism,* p. xii.

249. See Albert Einstein. "Science and Religion: A Symposium." Conference on Science, Philosophy and Religion in their Relation to the Democratic Way of Life, pp. 211–213. Edited by L. Bryson and L. Finkelstein, (N.Y., 1941).

250. Herskovitz, *Cultural Relativism*, p. 11.

251. Ibid., p. 97. See also section "A Cross-Cultural View of Bias and Values," pp. 97–109.

252. David Bidney, "Cultural Relativism," in *Encyclopedia of the Social Sciences*, p. 543.

253. Herskovitz, *Cultural Relativism*, pp. 32–34.

254. See Antonia Pantoja and Barbara Blourock, "Cultural Pluralism Redefined," in Pantoja et al., *Badges and Indicia of Slavery,* pp. 2-25. The authors disputed Horace M. Kallen's views on rejecting the "melting pot," which became the basis of a national colloquy. See Kallen's *Culture and Democracy in the United States* (New York: Liveright, 1924).

255. *United States Riot Commission Report,* Report of the National Advisory Commission on Civil Disorders (New York: Dutton and Co., 1968).

256. For example, see Kenneth B. Clark, "Problems of Power and Social Change; Toward a Relevant Social Psychology," *Journal of Social Issues* 21, no. 3 (1965): 420. Also, Margaret Mead, "Education As Cultural Growth," in *Social Foundations of Education: A Book of Readings,* Cole S. Brembeck and Marvin Grandstaff, eds. (New York: John Wiley, 1969), pp. 18–30. And David Riesman, "Some Questions About the Study of American Character in the Twentieth Century Life Styles," *Diversity in American Society*, Saul Feldman and Gerald W. Thielbar, eds. (Boston: Little, Brown and Co., 1972).

257. See National Institute of Education's *The Desegregation Literature: A Critical Appraisal,* July 1976, p. 5–8.

258. William Newman, *American Pluralism: A Study of Minority Groups and Social Theory* (New York: Harper and Row, 1973).

259. Ibid., pp. 271–272.

260. As quoted in William R. Hazard and Madelon Stent, "Cultural Pluralism and Schooling: Some Preliminary Observations," in Madelon D. Stent, William R. Hazard, and Harry N. Rivlin, eds., *Cultural Pluralism in Education: A Mandate for Change* (New York: Appleton-Century-Crofts, 1973), p. 14.

261. William Smith, "The Melting Pot Theory: Demise of Euphemism," in Stent et al., *Cultural Pluralism*, pp. 141–144. Also, John A. Carpenter and Judith V. Torney, "Overview: Beyond the Melting Pot to Cultural Pluralism."

262. Studies of race and ethnicity provided interesting information. Second-generation ethnic groups generally tended toward assimilation; however, research on second and third generations uncovered pluralistic patterns. See Newman, *American Pluralism;* Michael Novak, *The Rise of the Unmeltable Ethnics* (New York: Macmillan, 1972); Colin Greer, *The Great School Legend;* Andrew Greely, *Why Can't They Be Like Us?;* Murry Friedman, ed., *Overcoming Middle Class Rage;* and Irving Levine and Judith Herman, "The Life of White Ethnics," *Dissent*, Winter 1972.

263. David E. Washburn, "A Conceptual Framework of Multicultural Education," *The Florida FL Reporter*, Spring/Fall 1972, p. 27.

264. Title VII, a provision of the 1968 Elementary and Secondary Education Act (ESEA) of 1965 promoted languages in classrooms other than English; the Bilingual Education Act of the 1974 amendments of ESEA created an office to administer the provisions of the Act. The 1974 Supreme Court decision in *Lau* v. *Nichols* mandated bilingual activities to remedy language difficulties, Summary of Findings *Brown* v. *Califano* for Office of Civil Rights in HEW, see legislation on Affirmative Action, Civil Rights, Equal Employment Opportunity, and five court cases during 1952–1955 (schools in Sumerton, S.C.; Farmville, Va.; Topeka, Ka.; Wilmington, Del; and Washington, D.C.) and decision of *Brown* v. *Board of Education*, May 17, 1954.

265. James A. Banks, "The Implications of Multicultural Education for Teacher Education," in *Pluralism and the American Teacher: Issues and Case Studies*, F. Klassen and D. Gollnick, eds. p. 11. Also, for a comprehensive discussion of issues related to assimilationist, pluralist, and ethnicity, see pp. 1–30.

266. Ibid., p. 13.

267. Ibid., pp. 13–41.

268. John Hodge, Donald K. Struckmann, and Lynn Dorland Trost, *Cultural Bases in Racism and Group Oppression* (Berkeley, Calif.: Two Riders Press, 1975).

269. Ibid., p. 3, 5.

270. See Harry N. Rivlin and Dorothy M. Fraser, "Ethnic Labeling and Mislabeling," in *In Praise of Diversity: A Resource Book for Multicultural Education*, Milton J. Gold, Carl A. Grant, Harry N. Rivlin, eds. (Washington, D.C.: Association of Teacher Educators, 1977); Neil Postman and Charles Weingarten, *Teaching As a Suversive Activity* (New York: Delta Books, 1969); also, Bensen R. Snyder, *The Hidden Curriculum;* Robert Rosenthal and Lenore Jacobson, *Pygmalion in the Classroom: Teacher Expectations and Pupil's Intellectual Development* (New York: Holt, Rinehart, and Winston, 1968); Jerome B. Dusek, "Do Teachers Bias Children's Learning"; E. K. Wickman, *Children's*

Behavior and Teacher Attitudes; R. G. Rist, "Student Social Class and Teacher Expectations."

271. See Melville J. Herskovitz, "Education and the Sanctions of Custom," in *Cultural Relevance and Educational Issues: Readings in Anthropology and Education,* Francis A. J. Ianni and Edward Storey, eds. (Boston: Little, Brown and Co., 1973), pp. 29–47.

272. See Corliss Lamont, *The Philosophy of Humanism* (New York: Frederick Ungar Publishing Co., 1977), especially pp. 3–19. For an expanded definition, see the ten central propositions in humanist philosophy as outlined on pp. 12–14. Reason and science were crucial to humanistic thinking providing knowledge, while creative imagination was considered valid and significant determinants for both the individual and the social "good." See pp. 227–283.

273. Ibid., p. 22.

274. Eric Fromm, *Escape From Freedom* (Boston: Houghton Mifflin, 1941), p. 12.

275. Eric Fromm, *Man for Himself* (Boston: Houghton Mifflin, 1947), p. 60.

276. See William S. Sahakian, *Systematic Social Psychology* (New York: Chandler Publishing Co., 1974), especially chapter 13, "The Cultural Psychoanalysts," pp. 163–177. See also John Martin Rich, *Humanistic Foundations of Education* (Worthington, Ohio: Charles A. Jones Publishing Co., 1971), especially chapter 2, "The Student as a Person," pp. 63–91.

277. See John B. Watson, *Psychology From the Standpoint of a Behaviorist* (Baltimore: Penguin Books, 1974); B.F. Skinner modified this behavioristic view and differed from Watson in that concepts must be observable to the senses and did not explain physiological states but rather described functions. See B. F. Skinner, *Science and Human Behavior* (New York: Macmillan, 1953), p. 258.

278. See Paul Tillich, *The Courage to Be* (New Haven, Conn.: Yale University Press, 1952).

279. For components essential in humanistic learning, see *Humanistic Education Sourcebook,* Donald A. Read and Sidney B. Simon, eds. (New Jersey: Prentice Hall, 1975). Components include interpersonal relationships, relationships between ideas in learning and feelings, role of the teacher, and impact of experience.

280. "The Interpersonal Relationship in the Facilitation of Learning," in *Humanistic Education Sourcebook,* Carl Rogers, p. 6. Also, see Gerald Weinstein and Mario D. Fantini, eds., *Toward Humanistic Education: A Curriculum Affect* (New York: Praeger Publishers, 1970).

281. Abraham H. Maslow, "Creativity in Self-Actualizing People," in H. H. Anderson, ed., *Creativity and Its Cultivation* (New York: Harper and Bros., 1959); also, *The Farther Reaches of Human Nature* (New York: Penguin Books, 1971), pp. 40–51.

282. The profession of "school administration" developed by public school personnel who were vulnerable during the period as a reaction to business practice. The "Taylor System," after the engineer Frederick W. Taylor's ideas for manufacturing and corporate management, spread throughout the nation in the early twentieth century. It had its mark on school administrators who sought to apply the idea of increased productivity to the educational process.

See Raymond E. Callaghan, *Education and the Cult of Efficiency* (Chicago: University of Chicago Press, 1962).

283. See Michael B. Katz, "Bureaucracy and the Industrial Order," pp. 239–240; A. Richard King, "The Bureaucrat, The Martyr and The Artificial Self," pp. 247–251, and Anthony Oettinger, "Run Computer Run," pp. 264–268, in Miriam Wasserman, ed., *Demystifying School: Writings and Experiences* (New York: Praeger Publishers, 1974).

284. In American schooling, three main approaches had been influential in thinking; the "traditional," "classic education," copied from European practice; and "basic education," focusing primarily on fundamental skills such as reading, writing, and computation; and "progressive education" which promoted a child-oriented rather than subject-matter, teacher-directed education. In "progressive ideas," the emphasis was placed on mental health and sound socioemotional development as important goals in addition to "basic" aspects. It included art, music, and literature. See L. Joseph Stone and Joseph Church, *Childhood and Adolescence: A Psychology of the Growing Person* (New York: Random House, 1973), pp. 388–414.

The "child-study movement," which had been directed by the supposition that individual differences could be fully understood only in relation to each child's total personality, slowly deteriorated as standardization became the accepted doctrine. See Richard M. Brandt, "The Child-Study Movement," in *Cultural Pluralism and Social Change: A Collection of Position Papers*, Report V of the In-Service Teacher Education Project sponsored by the National Center for Education Statistics and Teacher Corps. The National Dissemination Center, Syracuse University, 123 Huntington Hall, Syracuse, New York 13210. Project Coordinators, Bruce R. Joyce and Lucy F. Peck, pp. 10–51.

285. See Irving Berlin, "Education for What?"

286. Gerald Weinstein and Mario D. Fantini, "Affect and Learning"; *Humanistic Education Sourcebook*, pp. 101–102. See also George Isaac Brown, "What Is 'Confluent Education'?" Ibid. pp 50–61.

287. Arthur W. Combs, "Humanistic Goals of Education," *Humanistic Education Sourcebook*, p. 91.

288. Jean-Paul Sartre, "Authentic and Inauthentic Man," in *The Substance of Sociology: Codes, Conduct and Consequences* (New York: Appleton-Century-Crofts, 1967), p. 215.

289. Paulo Freire, *Pedagogy of the Oppressed*, trans. Myra Bergman Ramor (New York: Seabury Press, 1970). See also Jean Piaget's works and the literature on humanistic education.

290. Fuller, *Utopia*, p. 6.

291. Meadows et al., *Limits of Growth*.

292. Ryan, *Blaming the Victim*, p. 11.

293. Freire, *Pedagogy*, p. 27.

294. Ibid., p. 28.

295. Ibid.,

296. Ibid., p. 30, footnote; as used throughout this book, the term "contradiction" denoted the dialectical conflict between opposing social forces. Translator's note.

297. Ibid., p. 31.

298. Ibid., p. 33.

299. Ryan, *Blaming the Victim*, p. 6.

300. Ibid., see chapter 1, "The Art of Savage Discovery."

301. Ibid., pp. 8–9. Ryan suggested that C. Wright Mills had examined the theoretical basis of those who wrote about social problems. His conclusion pointed to the relationship of their pointed to class interest and to perpetuation of the current social structures.

302. Ryan, "Community Care in Historical Perspective: Implications for Mental Health Services and Professionals," *Canada's Mental Health* supplement 60 (March-April, 1969).

Glossary

Many definitions and interpretations of the major terms of this study exist. The definitions reflect a condition and a concept specifically related to the value placed on them by this study.

Absolute. Those values that are perceived to be invariable, unchanging, that do not differ from culture to culture.

Acculturation. It is that process of culture change in the context of culture borrowing. It is the phenomena that results when members of a group having a different culture are in continuous direct contact, and the subsequent changes in the original culture patterns of either or both groups.

Anthropology. The study of human beings.

Assimilation. Is the process of integration of one group when it adapts the behavior patterns and values of a different cultural group. It results in the loss of its unique cultural characteristics. Usually groups that are in the minority take on the cultural characteristics of the dominant ethnic groups.

Basic patterns. The fundamental cultural aspects that characterize the whole culture.

Bias. A term used to describe the reactions and evaluations focused on the customs and beliefs of the group in which an individual has been enculterated. It is a form of ethnocentrism.

Common cultural heritage. The cultural products in different cultures that originate in a common underlying culture or the "social heredity" of a group.

Configuration. The concept that defines an arrangement or system in which the totality is more than the sum of its parts. At times, it refers to the dominant or unifying tendency within a larger whole.

Covert culture. The implicit, nonmanifest ideas and patterns.

Cross-cultural method. An anthropological method characterized by sampling different ethnic units all over the world to show the regularity of a custom, belief, social relationship, and so on.

Cultural anthropology. That branch of anthropology studying human culture, cultural materials. (It is the American counterpart of European ethnology.)

Cultural dynamics. The conditions of cultural change. It is a cultural process.

Cultural pattern. Cultural traits or complexes that are organized into an integrated unit. The "integrating principle" differentiates between trends that dominate in a value system and the configuration that refers to the quality and profile in a culture. The values shared by the group.

Cultural pluralism. The situation that recognizes and accepts the equal coexistence of distinct ethnic cultural groups that maintain their heritages within one nation made up of diverse cultures.

Cultural relativism. An anthropological concept and method to understand the nature and role of values in culture by interpreting and evaluating the appropriateness of any cultural manifestations within the cultural context of the given group.

Culture. It is the whole of ideological premises, learned behavior, mental, social, and material characteristics transmitted distinguishing a human social group. It is a generic concept with wide parameters and includes broad classifications and subgroupings. Culture is made up of all the elements that human society develops: its symbols, customs, institutions, behavior patterns, values, and beliefs that differentiate it from other human societies. (A. L. Kroeber and Clyde Kluckhohn, *Culture: A Critical Review of Concepts and Definitions.*)

Culture sense. A term created by the writer to connote knowledge of the dynamics of culture and its functions and the part it plays in the lives of human beings. It is the universal factors and the dynamics of differences and culture change knowable by people.

Custom. A behavior or behavior pattern considered right or good by the social group because of its conformity to the living cultural tradition.

Education. It is that part of the enculturative experience that, through the learning process, equips an individual to take a place as an adult member of the given society.

Education for cultural pluralism. The theoretical concepts in a model that serves as the foundation for developing alternative designs for including cultural dynamics in the learning process. The criteria are organized in such a manner as to serve as a prototype for future education programs at all levels of development.

Enculturation. It is that informal process that continues throughout life that transmits the traditions and values from one generation to the next.

Environment. The totality of external conditions and influences that affect human beings.

Ethics. Modes of thought that justify or criticize the morality.

Ethnicity. A term used as a concept and a behavioral system that distinct groups organize their lives. The ethnic group shares a common sense of identity, common sense of values, political view, economic interests, behavior patterns, and other cultural traits that distinguish them from other groups within a complex society. R. A. Schermerhorn defined ethnic groups as "a collectivity within a larger society having real or putative common ancestry; memories of a shared historical past, and a cultural focus on one or more symbolic elements . . . kinship patterns, physical continguity (as in localism or sectionalism), religious affiliation, language or dialect forms, tribal affiliations, nationally phenotypical features, or any combination of these." (*Ethnicity: A Conceptual Approach*, David E. Weinberg, ed., p. 5.)

Ethnocentrism. The viewpoint that the way of life to be preferred is the one that comes from the given group into which one is raised. It is cultural self-centeredness. Melville Herskovitz defines it as "the point of view that one's own way of life is to be preferred to all others. Flowing logically from the process of early enculturation, it characterizes the way most individuals feel about their own culture, whether or not they verbalize their feelings." (*Cultural Relativism: Perspective in Cultural Pluralism*, p. 21.)

Ethnography. It is the branch of cultural anthropology that is descriptive ethnology, which notes the data observed in the field.

Ethnology. The science of humankind as cultural beings. It is a division of anthropology devoted to analysis and systematic interpretation of cultural data (cultural anthropology).

Family. The (cultural) term designated to the minimal domestic groups that cooperate economically, are assigned to socialize and care for children by older members, and exchange offspring through marriage with other family units.

Frame of reference. The overall context in which a behavior response to an experience is organized, past experience, and learned expectation.

Function. Relation of an element or elements within a larger whole. The interconnections between cultural features, particularly the contribution made by a part of a culture to that whole culture.

Gestalt. An undivided, artificial whole that cannot be made up of mere addition of independent elements. It is a pattern or configuration implying that the whole is not analyzable into separate parts but that it is an integration.

Goal. The end result of an activity defined in advance by an observer; that for which the individual strives.

Heritage. The traits inherited from antecedents of a social group.

History or historical reference. Any process or developmental stages that can be reorganized through some satisfactory means. It is implied as being a working hypothesis (from Malinowski).

Humanistic education. A system through which individuals are provided the opportunity to develop fully, preparing for life, while fostering a social consciousness for one's group and society at large.

Institution. A term to denote a set of recurrent behavior patterns that serve to satisfy basic needs of a society.

Integration. The principle by which parts combine into a whole. In ethnology, the functional interrelations between cultural traits and systems as well as between culture and other factors.

Model. A device for the systematization of knowledge and theory built on empirical data but conceived as an abstract structure.

Multicultural education. Philosophical questions have been raised by endorsing concepts in which ethnic groups and the cultural heritage that characterizes the American society become a part of the educational system. An approach in which the educational environment enhances positive attitude toward those whose cultural groups have been victims of discrimination (from Banks).

Myth. Symbolic expressions that describe human existence, interests, and powers of entities. It has an explanatory function in which an order in the universe is depicted.

Needs. The basic forces behind cultural manifestations. Cultural need is the body of conditions that must be fulfilled for survival. Basic needs are biological, and derived needs are cultural responses to those basic needs. The positive force of the derived needs—that which calls forth the response—is termed "cultural imperatives" or instrumental imperatives of culture.

Open system. Living systems that are in continual interaction with an environment.

"Organic" or "physical" anthropology. Refers to the biological laws (heredity, cell development, evolution, and the outcome from disciplines such as physiology, embryology, zoology, etc.). Organic sciences are the foundations of sociocultural contexts.

Overt culture. The manifest forms of culture having at least three different orders: material, kinetic (overt behavior), and psychological.

Paradigm. The theory, application, or instrumentalization of scientific practice as a means through which scientific traditions are created (from Kuhn).

Primitive. The lower order in a complex. Primitive people are characterized by their mentality and their creative power. They do not produce, they merely reproduce.

Reality. That perception that an individual learns to feel and believe. The values held that are learned through direct and indirect experiences of acculturation—the individual's interpretation of the world. The perceptual components are interpreted through the senses and through abstract concepts. Matter, energy, time, space, and motion are also conceptual ways in which "reality" is understood.

Sanction. The validation and enforcing mechanism used for approving and endorsing a behavior or belief.

Schooling. Those processes of teaching and learning carried on at specific times in particular places by persons who are especially prepared for the task.

Social. Usually refers to phenomena that are nonorganic or "more than organic." It usually is attributed to both "social" and cultural phenomena.

Social system. Any functioning social unit.

Socialization. The process both conscious and unconscious of passing on the culture, that is, skills, knowledge, attitudes, values, and behavior, to the next generation. The process of becoming a member of a society.

Society. It is the largest and most complex system of human behavior consisting of active and latent cultural patterns. Culture and society have been used synonymously; however,

they differ even though they are closely related, according
to Frederik Bates and Clyde Harvey. Society is the ongoing,
largest, most complicated system of human behavior to
which people belong, and culture consists of learned behavior patterns acquired through socialization. They each refer
to *phases* rather than entities in the process of behavior.
"There is but one entity called *society* or the *social system.*
Its parts at any given time, exist in two states, an active
state and a latent state . . . active state, the parts of society
are observed as actively engaged in behavior . . . stored, latent behavior patterns awaiting the conditions which will
reactivate that portion of the social system" (*The Structure
of Social System*, pp. 40–41).

Sociocultural system. Refers as used in this study to the totality
of experiences as expressed through organization, including
the concept of social interactions as commonly used. The
interpretation of those phenomena that effect the innate
organic and acquired elements.

Socioculture. The superorganic configuration built up by society and culture in intimate interaction.

Status. A social pattern in a society.

Stereotype. Group of emotionally laden ideas on a scale of values so uncritically believed that they prevent unbiased observation or clear thinking in a situation.

Structure. Is a hypothetical construct that orders in space a set
of interconnected elements, each of which is named and each
of which has a part in the transformation of some social
process.

Style. The construct and recurrent pattern in culture, the
"spirit" or "essence" of culture.

Symbol. A form that is usually a fixed sensory signal to which
some permanent meaning is arbitrarily assigned.

Tonal feeling. A term created by the writer meant to denote
a mood or state of mind encompassing mental attitude, posture, outlook, and caring.

Tradition. Culture elements handed down from one generation
to another.

Trait. A minimum significant unit of a culture.

Transmission of cultural materials. The passing on of cultural materials from older times or from one place to another or from one social group (or class) to another.

Universal. A term that refers to those common factors identified from a range of diverse factors manifested from natural and cultural phenomena. The index of cultural aspects common to all cultures. Cultural forms and contents that, irrespective of historical connection, appear or *may* appear in any culture.

Universal culture affective model (UCAM). Is a meta-theory that uses the universality of classifications that become unique patterns that are revealed in all cultures. The model integrates culture knowledge, sensitivity to, and the recognition of different social realities through universal phenomena. It incorporates four major interrelated components that link holistic channels. It is the theoretical base to value cultural diversity.

Values (culture). It is the abstraction of the beliefs shared by each unique social group regarding right or wrong, moral and immoral, and good and bad. It is usually emotionally charged preferences or standards of worth.

Victim. Is someone who is seen as the cause of a social problem and is singled out for change.

Bibliography

Abell, Peter. *Model Building in Sociology*. New York: Schocken Books, 1971.

Albert, Ethel. "The Classification of Values." *American Anthropology* 58 (1956):221–248.

Alinsky, Saul. "The War on Poverty—Political Pornography." *Journal of Social Issues* 21, no. 1 (January 1965):41–47.

Alland, Alexander Jr. *Human Diversity*. New York: Anchor Press, 1973.

American Association of Colleges for Teacher Education. *No One Model American: A Statement on Multicultural Education*, Washington, D.C.: American Association of Colleges for Teacher Education, 1973.

American Educational Research Association (AERA). *Curriculum and Evaluation Monograph*. Chicago: Rand McNally, 1967.

American Jewish Committee. *Pluralism: Beyond the Frontier. Report of the San Francisco Consultation on Ethnicity 16-17 November 1971*. San Francisco, Calif.: American Jewish Committee, Nov. 16-17, 1971

Anastasi, Ann. "Heredity Environment and the Question of 'How?' " *Psychological Review* 65 (July 1958):197–208.

Angyal, A. "A Logic of Systems." In *Systems Thinking*, edited by E. F. Emery. Middlesex, England: Penguin Books, 1969, pp. 17–29.

Argyle, Michael. *Bodily Communication*. New York: International Universities Press, 1975.

Association for Childhood Education International. *Minorities Speak Out*. Washington, D.C.: Association for Childhood Education International, 1974.

Association for Supervision and Curriculum Development, NEA. *Learning More About Learning*, edited by Alexander Frazier. Washington, D.C.: Association for Supervision and Curriculum Development, 1959.

Ausubel, David Paul. "How Reversible are the Cognitive and Motivational Effects of Cultural Deprivation? Implications for Teaching the Culturally Deprived Child." *Urban Education* 1 (1964):16–39.

————. "Teaching Strategy for Culturally Deprived Pupils: Cognitive and Motivational Consideration." *Scholastic Review* 71 (1963):454–463.

Baker, Gwendolyn Calvert. "Multicultural Education: Two Preservice Training Approaches." *Journal of Teacher Education* 27 (May-June 1977):31–33.

Bandura, Albert. "Psychotherapy as a Learning Process." *Psychological Bulletin* 58:2 (March 1961):143–159.

Bandura, Albert; Ross, Dorothea; and Ross, Sheila. "A Comparative Test of the Status, Envy, Social Power, and Secondary Reinforcement Theories of Identificatory Learning." *Journal of Abnormal and Social Psychology* 67:6 (1963):527–534.

Banfield, E. C. *The Unheavenly City: The Nature and Future of Our Urban Crisis*. Boston: Little, Brown, 1970.

Banks, James A. "Cultural Pluralism and Contemporary Schools." *Integrated Education* 14 (January/February 1976):32–36.

———. "Ethnic Modification of the Curriculum." *Illinois Schools Journal*, vol. 55, no. 4 (winter 1975/6):24–31.

———. "Ethnic Studies as a Process of Curriculum Reform." Article based on a larger paper presented at the Conference on Pluralism in a Democratic Society. 4-6 April 1975, New York City, reprinted by National Council for the Social Studies. A National Affiliate of National Education Association.

———. "The Implications of Ethnicity for Curriculum Reform." *Educational Leadership* (December 1975):168–172.

———. "The Implications of Multicultural Education for Teacher Education." In *Pluralism and the American Teacher: Issues and Case Studies,* edited by Frank H. Klassen and Donna M. Gollnick. Washington, D.C.: Ethnic Heritage Center for Teacher Education of the American Association of Colleges of Teacher Education, 1977, pp. 1–30.

———. *Multicultural Education: Practices and Promises*. Bloomington, Ind.: Phi Delta Kappa Educational Foundation, Fastback 87, 1977.

———. *Teaching Ethnic Studies: Concepts and Strategies*. Washington, D.C.: National Council for the Social Studies. A National Affiliate of National Education Association, 43rd Yearbook, 1973.

———. *Teaching Strategies for Ethnic Studies*. Boston: Allyn and Bacon, 1975.

Baptiste, Prentice H. Jr. *Multicultural Education: A Synopsis*. Texas: College of Education University of Houston, 1976.

Baratz, Joan. "Language and Cognition Assessment of Negro Children." In *Demystifying School: Writings and Experiences,* edited by Miriam Wasserman. New York: Praeger Publishers, 1974, pp. 148-158.

Baratz, Joan, and Baratz, Stephan. "The Social Pathology Mode: Historical Bases for Psychology's Denial of the Existence of Negro Culture." Paper presented at the American Psychological Association, Washington, D.C., 1969.

Barclay, James R. *Controversial Issues in Testing: Guidance Monograph Series III*. Boston: Houghton Mifflin, 1968.

Barry, Herbert, III. "Cross-Cultural Research With Matched Pairs of Societies." *Journal of Social Psychology* 79 (first half October 1969):25–33.

Bates, Frederick L., and Harvey, Clyde E. *The Structure of Social Systems*. New York: Gardner Press, 1975.

Battle, S., and Rotter, J.B. "Children's Feelings of Personal Control As Related to Social Class and Ethnic Group." *Journal of Personality* 31 (1963):482–490.

Beals, Alan R., and Spindler, George and Louise. *Culture in Process*. New York: Holt, Rinehart, and Winston, 1967.

Beez, Victor. "Influence of Biased Psychological Reports on Teacher Behavior and Pupil Performance." *Proceedings of the 76th Annual Convention of the American Psychological Association*, 1968.

Benedict, Ruth. *Patterns of Culture*. Boston: Houghton Mifflin, 1934.

Bentley, Robert, Washington, Ernest, and Young, James. "Judging the Educational Programs of Young Children: Some Cautions." *Young Children* (November 1973):5–18.

Berlin, Irving N. "Education for What?" *The Record—Teachers College 70, no. 6 (March 1969):505–511*.

Bernbaum, Marcia. *Early Childhood Programs for Non-English Speaking Children*. Urbana, Ill.: ERIC Clearinghouse on Early Childhood Education, May 1971.

Bidney, David. "Cultural Relativism." In *International Encyclopedia of the Social Sciences*, edited by David L. Sills. New York: Macmillan and Free Press, 1968, pp. 543–544.

Black Student Organization. "Credo of Black Students." In *Toward Social Change: A Handbook of Those Who Will*, edited by Robert Buckhout and 81 Concerned Berkeley Students. New York: Harper and Row, 1957, p. 108.

"Blacks Challenge Placing of Retarded Based on I.Q. Tests." *Boston Globe*, 6 June 1978.

Bloom, B. S.; Davis, A.; and Hess, R. *Compensatory Education for Cultural Deprivation*. New York: Holt, Rinehart, and Winston, 1965.

Boas, Frans. *Race, Language and Culture*. New York: Macmillan, 1955 (original, 1896).

Borgatta, Edgar F., ed. *Social Psychology: Readings and Perspectives*. Chicago: Rand McNally, 1969.

Bowels, Samuel and Gintis, Herbert. "I.Q. in the United States Class Structure." *Social Policy* 3, no. 4 (November-December 1972 and January-February 1973):65–96.

Boyer, James B. and Boyer, Joe L., eds. *Curriculum and Instruction After Desegregation: Form, Substance and Proposals*. Manhattan, Kans.: AG Press Paperback, 1975.

Brace, Loring C., and Livingstone, Frank B. "On Creeping Jensenism." In *Rape and Intelligence*, edited by C. L. Brace, G. R. Gamble, and J. T. Bonds. Washington, D.C.: American Anthropology Association, 1971, pp. 64-75.

Brembeck, Cole S., and Grandstaff, Marvin. *Social Foundations of Education: A Book of Readings*. New York: John Wiley and Sons, 1969.

Brennen, J. "The Forgotten American: American Indians Remembered." New York Council on Social Work Education, New York: 1970.

Brickman, William, and Lehrer, Stanley. *Education and the Many Faces of Disadvantaged: Cultural and Historical Perspectives*. New York: John Wiley and Sons, 1972.

Brislin, Richard W., and Hammett, Michael, eds. *Topics in Culture Learning*. Honolulu: East-West Culture Learning Institute, 1977.

Brown, Ina Corine. *Understanding Other Cultures*. New Jersey: Prentice-Hall, 1963.

Brown v. Board of Education of Topeka, Shawnee County, Kansas et al. 347 U.S. 483 (1954).

Brown v. Califano. Summary of Findings: Brown v. Califano, Title VI of Civil Rights Act of 1973. October 5, 1977.

Brown, George Issac. "What Is Confluent Education?" In *Humanistic Education Sourcebook*, edited by Donald A. Read and Sidney B. Simon. New Jersey: Prentice-Hall, 1975, pp. 50-61.

Brown, Lester R. "Issues of Human Welfare." *The Humanist* (November, December 1974):17–21.

————.*The Twenty-Ninth Day: Accommodating Human Needs and Numbers to the Earth's Resources*. New York: W. W. Norton, 1978.

Brunner, Jerome S. "Culture, Politics, and Pedagogy." *Saturday Review* 18, May 1968, pp. 89, 90.

————. *The Relevance of Education*. New York: W. W. Norton, 1973.

Bryce-Laport, Roy Simon. "The American Slave Plantation and Our Heritage of Communal Deprivation." *American Behavioral Scientist* 12, no. 4 (March-April 1969):2-8.

Buckhout, Robert and 81 Concerned Berkeley Students. "The Education Game." In *Toward Social Change: A Handbook for Those Who Will*, edited by Robert Buckhout and 81 Concerned Berkeley Students. New York: Harper and Row, 1971, pp. 432–433.

Buckley, Walter, ed., *Modern Systems Research for the Behavioral Scientist*. Chicago: Aldine, 1968.

————. *Sociology and Modern Systems Theory*. New Jersey: Prentice-Hall, 1967.

Burleigh, Seaver W. "Effects of Naturally Induced Teacher Expectations." *Journal of Personality and Social Psychology* 28:3 (November 3, 1973):333–342.

Busch, Ronald J. "Ethnic Assimilation Vs. Cultural Pluralism: Some Political Implications." In *Ethnicity: A Conceptual Approach*. Edited by Daniel Weinberg. Cleveland: Cleveland Ethnic Heritage Studies, Cleveland State University, 1976, pp. 175–189.

Bush, Robert N. "Facing the Future: Focus Upon an Entire School." *Journal of Teacher Education* 26:2 (September 1975):148–149.

Buss, William. "Procedural Due Process for School Discipline: Probing the Constitutional Outline." *University of Pennsylvania Law Review* 119 (February 1971):577.

Callahan, Raymond E. *Education and the Cult of Efficiency*. Chicago: University of Chicago Press, 1962.

Campbell, Joseph. *Myths to Live By*. New York: Bantam, 1973.

Cardenas, José A. *An IDRA Response With a Summary by Dr. Jose A. Cardenas*. San Antonio, Tex.: Intercultural Development Research Association, June 1977.

Carlson, Paul E. "Toward A Definition of Local-Level Multicultural Education." *Anthropology and Education Quarterly* 7:4 (November 1976):26–29.

Carmichael, Stokeley, and Hamilton, Charles V. "White Power: The Colonial Situation." In *Toward Social Change: A Handbook for Those Who Will*, edited by Robert Buckhout and 81 Concerned Berkeley Students. New York: Harper and Row, 1971, pp. 97–102.

Carnoy, Martin. *Education as Cultural Imperialism*. New York: David McKay, 1974.

Caro, Francis G. "Issues in the Evaluation of Social Programs." *Review of Educational Research* 41 (1971):87–114.

Carpenter, John, and Plaza, Galo. *The Intercultural Imperative.* New York: American Association of State Colleges and Universities, Council for Intercultural Studies and Programs, Educational Research Center, University of the State of New York, 1972.

Carpenter, John, and Torney, Judith V. "Overview Beyond the Melting Pot to Cultural Pluralism." In *Overview and Research In Children and Intercultural Education Part II*, edited by Patricia Maloney Markun and Joan Troussaint Lane. Washington, D.C.: Association for Childhood Education International, 1973-1974 (Annual Bulletin Order), pp. 14–23.

Castañeda, Alfredo. "Persisting Ideological Issues of Assimilation in America," in *Cultural Pluralism,* edited by Edgar C. Epps. Berkeley, California: McCutchan, 1974, pp. 56–70.

Castañeda, Alfredo, James, Richard L., and Robbins, Webster. *The Educational Needs of Minority Groups.* Lincoln, Neb.: Professional Educators Publications, 1974.

Caudill, William, and DeVos, George. "Achievement, Culture, and Personality: The Case of the Japanese Americans." *American Anthropologist* 58 (1956):1102–1126.

Children's Defense Fund. *Children Out of School in America.* Washington, D.C.: Washington Research Project, 1974.

Children's Defense Fund and Five Other Organizations. *The Emergency School Assistance Program: An Evaluation.* Washington, D.C.: Washington Research Project, November 1970.

———. *It's Not Over in the South.* Written by the American Friends Service Committee with Children's Defense Fund and four other organizations. Washington, D.C.: Washington Research Project, May 1972.

———. *The Status of School Segregation in the South 1970.* Washington, D.C.: Washington Research Project and five other organizations, May 1972.

Clarizio, Harvey F., Craig, Robert C., and Mehrens, William A. *Contemporary Issues in Educational Psychology.* Boston: Allyn and Bacon, 1974.

Clark, Kenneth B. "Problems of Power and Social Change: Toward a Relevant Social Psychology." *Journal of Social Issues* 21:3 (1965):4-20.

Clasby, Miriam; Webster, Maureen; and White, Naomi. *Laws, Tests, and Schooling.* New York: Syracuse University Research Corp. October, 1973.

Clausen, John A., ed. *Socialization and Society.* Boston: Little Brown, 1968.

Claydon, Leslie; Knight, Tony; and Rado, Marta. *Curriculum and Culture: Schooling in a Pluralist Society.* London: George Allen and Unwin, 1977.

Clayton, Stafford A. "Education and Some Moves Toward a Value Methodology." *Educational Theory* 19:2 (spring 1969).

Cohen, Monroe D., and Martin, Lucy Prete, eds. *Testing and Evaluation: New Views.* Washington, D.C.: Association for Childhood Education International, 1975.

Cole, Michael, and Scribner, Sylvia. *Culture and Thought: A Psychological Introduction.* New York: John Wiley and Sons, 1974.

Cole, Michael; Glick, Gay J.; and Sharpe, D. *The Cultural Context of Learning and Thinking: An Exploration in Experimental Anthropology.* New

York: Basic Books, 1971.

Combs, Arthur W. "Humanistic Goals of Education." In *Humanistic Education Sourcebook,* edited by Donald A. Read, Sidney B. Simon. New Jersey: Prentice-Hall, 1975, pp. 91–101.

Cordasco, Francesco, and Bucchioni, Eugene, eds. *The Puerto Rican Experience.* Totowa, N.J.: Littlefield Adams, 1973.

Cordasco, Francesco; Hillson, Maurie; and Bullock, Henry A. *The School in the Social Order: A Sociological Introduction to Educational Understanding.* Scranton, Pennsylvania: Intext Publishers, 1972.

Cortes, Fernando; Przeworski, Adam; and Sprague, John. *Systems Analysis for Social Scientists.* New York: John Wiley and Sons, 1974.

Corwin, Ronald G.; Edelfelt, Roy A.; Andrew, Theodore E.; and Bryant, Brenda L., eds. *Perspectives on Organization: The School as a Social Organization.* Washington, D.C.: American Association of Colleges for Teacher Edcuation and Association of Teacher Education, 1977.

Craig, James H. and Marge. *Synergic Power: Beyond Domination and Permissiveness.* Berkeley: Pro Active Press, 1974.

Crandall, V. J.; Katlowsky, W.; and Preston, A. "Motivation and Ability Determinants of Young Children's Intellectual Achievement Behaviors." *Child Development* 33 (1962):643–661.

Cross, Dolores E.; Baker, Gwendolyn C.; and Stiles, Lindley J. *Teaching in a Multicultural Society.* New York: Free Press, 1977.

Cruz, Josue. "Growing Up in the Barrio," pp. 6–8. In *Some Minorities Speak Out.* Association for Childhood Education International. Washington, D.C.: Association for Childhood Education International, 1974.

Cubberley, Elwood. Quoted in Roman Pucinski, "Ethnic Studies and Urban Reality." In *Pieces of a Dream,* edited by Michael Wenk, S. M. Thomasi, and Geno Baroni. New York: The Center for Migration Studies, 1972, p. 78.

Dahn, Robert. *Pluralist Democracy in the United States.* Chicago: Rand McNally, 1967.

Dawson, Martha E. "Are There Unwelcome Guests in Your Classroom?" In *Are There Unwelcome Guests in Your Classroom?,* edited by Martha E. Dawson. Washington, D.C.: Association for Childhood International, 1971, pp. 36–39.

Davis, Renée A. "A Case for Multi-Cultural Intercultural Education: A Philosophical View and Approach to Work with Young Children," 1975 (unpublished).

————. "Cultural Imperatives for Education in Head Start: A Position Paper," 1977 (unpublished).

————. "Cultural Pluralism in the Education of Children." Presented at the Rhode Island Conference for Early Childhood Education 7–8 April 1978.

————. "Culture and Education: A Case for Multi-Cultural Education: A Philosophy and Self-Development Model," 1976.

————. "Diversity and Values: Implications for Education," 1976

————. "Report on a Speech by Dr. Chester Pierce, 'Beyond the Horizon: Quest for Meaning.' Presented at the ACEI Conference 2-7 April 1972" (unpublished).

Dentan, Robert K. *The Semai: A Nonviolent People of Malaya.* New York: Holt,

Rinehart, and Winston, 1968.

de Price, Derek J. *Little Science Big Science*. New York: Columbia University Press, 1963.

de Tocqueville, Alexis. *Democracy in America*. Translated by Henry Reeve. New York: D. Appleton, 1901, p. 285, as quoted in *Culture Against Man* by Jules Henry. New York: Vintage, 1965, p. 5.

Deutsch, Cynthia P. "Auditory Discrimination and Learning Social Factors." *Merrill-Palmer Quarterly of Behavior and Development* 10:3 (1964):277–296.

Deutsch, Martin. "The Disadvantaged Child and the Learning Process." In *Education in Depressed Areas*, edited by A. H. Passow. New York: Teachers College Press, 1963, pp. 163–179.

———. "Facilitating Development in the Preschool Child: Social and Psychological Perspectives," *Merrill-Palmer Quarterly of Behavior and Development* 10:3 (1964):249–264.

———. "Heredity and Intelligence." Paper developed at the Social Policy Conference on I.Q. New York, May 1973.

Dimen-Schein, Muriel. *The Anthropological Imagination*. New York: McGraw-Hill, 1977.

Dinges, Norman. "Interdisciplinary Collaboration in Cross-Cultural Social Science Research." In *Topics in Culture Learning*, edited by Richard W. Brislin and Michael P. Hammett. Honolulu: East-West Culture Learning Institute, 1977, pp. 136–143.

Dinnerstein, Leonard, and Reimer, David M. *Ethnic Americans: A History of Immigration and Assimilation*. New York: Dodd, Mead and Co., 1975.

Downs, James F. *Cultures in Crisis*. London: Glencoe Press, 1975.

Dunfee, Maxime., ed. *Eliminating Ethnic Bias in Instructional Material: Comment and Bibliograpny*. Washington, D.C. Association for Supervision and Curriculum Development, 1974.

———. *Ethnic Modification of the Curriculum*. Report of a Conference on Ethnic Modification of the Curriculum, 20-22 November 1969. Washington, D.C.: Association for Supervision and Curriculum Development, NEA, 1970.

Durkheim, Emile. *Sociology and Philosophy*. New York: Free Press, 1974.

Durrett, Mary Ellen; O'Bryant, Shirley; and Pennebaken, James W. "Child Roaring Reports on White, Black, and Mexican-American Families." *Developmental Psychology* 2, no. 6 (1975):871.

Dusek, Jerome B. "Do Teachers Bias Children's Learning." *Review of Educational Research* 45, no. 4 (fall 1975):679–680.

Dusek, Jerome B.; Summers, Anita A.; and Wolf, Barbara. *Equality of Opportunity Quantified: A Production Function Approach*. Philadelphia: Department of Research Federal Reserve Bank of Philadelphia, 1975.

Dworkin, Susan. "Notes on Carter's Family Policy—How It Got That Way: What Happened to His White House Conference and Some Warnings for the Future . . . " *Ms. Magazine* (September 1978):63, 93.

Dyer, H. S. *The Discovery and Development of Educational Goals. Proceedings of the Invitational Conference on Testing Problems*: pp. 12–24. Educational Testing Service, 1966, Princeton, N.J.

Educational Policies Commission. "The Central Purpose of American Education." In *Curriculum Planning: A New Approach*, edited by Glen Hass, Joseph Bondi, and Jon Wiles. Boston: Allyn and Bacon, 1974, pp. 211–216.

Egashira, Pam. "An Asian American Perspective." *Journal of Teacher Education*. 26:2 (September 1975):131–132.

Einstein, Albert. "Science and Religion: A Symposium." *Conference on Science, Philosophy, and Religion in Their Relation to the Democratic Way of Life*, edited by L. Bryson and L. Finkelstein. New York, 1941, pp. 211–213.

Ellul, Jacques. "Search for an Image." *The Humanist* (November-December 1973):22–25.

Emery, R. E. *Systems Thinking*. Middlesex, England: Penguin Books, 1972.

Engle, Patricia L. "Language Medium in Early School Years for Minority Language Groups." *Review of Educational Research* 45:2 (1975):283 325.

Epps, Edgar G. *Cultural Pluralism*. Berkeley, Calif.: McCutchan, 1974.

Epstein, Noel. *Language, Ethnicity, and the Schools: Policy Alternatives for Bilingual Bicultural Education*. Washington, D.C.: Institute for Educational Leadership, the George Washington University, 1977.

Ethnic Millions Political Action Committee (EMPAC) 12, June 1977.

Etzioni, Amitai. "Man and Society: The Inauthentic Condition." In *Toward Social Change: A Handbook for Those Who Will*, edited by Robert Buckhout and 81 Concerned Berkeley Students. New York: Harper and Row, 1971, pp. 24–28.

Evans, Ellis D. *Contemporary Influences in Early Childhood Education*. New York: Holt, Rinehart, and Winston, 1971.

"Extension Support Grows." in *NOW Times*, April/May 1978

Fantini, Mario D. *Alternative Education: A Source Book for Parents, Teachers, and Administrators*. New York: Anchor Books, 1976.

Fantini, Mario, and Weinstein, Gerald. *The Disadvantaged: Challenge to Education*. New York: Harper and Row, 1968.

———. "Taking Advantage of the Disadvantaged." *The Record* 69:2 (November 1967):103–115.

Far West Laboratory for Educational Research and Development. *School Desegregation and Cultural Pluralism: Perspectives on Progress*. Selected Presentation of the 1974-75 Workshops. San Francisco: Far West Laboratory for Educational Research and Development, 1975.

Faulkingham, Ralph H. "Where the Lifeboat Ethic Breaks Down." *Human Nature* (October 1978):32–29.

Featherstone, Joseph. "Experiments in Learning." *The New Republic*, 14 December 1968.

———. *Schools Where Children Learn*. New York: Liveright, 1971.

Feld, S. C., and Lewis, J. *The Assessment of Achievement Anxieties*. Washington, D.C.: Mental Health Center, National Institute of Mental Health, 1967.

Feldman, Saul D., and Thielbar, Gerald W. *Life Styles: Diversity in American Society*. Boston: Little, Brown, 1972.

Fitzpatrick, Joseph P. "The Importance of 'Community' in the Process of Immigrant Assimilation." In *Ethnicity*, edited by Daniel Weinberg. Cleveland: Cleveland Ethnic Heritage Studies, Cleveland State University, 1976, pp. 81–89.

Forbes, Jack D. *Education of the Culturally Different: A Multicultural Approach*. Berkeley, Calif.: Far West Laboratory for Educational Research and Development, 1968.

Francoeur, Robert T. "Human Nature and Human Relations." *The Humanist* (November, December 1973):32–34.

Franklin, John Hope. *From Slavery to Freedom: A History of Black Americans*. New York: Vintage Books, 1969.

Freilich, Morris., ed. *The Meaning of Culture: A Reader in Cultural Anthropology*. Lexington, Mass.: Xerox College Publishing, 1972.

Freire, Paulo. *Pedagogy of the Oppressed*. Translated from the original Portuguese manuscript 1968. New York: Seabury Press, 1970.

Friedman, Murry, ed. *Overcoming Middle-Class Rage*. Philadelphia: Westminister, 1971.

Fromm, Eric. *Escape From Freedom*. Boston: Houghton Mifflin, 1941.

————. *Man for Himself*. Boston: Houghton Mifflin, 1947.

Fuller, Buckminster. *Earth Inc*. New York: Anchor Book, 1973.

————. *Utopia or Oblivion: The Prospects for Humanity*. New York: Bantam Books, 1969.

Gall, Meredith Damian. "The Importance of Context Variables in Research on Teaching Skills." *Journal of Teacher Education* 23, no. 3 (May-June 1977):43–54.

Garcia, Chris F. "Politics and Multicultural Education Do Mix." *Journal of Teacher Education* 28, no. 3 (May-June 1977):21–25.

Garcia, Ernest. "Chicano Cultural Diversity: Implications for Competency-Based Teacher Education." In *Multicultural Education Through Competency-Based Teacher Education*, edited by William Hunter. Washington, D.C.: American Association of Colleges for Teacher Education, 1974, pp. 146–157.

Gartner, Alan; Greer, Colin; and Reissman, Frank., eds. *The New Assault on Equality: I.Q. and Social Stratification*. New York: Harper and Row, 1974.

Geertz, Clifford. *The Interpretation of Cultures*. New York: Basic Books, 1973.

George, Frank. *Models of Thinking*. Cambridge, Mass.: Schenkman Publishing, 1970.

Gibson, Margaret A. "Approaches to Multicultural Education in the United States: Some Concepts and Assumptions." *Anthropology and Education Quarterly* 7:4 (November 1976):7–18.

Giese, James; Gold, Milton J.; and Grant, Carl A., eds. *Multicultural Education: A Functional Bibliography for Teachers*. Omaha, Nebraska: Teacher Corps Center for Urban Education, 1977.

Giles, Raymond H., and Gollnick, Donna. "Ethnic/Cultural Diversity as Reflected in State and Federal Educational Legislation and Policies." In *Pluralism and the American Teacher: Issues and Case Studies*, edited by Frank Klassen and Donna Gollnick. Washington, D.C.: Ethnic Heritage Center for Teacher Education of the American Association of Colleges for Teacher Education, 1977, pp. 115–162.

Giordano, Joseph. *Ethnicity and Mental Health: Research and Recommendations*. New York: National Project on Ethnic America of the American Jewish Committee, Institute of Human Relations, 1973.

Giordano, Joseph, and Giordano, Grace Pineiro. *The Ethno-Cultural Factor*.

In Mental Health: A Literature Review and Bibliography. New York: Institute on Pluralism and Group Identity of the American Jewish Committee, 1977.

Giordano, Joseph, and Levine, Irving M. "Is the Family Dead?" *Journal of Current Social Issues* (winter 1977):49–52.

Glazer, Nathan, and Moynihan, Daniel Patrick. *Beyond the Melting Pot: The Negros, Puerto Ricans, Jews, Italians, and Irish of New York City.* Cambridge, Mass.: Massachusetts Institute of Technology Press, 1963.

Glazer, Nona Y., and Creedon, Carol F. *Children and Poverty: Some Sociological and Psychological Perspectives.* Chicago: Rand McNally, 1970.

Gold, Milton J.; Grant, Carl A.; and Rivlin, Harry N., eds. *In Praise of Diversity: A Resource Book for Multicultural Education.* Washington, D.C.: Teacher Corps and Association of Teacher Educators, 1977.

Gollnick, Donna. *State Legislation, Provisions and Practices Related to Multicultural Education. Report to the National Institute of Education January 1978* (unpublished).

Gollnick, Donna; Cyr, Ralph; and Jonas, Sheila. *Multicultural Education: Preliminary Findings of Three Surveys: Multicultural Education in Teacher Education: Preliminary Findings of a National Survey, Multicultural Education As Addressed by the States and Territories of the United States, Multicultural Activities of Professional Education Associations.* Prepared for National Institute on Multicultural Teacher Education Standards. Sponsored by the American Association of Colleges of Teacher Education and National Institute of Education (not for dissemination).

Gollnick, Donna; Klassen, Frank; and Yff, Joost. *Multicultural Education and Ethnic Studies in the United States: An Analysis and Annotated Bibliography of Selected ERIC Documents.* Washington, D.C.: American Association of Colleges for Teacher Education, 1976.

Golub, Judith S. *Facing the Future: Issues in Education and Schooling (Papers of John I. Goodland).* New York: McGraw-Hill, 1976.

Gonzalez, Jose M. *Growth Pains in Bilingual Bicultural Education Since '66.* Report on Bilingual Bicultural Institute. Washington, D.C., National Education Association Conference, 28 November 1-December 1973.

Goodenough, Ward. "Multiculturalism as the Normal Human Experience." *Anthropology and Education Quarterly* 7:4 (November 1976):4–6.

Goodman, Mary Ellen. *The Culture of Childhood: Child's Eye View of Society and Culture.* New York: Teachers College Press, 1970.

Gordon, Milton M. "Assimilation in America: Theory and Reality." *Daedalus* 90:2 (spring 1961):263–285.

———. *Assimilation in American Life: The Role of Race, Religion, and National Origins.* New York: Oxford University Press, 1964.

Gordon, William J. *Synectics: The Development of Creative Thinking.* New York: Collier Books, 1961.

Graham, Grace. "Influences of Social Class Differences in Schools." In *Foundations of Education: A Social View,* edited by Albert W. Vogel, David L. Bachelor, and John T. Zepper. Albuquerque: University of New Mexico Press, 1970, pp. 127–147.

Grant, Carl A. "Exploring the Relationship Between Teacher Corps and Multicultural Education." *Journal of Teacher Education* 26:2 (September 1975):119–120.

———. *Sifting and Winnowing: An Exploration of the Relationship Between Multicultural Education and CBTE*. Washington, D.C.: Teacher Corps and University of Wisconsin-Madison, 1975.

Grant, Gloria, ed. In *Praise of Diversity: Multicultural Classroom Applications*. Omaha: Center for Urban Education University of Nebraska Teacher Corps., 1977.

Grant, Jack; South, Oron; and Hansen, John H. *Temporary Systems*. Florida: James L. Grant, Oron South, and John H. Hansen. P.O. Box 2011, Tallahassee, Florida 32304, 1977.

Greely, Andrew M. *Why Can't They Be Like Us? Facts and Fallacies About Ethnic Differences and Group Conflicts in America*. New York: American Jewish Committee, 1969.

Green, Thomas F. *Work, Leisure, and the American School*. New York: Random House, 1968.

Greer, Colin. *The Great School Legend: A Revisionist Interpretation of American Public Education*. New York: Viking, 1972.

Grotberg, Edith, ed. *Critical Issues in Research Related to Disadvantaged Children. Proceedings of Six Head Start Research Seminars*. Princeton, N.J.: Educational Testing Service. 1969.

———. *200 Years of Children*. Washington, D.C.: United States Department of Health, Education, and Welfare, Office of Child Development, Division of Research and Evaluation, 1977.

Grove, Cornelius Lee. *Communication Across Cultures: A Report on Cross Cultural Research*. Washington, D.C.: National Education Association, 1976.

Gurda, John. "The Born-Again Ethnic." In *EMPAC! Newsletter of the Ethnic Millions Political Action Committee* 12 (June 1977):11–14.

Gutek, Gerald Lee. *Philosophical Alternatives in Education*. Columbus, Ohio: Charles E. Merrill, 1974.

Hall, Edward T. *Beyond Culture*. New York: Anchor Press, 1976.

———. *The Hidden Dimension*. New York: Anchor Book, 1969.

———. *The Silent Language*. New York: Anchor Book, 1973.

Hallowell, Irving A. *Culture and Experience*. Philadelphia: University of Pennsylvania Press, 1974.

Handlin, Oscar. *The Uprooter: The Epic Story of the Great Migration That Made American People*. New York: Grosset and Dunlap, 1973.

Hansen, Judith Friedman. *Sociocultural Perspectives on Human Learning: An Introduction to Educational Anthropology*. Englewood Cliffs, N.J.: Prentic-Hall, 1979.

Harris, Marvin. *Cows, Pigs, Wars and Witches: The Riddles of Culture*. New York: Vintage, 1975.

Hartup, Willard W., ed. *The Young Child: Reviews of Research*, vol 2. Washington,D.C.: National Association for the Education of Young Children. 1967, 1970.

Hass, Glen. *Curriculum Planning: A New Approach*, 2nd ed. Boston: Allyn and Bacon, 1977.

Hass, Glen; Bondi, Joseph; Wiles, Jon. *Curriculum Planning: A New Approach*.

Boston: Allyn and Bacon, 1977.

Havighurst, R. J. and Breese, F. H. "Relation Between Ability and Social Status in Midwestern Community III. Primary Mental Abilities." *Journal of Educational Psychology* 38 (1947):241–247.

Haviland, William A. *Cultural Anthropology*. New York: Holt, Rinehart, and Winston, 1975.

Hawkins, David. "Square Two Square Three." *Forum for the Discussion of New Trends in Education* 12, no. 1 (autumn 1969):4–6.

Hawthorne, Phyllis. *Legislation by States: Accountability and Assessment in Education*. Revised April 1973. Denver: Cooperative An Accountability Project Colorado Department of Education, 1973.

Hayakawa, S. I. *Symbol, Status, and Personality*. New York: Harvest Book, 1963.

Hazard, William R., and Stent, Madelon. "Cultural Pluralism and Schooling: Some Preliminary Observations." In *Cultural Pluralism in Education: A Mandate for Change*, edited by Madelon Stent, William R. Hazard, and Harry Rivlin. New York: Appleton-Century-Crofts, 1973, pp. 13–25.

Hechinger, Fred M. "Reappraising the Open Classroom." *Saturday Review* 19 March 1977), pp. 6–10.

Hecht, Kathy A. "Teacher Ratings of Potential Drop-Outs and Academically Gifted Children: Are They Related?" *Journal of Teacher Education* 26, no. 2 (summer 1975):172–175.

Hedgepeth, William. "America's Indians: Reawakening in a Concerned People." *Look Magazine* 2 June 1970), p. 23.

Heilbroner, Robert L. *The Future as History*. New York: Harper, 1960.

Hellmuth, Jerome, ed. *Compensatory Education: A National Debate*. New York: Brunner/Mazel, 1970.

Henderson, George. "Opportunity and Alienation in Public Schools." *The Record Columbia University* 69, no. 2 (November 1967):151–159.

Henry, Jules. *Culture Against Man*. New York: Random House, 1963.

————. *On Education*. New York: Vintage, 1972.

————. "Reading For What?" *Claremont Reading Conference 28th Yearbook*. Claremont: Claremont College Laboratory pp. 19-35, 1961.

Herman, Judith, ed. *The Schools and Group Identity*. New York: Institute on Pluralism and Group Identity, 1974.

Herrenstein, Richard. "I.Q." *Atlantic Monthly*, September 1971, pp. 43–64.

Herskovitz, Melville J. *Cultural Relativism: Perspectives in Cultural Pluralism*. New York: Vintage, 1973.

Higham, John. *Strangers in the Land: Patterns of American Nativism 1860-1925*. New York Atheneum, 1972.

Hikirk, Diana and Goon, Susan. "Desegregation and the Cultural Deficit Model: An Examination of the Literature." *Review of Educational Research* 45, no. 3 (August 1970):411–451.

Hill, K.T., and Sarason, S.B. "The Relation of Test Anxiety and Defensiveness to Test and School Performance Over the Elementary School Years: A Further Longitudinal Study." *Monographs of the Society for Research in Child Development* 31, no. 2 (1966):1–76.

Hilliard, Asa III. "Giving Families a 'Head Start'." Keynote Address, National Head Start Association Fifth Annual Conference Cleveland, Ohio, May 1978.

Hing, Alex. "The Need for a United Asian-American Front." In *Toward Social Change: A Handbook for Those Who Will,* edited by Robert Buckhout and 81 Concerned Berkeley Students. New York: Harper and Row, 1971, pp. 115–116.

Hirschfeld, Gerhard. "Teachers Should Understand Mankind." *The Record–Teachers College* 70, no. 6 (March 1969):541–548.

Hodge, John; Struckmann, Donald K.; and Trost, Lynn Dorland. *Cultural Bases of Racism and Group Oppression: An Examination of Traditional "Western" Concepts, Values, and Institutional Structures Which Support Racism, Sexism, and Elitism.* Berkeley, California: Two Riders Press, 1975.

Hogg, Thomas C., and McComb, Marlin R. "Cultural Pluralism: Its Implications for Education." In *Foundations of Education: A Social View,* edited by Albert W. Vogel, David L. Bachelor, and John T. Zepper. Albuquerque: University of New Mexico Press, 1970, pp. 32†37.

Hollinghead, August. "Caste and Class in Elmtown." In *Demystifying School: Writings and Experiences,* edited by Miriam Wasserman. New York: Praeger, 1974, pp. 74–80.

Holmen, Milton G. and Doctor, Richard F. *Educational and Psychological Testing: A Study of the Industry and Its Practices.* New York: Russell Sage Foundation, 1972.

Holt, John. *How Children Fail.* New York: Pitman, 1964.

Homans, George C. *The Nature of Social Science.* New York: Harcourt, Brace and World, 1967.

Honigmann, John J. *Understanding Culture.* New York: Harper and Row, 1963.

Hourihan, John J., and Chapin, Dexter. "Multicultural Education in a Pluralistic Society: Group vs. Individual." *Anthropology and Education Quarterly* 7, no. 4 (November 1976):23–25.

Hovey, Esther. *Ethnicity and Early Education.* Urbana: ERIC Clearinghouse on Early Childhood Education, April 1975.

Howsam, Robert B.; Corrigan, Dean C.; Denemark, George W.; and Nash, Robert J. *Educating a Profession.* Washington, D.C.: American Association of Colleges for Teacher Education, 1976.

Huizinga, Johan. *Homo Ludens: A Study of the Play Element in Culture.* Boston: Beacon Press, 1955.

Hultkrantz, Ake. *General Ethnological Concepts: International Dictionary of Regional European Ethnology and Folklore.* Copenhagen: Rosenkilde and Bagger, 1960.

Hunt, Joseph. *Intelligence and Experience.* New York: Ronald Press, 1961.

———. "The Psychological Bases for Using Preschool Enrichment as an Antidote for Cultural Deprivation." *Merrill-Palmer Quarterly of Behavior and Development* 10, no. 3 (1964):209–248.

Hunter, William. "Antecedents to Development of and Emphases on Multi-Cultural Education!" In *Multicultural Education: Through Competency-Based Teacher Education,* edited by William Hunter. Washington, D.C.: American Association of Colleges for Teacher Education, 1974, pp. 35–99.

Hutchings, Robert W. "Education as Cultural Therapy." In *Social Foundations of Education: A Book of Readings,* edited by Cole S. Brembeck and Marvin Grandstaff. New York: John Wiley and Sons, 1969, pp. 24–30.

Ianni, Francis A. J., and Storey, Edward., eds. *Cultural Relevance and Educational Issues: Readings in Anthropology and Education*. Boston: Little Brown, 1973.

Illich, Ivan. *Deschooling Society*. New York: Harper and Row, 1971.

Itzkoff, Semour W. "Curriculum Pluralism in Urban Education." *School and Society* 94:2281 (1966):385.

Jacobs, Paul, and Landau, Saul, with Eve Pell. *To Serve the Devil: A Documentary Analysis of America's Racial History and Why It Has Been Kept Hidden*, 2 vols. New York: Vintage Books, 1971.

James, Richard. "Multicultural Education From a Black Educator's Perspective." In *Multicultural Education: Through Competency-Based Teacher Education*, edited by William Hunter, Washington, D.C.: American Association of Colleges for Teacher Education, 1974, pp. 35–39.

Jenks, Christopher, and others. *Inequality: A Reassessment of the Effects of Family and Schooling in America*. New York: Basic Books, 1972.

Jensen, Arthur. "Can We and Should We Study Race Difference?" In *Compensatory Education: A National Debate*, edited by Jerome Hellmuth. New York: Brunner/Mazel Publishers, 1970, pp. 124–157.

————. "How Much Can We Boost I.Q. and Scholastic Achievement?" *Harvard Educational Review* 39 (1969):1–233.

————. "Reducing the Heredity Environment Uncertainty: A Reply." *Harvard Educational Review* 39 (Spring 1961):273–356.

John, Vera P. Position on *Pre-School Programs: A Brief Survey of Research on the Characteristics of Children From Low-Income Backgrounds*. Disadvantaged Document ED001816, ERIC, U.S.H.E.W.

John V.P., and Goldstein, L.S. "The Social Context of Language Acquisition." *Merrill-Palmer Quarterly of Behavior and Development* 10, no. 30 (1964):265–276.

Johnson, Jacqueline W. "Human Relation Preparation in Teacher Education: The Wisconsin Experience." In *Pluralism and the American Teacher: Issues and Case Studies*, edited by Frank H. Klassen and Donna M. Gollnick. Washington, D.C.: Ethnic Heritage Center for Teacher Education of the American Association of Colleges of Teacher Education, 1977, pp. 185–203.

Johnson, Norris Brock. "On the Relationship of Anthropology to Multicultural Teaching and Learning." *Journal of Teacher Education* 27 (May-June 1977):10–15.

Jones, Maldwyn Allen. *American Immigration*. Chicago: University of Chicago Press, 1960.

Kallen, Horace M. *Cultural Pluralism and the American Idea*. Philadelphia: University of Pittsburgh Press, 1956.

————. *Culture and Democracy in the United States*. New York: Boni and Liveright, 1924.

Katz, Michael B. "Bureaucracy and the Industrial Order." In *Demystifying School: Writings and Experiences*, edited by Miriam Wasserman. New York: Praeger, 1974, pp. 239–240.

Kauffman, Draper L., Jr. "Futurism: And Future Studies." In *Learning for Tomorrow: The Role of the Future*, edited by Alvin Toffler. New York: Vintage, 1975, pp. 29–42.

————. *Teaching the Future: A Guide to Future-Oriented Education*. Palm Springs, Calif.: ETC Publication, 1976.

Kellog, Mark. "Indian Rights: Fighting Back With White Man's Weapons." *Saturday Review*, 25 November 1978, pp. 24–27.

Kent, James K. "Race, Class, and Education." In *Social Foundations of Education: A Book of Readings*, edited by Cole S. Brembeck and Marvin Grandstaff. New York: John Wiley, 1969, pp. 150–168.

Kerner, Otto. *National Advisory Commission on Civil Disorders Report*. Washington, D.C.: U.S. Government Printing Office, 1968.

Kiev, Ari. *Transcultural Psychiatry*. New York: Free Press, 1972.

Kimball, Solon T. *Culture and the Educative Process: An Anthropological Perspective*. New York: Teachers College Press, Columbia University, 1974.

King, Richard A. "The Bureaucrat, the Martyr and the Artificial Self." In *Demystifying Education: Writings and Experiences*, edited by Miriam Wasserman. New York: Praeger, 1974, pp. 247–251.

Kirschenbaum, Howard, and Simon, Sidney B. "Values and the Future Movement in Education." In *Learning for Tomorrow: The Role of the Future*, edited by Alvin Toffler. New York: Vintage, 1975, pp. 257–270.

Kluckhohn, Clyde. *Mirror for Man: Anthropology and Modern Life*. New York: McGraw-Hill, 1971.

————. "Parts and Wholes in Cultural Analysis." In *Parts and Wholes*, edited by Daniel Learner. New York: Free Press, 1963, pp. 111–133.

Kneller, George F. *Educational Anthropology: An Introduction*. New York: John Wiley and Sons, 1965.

Koehler, W. "Closed and Open Systems." In *Systems Thinking*, edited by F. E. Emery. Middlesex, England: Penguin Books, 1972, pp. 59–69.

Koemer, James. *The Miseducation of American Teachers*. Boston: Houghton Mifflin, 1963.

Kohl, Herbert R. *The Open Classroom*. New York: Vintage, 1970.

Köhler, Wolfgang. *The Place of Value in a World of Facts*. New York: Liveright, 1976.

Kopan, Andrew T. "Melting Pot: Myth or Reality." In *Cultural Pluralism*, Edited by Edgar G. Epps. pp. 37-55. Berkeley, Calif.: McCutchan, 1974.

Kozol, Jonathan. "Free Schools: A Time for Candor." *Saturday Review*, 4 March 1972, pp. 51–54.

Kroeber, Alfred L. *Anthropology: Culture Patterns and Processes*. New York: Harcourt, Brace and World, 1963.

————. *The Nature of Culture*. Chicago: University of Chicago Press, 1952.

Kroeber, Alfred L., and Kluckhohn, Clyde. *Culture: A Critical Review of Concepts and Definitions*. New York: Vintage, 1972.

Krug, Mark M. "Cultural Pluralism—Its Origins and Aftermath." *Journal of Teacher Education* 28, no. 3 (May-June 1977):5–9.

Kuhn, Thomas S. *The Structure of Scientific Revolutions*. Chicago: University of Chicago Press, 1970.

Kunkel, John H. *Behavior, Social Problems and Change: A Social Learning Approach*. Englewood Cliffs, N.J.: Prentice-Hall, 1975.

Lake, Ernest G. "The Case Against External Standardized Tests: They Create an Elite and Slur Our Average Students!" *The Nation's Schools* 70, no. 2 (August 1962):51–54.

Lamont, Corliss. *The Philosophy of Humanism.* New York: Frederick Ungar Publishing, 1977.

Laosa, Luis. "Multicultural Education—How Psychology Can Contribute." *Journal of Teacher Education* 27 (May-June 1977):26–30.

Lau v. Nichols, 414 U.S. 563 (1974).

Laurencall, Charles. "The Bakke Case: Are Racial Quotas Defensible?" *Saturday Review,* 15 October 1977, pp. 11–16.

Lawrence, Theodora J., and Singleton, John. "Multiculturalism in Social Context: Conceptual Problems Raised by Educational Policy Issues." *Anthropology and Education Quarterly* 7, no. 4 (November 1976): 19–22.

Lazar, Irving; Hubbell, Virginia Ruth; Murry, Harry; Rosche, Marilyn; and Royce, Jacqueline. *The Persistence of Preschool Effects.* Washington, D.C.: Health, Education and Welfare, Administration for Children, Youth, and Families, 1977.

Leach, Edmund. *Culture and Communication: The Logic by Which Symbols Are Connected.* Cambridge: Cambridge University Press, 1976.

Leacock, E. B., ed. *The Culture of Poverty: A Critique.* New York: Simon and Schuster, 1971.

Lechtman, Heather, and Merrill, Roberts, eds. *Material Culture: Styles Organization, and Dynamics of Technology.* St. Paul: West Publishing, 1977.

LeCompte, Margaret. "Learning to Work: The Hidden Curriculum." *Anthropology and Education Quarterly* 9, no. 1 (spring 1978):22–37.

Lee, Dorothy. *Freedom and Culture.* New Jersey: Prentice-Hall, 1959.

Leicher, Hope Jensen, ed. *The Family as Educator.* New York: Teachers College Press, 1974.

Lerner, Daniels, ed. *Parts and Wholes: The Hayden Colloquium on Scientific Method and Concept.* New York: Free Press, 1963.

Lesser, Gerald S. "The Need for Diversity in American Day Care." In *Day Care: Resources for Decisions,* edited by Edith Grotberg. Washington, D.C.: Office of Economic Opportunity Pamphlet, 1971, pp. 50–57.

Lesser, Gerald; Fifer, G.; and Clark, D.H. "Mental Abilities of Children From Different Social-Class and Cultural Groups." *Monographs of Society for Research in Child Development.* 30:4 (whole no. 102).

Levenson, William B. "Compensatory Education Programs." In *Foundations of Education: A Social View,* edited by Albert Vogel, David L. Bachelor, and John T. Zepper. Albuquerque: University of New Mexico Press, 1970, pp. 301–317.

Leventhal, Howard. "Attitudes: Their Nature, Growth, and Change." In *Social Psychology: Classic and Contemporary Integrations,* edited by Charles Nemeth. Chicago: Rand McNally, 1974, pp. 52–126.

Levine, Daniel U. "The Integration-Compensatory Education Controversy." In *Foundations of Education: A Social View.* Albuquerque: University of New Mexico Press, 1970, pp. 338–346.

Levine, Irving M. "Appreciating Group Differences." *The Journal of Intergroup Relations (Spring 1973).* Address presented to the 25th Anniversary Conference of the National Association of Human Rights Workers, October 1, 1972.

———. *Ethnicity and American Education.* New York: Institute on Pluralism and Group Identity, May 1971.

————. *Social Policy and Multi-Ethnicity in the Seventies*. New York: Institute on Pluralism and Group Identity. Working Paper Series 1, January 1975.

Levine, Irving, and Levine, Judith. "The Life of White Ethnics." *Dissent* (Winter 1972):286–295.

Levine, Robert A., ed. *Culture and Personality: Contemporary Readings*. Chicago: Aldine, 1974.

Lewis, Diane K. "The Multicultural Education Model and Minorities: Some Reservations." *Anthropology and Education Quarterly* 7, no. 4 (November 1976):32–36.

Lewis, Hylan. *Culture, Class, and Poverty: Three Papers From the Child Rearing Study of Low-Income District of Columbia Families*. Sponsored by the National and Welfare Council of the National Capitol. Washington, D.C.: National Institute of Mental Health, February, 1967.

Linton, Ralph, ed. *The Science of Man in the World Crisis*. New York: Columbia University Press, 1945.

Lippitt, Ronald. "Improving the Socialization Process." In *Socialization and Society*, edited by John A. Clausen. Boston: Little, Brown, 1968, pp. 321–374.

Litwack, Leon F. "The Federal Government and the Free Negro, 1790–1860." In *Majority and Minority*, edited by Norman R. Yetman and C. Hoy Steele. Boston: Allyn and Bacon, 1974, pp. 178–192.

Longstreet, Wilma S. *Aspects of Ethnicity: Understanding Differences in Pluralistic Classrooms*. New York: Teachers College Press, 1978.

McAdoo, Harriette Pipes. "A Different View of Race Attitudes and Self-Concepts in Black Preschool Children." Paper presented at the Annual Meeting of the Association of Black Psychology Symposium on Cultural and Political Aspects of Child Development. Detroit, Michigan. August 1973.

McDavid. John W., and Harari, Herbert. *Psychology and Social Behavior*. New York: Harper and Row, 1974.

Macdonald, James B.; Wolfson, Bernice J.; and Zaret, Esther. *Reschooling Society: A Conceptual Model*. Washington, D.C. Association for Supervision and Curriculum Development, 1973.

McKibbin, Michael; Weil, Marsha; and Joyce, Bruce. *Teaching and Learning: Demonstrations of Alternatives*. Washington, D.C. Association of Teacher Education, 1977.

McLuhan, Marshall. *Understanding Media: The Extension of Man*. New York: McGraw-Hill, 1966.

Mahan, James M. "Employment Success." *Journal of Teacher Education* 27 (May-June 1977):39–42.

Malcolm X. "You've Got to Be Realistic About Being a Nigger." In *Demystifying School: Writings and Experiences*, edited by Miriam Wasserman. New York: Praeger Press, 1974, pp. 81–82.

Malec, Michael A., ed. *Attitude Change*. Chicago: Markham Publishing, 1971.

Malinowski, Bronislaw. *Magic, Science, and Religion*. New York: Anchor Books, 1954.

————. *A Scientific Theory of Culture and Other Essays*. Chapel Hill: University of North Carolina Press, 1944.

Margolin, Edythe. *Sociocultural Elements in Early Childhood Education*. New

York: Macmillan, 1974.

Marx, Melvin H, and Hillix, William A. *Systems and Theories in Psychology.* New York: McGraw-Hill, 1963.

Maslow, Abraham H. "Creativity in Self-Actualizing People." In *Creativity and Its Cultivation,* edited by H. H. Anderson. New York: Harper and Brothers, 1959, pp. 83–96.

————. *The Farther Reaches of Human Nature.* New York: Penguin Books, 1977.

————. *Toward a Psychology of Being.* New York: D. Van Nostrand, 1968.

Matzkin, Carol. "$6,000 Degree in Boredom." In *Toward Social Change: A Handbook for Those Who Will,* edited by Robert Buckhout and 81 Concerned Berkeley Students. New York: Harper and Row, 1971, pp. 433–434.

Mead, Margaret, ed. *Cultural Patterns and Technical Change.* New York: Mentor Book, 1955.

————. "Education as Cultural Growth." In *Social Foundations of Education: A Book of Readings,* edited by Cole S. Brembeck and Marvin Grandstaff. New York: John Wiley, 1969, pp. 18–30.

Mead, Margaret, and Wolfenstein, Martha, eds. *Childhood in Contemporary Cultures.* Chicago: University of Chicago Press, 1974.

Meadows, Donella H.; Meadows, Dennis; Randers, Jorgen; and Behrens, William III. *The Limits to Growth: A Report for the Club of Rome's Project on the Predicament of Mankind.* New York: Signet, 1974.

Meier, August, and Rudwich, Elliot. *From Plantation to Ghetto.* New York: Hill and Wang, 1970.

Meir, Matt S., and Rivera, Feliciano. *The Chicanos: A History of Mexican Americans.* New York: Hill and Wang, 1972.

Mercer, Jane R. "A Policy Statement on Assessment Procedures and the Rights of Children." *Harvard Educational Review* 44 (February 1974):137.

Merton, Robert K. "Self-Fulfilling Prophecy." In *Children and Poverty: Some Sociological and Psychological Perspectives,* edited by Nona Y. Glazer and Carol F. Creedom. Chicago: Rand McNally, 1970, pp. 16–20.

Middleton, John, ed. *Studies in Social and Cultural Anthropology.* New York: Thomas Y. Crowell, 1969.

Miles, Matthew W., and Charters, W. W. Jr. *Learning in Social Settings.* Boston: Allyn and Bacon, 1970.

Milner, E. "A Study of the Relationship Between Reading Readiness in Grade One School Children and Patterns of Parent-Child Interactions." *Child Development* 22 (1951):95–122.

Montagu, Ashley. *Culture and Human Development: Insights Into Growing Human.* Englewood Cliffs, N.J.: Prentice-Hall, 1974.

————. *Man's Most Dangerous Myth: The Fallacy of Race.* London: Oxford University Press, 1974.

Morales, Royal Makibaka, S. *The Philippine American Struggle.* Los Angeles: Mountainview Press, 1974.

Munro, Donald J. "The Chinese View of Modeling." *Human Development* 18:5 (1975):333–352.

Munroe, Robert L., and Munroe, Ruth. *Cross-Cultural Human Development.* New York: Jason Aronson, 1977.

Murdock, George Peter. "The Common Denominator of Cultures." In *The Science of Man in the World Crisis*, edited by Ralph Linton. New York: Columbia University Press, 1945.

National Advisory Countil on Bilingual Education Second Annual Report to the Congress and the President of the United States. By Inter-America Research Associates. Washington, D.C.: Inter-America Associates, 1976.

National Association of the Education of Young Children. *Preparing Teachers of Disadvantaged Young Children: Summary of a Conference of National Defense Education Act Institutes*, edited by Bernard Spodek. Washington, D.C.: Institute for Teachers of Disadvantaged Youth, 1965.

National Coalition for Cultural Pluralism. "Statement by Steering Committee." In *Cultural Pluralism in Education: A Mandate for Change*. p. 150. Edited by Madelon Stent, William Hazard, and Harry Rivlin. New York: Appleton-Century-Crofts, 1973.

National Council for Accreditation of Teacher Education. *Standards for Accreditation of Teacher Education: The Accreditation of Basic and Advanced Preparation Programs for Professional School Personnel*. Washington, D.C.: NCACTE, 1977.

National Council for the Social Studies. *Curriculum Guidelines for Multiethnic Education: Position Statement*. Written by the NCSS Task Force on Ethnic Studies Curriculum Guidelines, James A. Banks, chairperson, 1976.

National Education Association. *Certain American Truths. Report of the Task Force on Human Rights*. Washington, D.C.: NEA, 1968.

————. *Educational Neglect: Thirteenth Annual NEA Conference on Civil and Human Rights in Education*. Washington, D.C., 1975.

————. *Desegregation/Integration: Planning for School Change*. Washington, D.C.: NEA, 1974.

————. *Ethnic Heritage Studies Program: Assessment of the First Year July 1, 1974-June 30, 1975*. Washington, D.C.: National Education Association, 1977.

————. *Guidelines for Building an Affiliate Awareness and Action Planning Program in Bilingual Multi-Cultural Education*. Washington, D.C.: October 1975.

————. *Learning More About Learning: Papers and Reports From the Third ASCD Research Institute*. Washington, D.C.: National Education Association, 1959.

————. *The Multicultural Multiracial Task Force on Bilingual/Bicultural Education*. NEA Conference 28 Nov-Dec, 1973.

————. *Report of the NEA Task Force on Testing 2-8 July 1975*. Los Angeles, California.

————. *Report of the NEA Task Force on Bilingual/Multicultural Education. Presented to and Received by the Fifty-fourth Representative Assembly and Referred to the NEA Board of Directors for Implementation, July 1975*.

————. *Roots in America*. Washington, D.C.: National Education Association, 1975.

————. *NEA Task Force on Bilingual/Bicultural Education 53rd Representative Assembly*. Washington, D.C.: NEA, July 2, 1974.

————. *Values Education and the Study of Other Cultures*. Washington, D.C.: National Education Association, 1976.

————. *Violations of Human Rights: Tests and Use of Tests: A Report of the Tenth National Conference on Civil and Human Rights in Education. 18-20 February 1972*. Washington, D.C.: NEA, 1972.

National Research Council National Academy of Sciences. *Toward a National Policy for Children and Families*. Washington, D.C.: Advisory Committee on Child Development Assembly of Behavioral and Social Sciences, 1976.

Nemeth, Charlan. *Social Psychology: Classic and Contemporary Integrations*. Chicago: Rand McNally College, 1974.

Newman, William M. *American Pluralism: A Study of Minority Groups and Social Theory*. New York: Harper and Row, 1973.

Nicholson, Clara K. *Anthropology and Education*. Columbus, Ohio: Charles E. Merrill, 1968.

Nieburg, H. L. *Culture Storm: Politics and the Ritual Order*. New York: Saint Martin's Press, 1973.

"No One Model American: Statement on Multicultural Education." *The Commission on Multicultural Education American Association of Colleges of Teacher Education*. Washington, D.C.: AACTE, Nov. 1972.

"Non-Verbal Communication." *Theory Into Practice-Journal of College of Education*, Ohio State University 16, no. 3 (June 1977): 129–219.

Novak, Michael. "Among Middle-Class Ethnics: A Great Deal of Bitterness." *Interview with Michael Novak, Philosopher and Social Critic. Special Report U.S. News and World Report*. Reprinted by EMPAC, Ethnic Millions Political Action Committee, 1974.

————. "One Species, Many Cultures." *The American Scholar* 43, no. 1 (winter 1973–1974):119.

————. *The Rise of the Unmeltable Ethnics*. New York: Macmillan, 1972.

Noyes, Katherine Johnson, and McAndrew, Gordon L. "Is This What Schools Are for?" *Saturday Review*, 21 December 1968, p. 65.

Oestreich, Nancy Lurie. "The American Indian: Historial Background." In *Majority and Minority: The Dynamics of Racial and Ethnic Relations*, edited by Norman Yetman and C. Hoy Steele. Boston: Allyn and Bacon, 1974, pp. 207–229.

Oettinger, Anthony. "Run Computer Run." In *Demystifying School: Writings and Experiences*, edited by Miriam Wasserman. New York: Praeger Press, 1974, pp. 264–268.

Olson, Paul A. "Introduction." In *Badges and Indicia of Slavery: Cultural Pluralism Redefined*, edited by Antonia Pantoja, Chairman Study Commission on Undergraduate Education and the Education of Teachers. Lincoln, Neb.: University of Nebraska Printing and Duplicating Service, 1975, pp. vi–xxvi.

Pacheco, Arturo. "Cultural Pluralism: A Philosophical Analysis. *Journal of Teacher Education* 28, no. 3 (May-June 1977):16–20.

Pap, Michael. *Why Title IX? Why Do We Need an Ethnic Heritage Studies Program?* Remarks at the First National Meeting of Ethnic Heritage Studies Program Directors. Washington, D.C.: 22 October 1974.

Park, George. *The Idea of Social Structure.* New York: Anchor, 1974.

Park, Robert Ezra. *Race and Culture: Essays in the Sociology of Contemporary Man.* New York: Free Press, 1950.

Perlmutter, Phillip. "Ethnic Education: Can It Be Relevant?" *Massachusetts Teacher,* February 1974.

Perry, Sir Walter. "How to Save the Educational System." *Human Nature* (September 1978):68–75.

Peterson, William. *Japanese Americans: Oppression and Success.* New York: Random House, 1971.

Philips, Susan U. "Commentary: Access to Power and Maintenance of Ethnic Identity as Goals of Multicultural Education: Are They Compatible?" *Anthropology and Education Quarterly* 7, no. 4 (1976):30–31.

Plog, Fred; Jolly, Clifford; and Bates, Daniel. *Anthropology: Decisions, Adaptation, and Evolution.* New York: Alfred A. Knopf, 1976.

Polak, Fred L. "Responsibility for the Future." *The Humanist* (November-December 1973):14–16.

Postman, Neil, and Weingartner, Charles. *Teaching as a Subversive Activity.* New York: Delta Book, 1969

Practicing Anthropology: A Career-Oriented Publication of the Society for Applied Anthropology. Tampa, Fl.: Department of Anthropology, University of Southern Florida, 1978.

Pritzkau, Philo T. *On Education for the Authentic.* Scranton, Penn.: International Textbook, 1970.

Public Citizen. Headline, "Some Winners Some Losers," "Federal Taxes." By Robert S. McIntyre. "State and Local Taxes." By Diane Fuch. Issue 8 Winter, 1978.

Pucinski, Roman. "Ethnic Studies and Urban Reality." In *Pieces of A Dream,* edited by Michael Wenk, S. M. Thomasi, and Geno Baroni. New York: The Center for Migration Studies, 1972, pp. 73–88.

Qualey, Carlton C. "Ethnicity and History." In *Ethnicity: A Conceptual Approach,* edited by Daniel E. Weinberg. Cleveland: Ethnic Heritage Studies, Cleveland State University, 1976, pp. 27–37.

Ramirez, Manuel, III, and Castañeda, Alfredo. *Cultural Democracy, Biocognitive Development and Education.* New York: Academic Press, 1974.

Rand, Helen. "Experimental Learning Reevaluated." *Young Children.* Vol 25 (September 1970):363–366.

Rathbone, Charles H. *Open Education: The Formal Classroom.* New York: Citation Press, 1971.

Read, Donald A., and Simon, Sidney B., eds. *Humanistic Education Sourcebook.* New Jersey: Prentice-Hall, 1975.

Redman, George L. "A Model for Human Relations In-Service Training." *Journal of Teacher Education* 27 (May-June 1977):34–38.

Reischuauer, Edwin O. *Toward the 21st Century: Educating for a Changing World.* New York: Alfred A. Knopf, 1973.

Reluctant Guardians: A Survey of Federal Civil Rights Laws, PB 192 346. Springfield, Virginia: Clearinghouse for Federal Scientific and Technical Information, December, 1969.

Report to the President: White House Conference on Children, 1970. Washington, D.C.: U.S. Government Printing Office, 1970.

Rescher, Nicholas. *Introduction to Value Theory*. Englewood Cliffs, N.J.: Prentice-Hall, 1969.

Reuter, Edward Byran. *Race Mixture: Studies in Intermarriage and Miscegenation*. New York: McGraw-Hill, 1931.

Rich, John Martin. *Humanistic Foundations of Education*. Worthington, Ohio: Charles A. Jones, 1971.

Riesman, David. "Some Questions About the Study of American Character in the Twentieth Century Life Styles." In *Diversity in American Society*, edited by Saul Feldman and Gerald Withielbar. Boston: Little Brown, 1972.

Riessman, Frank. *The Culturally Deprived Child*. New York: Harper, 1962.

Rist, Ray C. "Students, Social Class, and Teacher Expectations: The Self-Fulfilling Prophecy in Ghetto Education." *Harvard Educational Review* 40, no. 3 (August 1970):411–451.

Rivlin, Harry N. "General Perspectives on Multiculturalism." *Journal of Teacher Education* 26, no. 2 (September 1975):121–122.

———. "Research and Development in Multicultural Education." In *Pluralism and the American Teacher: Issues and Case Studies*, edited by Frank Klassen and Donna Gollnick. Washington, D.C.: Ethnic Heritage Center for Teacher Education of the National Association of Colleges for Teacher Education, 1977, pp. 81–86.

Rivlin, Harry N., and Fraser, Dorothy M. "Ethnic Labeling and Mislabeling." In *In Praise of Diversity: A Resource Book for Multicultural Education*, edited by Milton J. Gold, Carl A. Grant, and Harry N. Rivlin. Washington, D.C.: Teacher Corps and Association of Teacher Education.

Roberts, S. O., and Robinson, J. M. "Intercorrelations of Primary Mental Abilities Test for Ten-Year-Olds by Socioeconomic Status, Sex and Race. *American Psychology* 7 (1952):304–305.

Rogers, Carl. "The Interpersonal Relationship in the Facilitation of Learning." In *Humanistic Education Sourcebook*, edited by Donald A. Read and Sidney B. Simon. Englewood Cliffs, N.J.: Prentice-Hall, 1975, pp. 3–19.

Rohwer, William D. Jr. "Learning, Race, and School Success." *Review of Educational Research* 41, no. 3 (June 1971):191–211.

Rose, Peter I. *They and We: Racial and Ethnic Relations in the United States*. New York: Random House, 1974.

Rosenthal, Robert. "Self-Fulfilling Prophecy." In *Readings in Psychology Today*. Delmar, Calif.: Communications/Research/Machines, 1969, pp. 466–471.

Rosenthal, Robert, and Jacobson, Lenore. *Pygmalion in the Classroom: Teacher Expectations and Pupils' Intellectual Development*. New York: Holt, Rinehart and Winston, 1968.

Rosenshine, B., and Furst, N. R. "Research on Teacher Performance Criteria." In *Research in Teacher Education: A Symposium*. New Jersey: Prentice-Hall, 1971.

Rossi, Ino, ed. *The Unconscious in Culture: The Structuralism of Claude Levi-Strauss in Perspective*. New York: Dutton, 1974.

Rothstein, Richard. "How Tracking Works." In *Demystifying School: Writings and Experiences,* edited by Miriam Wasserman. New York: Praeger, 1974, pp. 61–73.

Rubin, Israel. "Ethnicity and Cultural Pluralism." In *Ethnicity: A Conceptual Approach.* Cleveland: Cleveland Ethnic Heritage Studies, Cleveland State University, 1976, pp. 94–95.

Rubin, Jerry. "Burn Down the Schools." In *Toward Social Change: A Handbook for Those Who Will,* edited by Robert Buckhout and 81 Concerned Berkeley Students. New York: Harper and Row, 1971, pp. 434–436.

Ryan, William. *Blaming the Victim.* New York: Vintage, 1976.

Sahakian, William S. *Systematic Social Psychology.* New York: Chandler, 1974.

Saint Lawrence, Theodora J., and Singleton, John. "Multuculturalism in Social Context: Conceptual Problems Raised by Educational Policy Issues." *Anthropology and Education Quarterly* 7, no. 4 (November 1976):19–23.

Sanday, P. R. "The Relevance of Anthropology to United States Social Policy." *Council on Anthropology and Education Newsletter III.* 3 (1972).

Sapir, Edward. "Culture—Genuine and Spurious." *American Journal of Sociology* 29 (1924):401–429.

Sarason, Seymour. *The Culture of the School and the Problem of Change.* Boston: Allyn and Bacon, 1971.

Sarte, Jean-Paul. "Authentic and Inauthentic Man." In *The Substance of Sociology: Codes, Conduct, and Consequences.* New York: Appleton-Century-Crofts, 1967, pp. 215–219.

Schermerhorn, R. A. *Comparative Ethnic Relations: A Framework for Theory and Research.* New York: Random, 1970.

––––––. "Ethnicity in the Perspective of the Sociology of Knowledge." In *Ethnicity: A Conceptual Approach,* edited by Daniel E. Weinberg. Cleveland: Cleveland State University, 1976, pp. 5–17.

Schumacher, E. F. *Small Is Beautiful: Economics as if People Mattered.* New York: Harper and Row, 1973.

Scott, Myrtle, and Grimmett, Sadie, eds. *Current Issues in Child Development.* Washington, D.C.: National Association for the Education of Young Children, 1977.

Srinivas, M. N., ed. *A.R. Radcliff-Brown. Methods in Social Anthropology: Selected Essays and Addresses.* Chicago: University of Chicago Press, 1958.

Scriven, Michael, ed. *Methods in Social Anthropology: Selected Essays and Addresses.* Chicago: University of Chicago Press, 1958.

––––––. "The Methodology of Evaluation." In *Perspectives of Curriculum Evaluation.* Edited by Ralph W. Tyler, Robert M. Gagne, and Michael Scriven. Chicago: Rand McNally, 1967.

Sears, Robert R.; Maccoby, Eleanor E.; and Levin, Harry. *Patterns in Child Rearing.* Stanford, Calif.: Stanford University Press, 1957.

Seelig, Jerome M. *The Cultural Dimension in Learning and Child Development: New Policy Implications.* New York: Institute on Pluralism and Group Identity, 1975.

Seifer, Nancy. *Education and the New Pluralism: A Preliminary Survey of Recent Progress in the Fifty States.* Presented to Annual Meeting of the National Coordinating Assembly on Ethnic Studies held in Conjunction with Ethnic Conference IV. Ethnic Heritage Center, Detroit, Michigan, May 19, 1973.

————. *The New Jersey Consultation on Ethnic Factors in Education.* New York: Institute on Pluralism and Group Identity, 1973.

Serna v. Portales, Municipal Schools 351 F Supp (D.N.M. 1972).

Service, Elma R. *Profiles in Ethnology.* New York: Harper and Row, 1978.

Shane, Harold G. *Curriculum Change: Toward the 21st Century.* Washington, D.C.: National Education Association, 1977.

Shockley, William. "Negro I.Q. Deficit: Failure of a 'Malicious Coincidence' Model Warrants New Research Proposals." *Review of Education Research* 41, no. 3 (June 1971):227–248.

Silberman, Charles E. *Crisis in the Classroom.* New York: Random House, 1970.

Skinner, B. F. *Science and Human Behavior.* New York: Macmillan, 1953.

Smith, Othaniel B.; Cohen, Saul B.; and Pearl, Arthur. *Teachers for the Real World.* For the Task Force of the NDEA National Institute for Advanced Study in Teaching Disadvantaged Youth. The American Association of Colleges for Teacher Education, 1969.

Smith, Philip G., ed. *Theories of Value and Problems of Education.* Urbana: University of Illinois Press, 1970.

Smith, William. "The Melting Pot Theory: Demise of Euphemism." In *Cultural Pluralism in Education: A Mandate for Change,* edited by Madelon Stent, William Hazard, and Harry Rivlin. New York: Appleton-Century-Crofts, 1973, pp. 141–144.

Snyder, Benson R. *The Hidden Curriculum.* Cambridge, Mass.: MIT Press, 1973.

Sobel, Harold. "The Anachronistic Practices of American Education As Perpetuated by an Unenlightened Citizenry and Misguided Pedagogues Against the Inmates of the Public Schools." In *Foundations of Education: A Social View,* edited by Albert W. Vogel, David L. Bachelor, and John T. Zepper. Albuquerque: University of New Mexico Press, 1970, pp. 26–31.

Social Research Group. *Research Problems and Issues in Areas of Socialization.* Prepared for the Inter-Agency Panel on Early Childhood Research and Development. Washington, D.C.: George Washington University, September 1972.

Sowder, Barbara J., and Lazar, Joyce B. *Research Problems and Issues in the Area of Socialization.* Prepared for the Interagency Panel on Early Childhood Research and Development. Washington, D.C. Social Research Group George Washington University, 1972.

Spindler, George Dearborn, ed. *Education and Cultural Process: Toward an Anthropology of Education.* New York: Holt, Rinehart, and Winston, 1974.

Spiro, Melford E. "Religion: Problems of Definition and Explanation." In *Anthropological Approaches to the Study of Religion,* edited by Michael Bauton. London: Tamstock, 1966, pp. 85–125.

Spradley, James P., and McCurdy, David W. *Conformity and Conflict: Readings in Cultural Anthropology.* Boston: Little, Brown, 1974.

————. *The Cultural Experience: Ethnography in Complex Society*. Chicago: Science Research Associates, 1972.

State Legislation Provisions and Practices Related to Multicultural Education. Report Prepared for the National Institute of Education. January 1978. Prepared in part from a report by Raymond Giles under contract #400-76-0127 (unpublished).

Starr, James B., and Wilson, Suzanne F. "Some Epistemological and Methodological Issues in the Design of Cross-Cultural Research." In *Topics in Cultural Learning,* edited by Richard P. Brislin and Michael P. Hammett. Honolulu, Hawaii: East-West Learning Institute, August 1977, pp. 125–135.

Steinberg, Erwin R. "Class and Educational Meaning." In *Social Foundations of Education: A Book of Readings,* edited by Cole S. Brembeck and Marvin Grandstaff. New York: John Wiley and Sons, 1969, pp. 169–177.

Stone, Joseph, and Church, Joseph. *Childhood and Adolescence: A Psychology of the Growing Person*. New York: Random House, 1973.

Strom, Robert D., and Torrance, Paul E., eds. *Education for Affective Achievement*. Chicago: Rand McNally, 1973.

Sung, S. W. *Chinese in American Life: Some Aspects of Their History, Status, Problems, and Contributions*. Seattle: University of Washington Press, 1962.

Superka, Douglas; Ahrens, Christine; Hedstrom, Judith E.; with Ford, Luther J.; and John, Patricia L. *Values Education Sourcebook*. Boulder, Colo.: Social Science Education Consortium, 1976.

Sutherland, John W. *A General Systems Philosophy for the Social and Behavioral Sciences*. New York: George Braziller, 1973.

Taba, Hilda, and Elkins, Deborah. *Teaching Strategies for the Culturally Disadvantaged*. Chicago: Rand McNally, 1966.

Theory Into Practice (TIP) Journal of College of Education Ohio State University. Nonverbal Issue 16, no. 3 (June 1977).

Tillich, Paul. *The Courage to Be*. New Haven: Yale University Press, 1952.

"Tio Taco Is Dead," *Newsweek,* 29 June 1970, reprinted in *Toward Social Change: A Handbook for Those Who Will.* pp. 22–28, edited by Robert Buckhout and 81 Concerned Berkeley Students. New York: Harper and Row, 1971.

Toffler, Alvin, ed. *Future Shock*. New York: Bantam, 1971.

————. *Learning for Tomorrow: The Role of the Future in Education*. New York: Vintage Books, 1974.

Travieso, Lourdes. "Puerto Ricans and Education." *Journal of Teacher Education* 26, no. 2 (September 1975):128–130.

Trujillo, Rupert A. "Multiculturalism." *Journal of Teacher Education* 26:2 (September 1975):125–126.

Tsukamoto, Mary. "An American With a Japanese Face." In *Some Minorities Speak Out*. Association for Childhood Education International. Washington, D.C. Children and Intercultural Education Series, 1974, pp. 2–5.

Tumin, Melvin. "Teaching in America." In *The School in the Social Order: A Sociological Introduction to Educational Understanding,* edited by Francisco Cordasco, Maurie Hillson, and Henry Bullock. Scranton, Penn.:

Intext Publication, 1972, pp. 39–45.

Tyack, David T. *The One Best System: A History of American Urban Education.* Cambridge, Mass.: Harvard University Press, 1974.

Tylor, Sir Edward B. *Anthropology.* Michigan: University of Michigan Press, 1970.

———. *Primitive Culture: Researches Into the Development of Mythology, Philosophy, Religion, Art, and Custom. 2 vols.: vol. 1 Origins of Culture and vol. 2 Religion in Primitive Culture.* Gloucester, Massachusetts: Smith, 1958 (original, 1871).

Tylor, Ralph; Gagne, Robert; and Scriven, Michael. "Perspectives of Curriculum Evaluation." *AERA Monograph* 1 (1967):39–83.

Ueda, Reed. "The Americanization and Education of Japanese Americans: A Psychodramatic and Dramaturgical Perspective." In *Majority and Minority: The Dynamics of Racial and Ethnic Relations,* edited by Norman Yetman, and C. Hoy Steele. Boston: Allyn and Bacon, 1974, pp. 71–90.

U.S. Commission on Civil Rights. *A Better Chance to Learn: Bilingual Bicultural Education.* No. 51 (May 1975).

———. *Racial Isolation in the Public Schools.* 2 vols. (Washington, D.C.: Government Printing Office, 1967).

———. *Task Force Findings Specifying Remedies Available for Eliminating Past Educational Practices Ruled Unlawful Under Lau v. Nichols.* (Summer 1975).

U.S. Congress. *Bilingual Education Act Pub. L. 90-247, Pub. L. 93-80, As Amended Sec. 701-742, HR 7571, HRR 9419, 95th Cong. 1st session, 1977.*

———. *Elementary and Secondary School Act of 1965 Pub. L. 89-10, and amendments.*

———. *Equal Educational Opportunities: Hearings Before the Select Committee on Equal Educational Opportunity of the U.S. Senate, 1971-1972.*

———. *Justice for Children.* Select Committee on Equal Educational Opportunity. Walter Mondale, Chairman. U.S. Government Printing Office, 1972.

———. Senate. *Child Care: Data and Materials.* Russel B. Long, Chairman, October, 1974.

U.S. Department of Health, Education, and Welfare. National Institute of Education. *Cognitive Development in Young Children: A Report for Teachers.* Prepared by Nancy Ewald Jackson, Halbert B. Robinson, and Philip S. Dale, January 1976.

———. National Institute of Education. *The Desegregation Literature: A Critical Appraisal,* July 1976.

———. National Institute of Education. *Educational Research in America. National Council on Education Research-Annual Report,* 1975.

———. National Institute of Education. *A Fieldwork Manual for Studying Desegregated Schools.* By Joan Cassell. Washington, D.C.: National Institute of Education, 1978.

———. National Institute of Education. *Minority Students: A Research Appraisal.* Prepared by Meyer Weinberg, March 1977.

———. National Institute of Education. *Multicultural Bilingual Division Fiscal Year 1977-1978 Program Plan.*

————. National Institute of Education. *School Desegregation and Cultural Pluralism: Perspectives on Progress. Selected Presentations of the 1974-75 STRIDE Workshops*. Prepared by Far West Laboratory for Educational Research and Development. San Francisco, California 94103.

————. National Institute of Education. *School Desegregation in Metropolitan Areas: Choices and Prospects*. A National Conference 15-16 March 1977.

————. Office of Education. *Cultural Pluralism and Social Change Report V: Collection of Position Papers. The In-Service Teacher Education Concepts Project*. By Bruce R. Joyce and Lucy F. Peck. Sponsored by National Center for Education Statistics and Teacher Corps. Syracuse: The National Dissemination Center, Syracuse University, 1977.

————. Office of Education. *Equality of Educational Opportunity*. By James Coleman and others. Government Printing Office, 1966.

————. Office of Education. *ESAA Regulations That Govern the Emergency School Aid Act. Title VII of the Education Amendments, as amended*.

————. Office of Education. *ESEA Title VII Joint Meeting: Directors of National Network Centers and State Bilingual Coordinators*. 5-7 December 1977.

————. Office of Education. *Federal Assistance to Desegregating School Districts: Emergency School Aid Aict, Title VII, PL 92-318, as amended (20 U.S.C. 1601 et seq.) A Report on Activities May-September 1976*.

————. Office of Education. *Instructional Strategies in Schools with High Concentration of Low-Income Pupils: A Report to the U.S. Office of Education National Task Force: Urban Education Rural and Migrant Education, Native American Education and Bilingual-Bicultural Education*. (no date)

————. Office of Education. *A Summary of Federal Aid Under the Emergency School Aid Act (Title V11 of PL 92-318) as amended by Education Amendments of 1974 (PL 93-380)*. August, 1976.

————. Office of Education. Citizen Education. *Citizen Education Today*. Report prepared by National Center for Voluntary Action, 1978. (draft)

————. Office of Education. Citizen Education. *Education and Citizenship: The National Conference on Education and Citizenship: Responsibilities for Common Good 20-23 September 1976*.

————. Office of Education Division of Bilingual Education. *The Condition of Bilingual Education in the Nation. First Report of the U.S. Commissioner of Education to the President and Congress, November 1976*.

————. Office of Education. Division of Bilingual Education. *First Annual National Title VII Bilingual Education Management Institute 20-23 October, 1977*.

————. Office of Education. Division of Bilingual Education. *National Advisory Council on Bilingual Education Second Annual Report, 1976*. By Inter-American Research Associates, Washington, D.C.

————. Office of Education. Division of Compensatory Education. *Acceleration of Intellectual Development in Early Childhood*. By Carl Bereiter, 1966.

————. Office of Education. Division of Compensatory Education. *Compensatory Educational Programs March 1977, Title 1 of Elementary and Secondary Education, Title IV Community Service Act: Program Descriptions and Status Reports*.

————. Office of Education. English as a Second Language Division. *Evaluation* of the Impact of ESEA Title VII Spanish/English Education Program April 1977.

————. Office of Education. Ethnic Heritage Branch. *Ethnic Heritage Studies Program in Fiscal Year 1974, 1975, and 1976: Facts and Figures.*

————. Office of Education. National Center for Educational Statistics. *The Condition of Education: A Statistical Report on the Condition of Education in the United States.* 1977 edition. Prepared by Mary A. Golladay, 1977.

————. Office of Education. National Center for Educational Statistics. *Report to the Congress by the Comptroller General of the United States. The National Assessment of Educational Progress: Its Results Need to be Made More Useful, July 20, 1976.*

————. Office of Education. Office of Planning, Budgeting, and Evaluation. *A Handbook for Integrated Schooling,* July 1976.

————. Office of Education. Teacher Corps. *Descriptions and Interpretations 1975 CMTI Impact Study: Report of CMTI Impact Study Team for Teacher Corps Recruitment and Technical Resources Center, University of Nebraska-Omaha, September 1976.*

————. Office of Human Development. Administration for Children, Youth, and Families. *Proceedings Bilingual/Bicultural Early Childhood Development Research Workshop, February 1976.*

————. Office of Human Development. Administration for Children, Youth, and Families. *Proceedings Bilingual Bicultural Preschool Projects Conference: Research, Staff Training, Curriculum Development, Resource Network 15-18 November 1977.*

————. Office of Human Development. Administration for Children, Youth, and Families. Head Start. *Transmittal Notices N-30-365 on Head Start Performance Standards and OCD-HS Notice N-364-4, July 1975 Head Start Performance Standards Manual.*

————. Public Health Service. National Institutes of Health. National Institute of Mental Health. *Early Childhood Education Studies and Education for Parenting Funded Projects Related to Early Language Development 1969-1974.*

————. Public Health Service. National Institutes of Health. *NIMH Research in the Service of Mental Health. Report of the Research Task Force of the National Institute of Mental Health Summary Report.* Prepared by Task Force and Coordinating Committee, Julius Segal and Donald S. Boomer, associate editors, 1977.

U.S. Department of Labor. *The Negro Family: The Case for National Action.* Prepared by Daniel P. Moynihan, U.S. Government Printing Office, 1965.

U.S. Department of State. Advisory Commission on International Education and Cultural Affairs. International Education and Cultural Exchange. *American Blacks . . . Involvement in Educational Exchange,* by Gilbert Anderson, Washington, D.C.: Commission on International Education and Cultural Affairs. Fall 1972.

U.S. Government Federal Register. Office of Education. *Bilingual Education Programs. Criteria for Governing Grant Awards Part III, June 11, 1976.*

U.S. National Institute of Education. *Evaluating Compensatory Education: An*

Interim Report on the NIE Compensatory Study 30 December 1976.

U.S. National Technical Information Service. Clearinghouse for Federal Scientific and Technical Information. 5285 Port Royal Rd., Springfield, Va. 22161. *Reluctant Guardians: A Survey of Federal Civil Rights Laws, P B 192 346. December 1969.*

U.S. Public Health Service. National Institutes of Health. National Institute of Mental Health. Center for Studies of Child and Family Mental Health. *Teachers Talk About Their Feelings,* 1973.

Valentine, Charles A. *Culture and Poverty: Critique and Counter Proposals.* Chicago: University of Chicago Press, 1972.

Van Til, Williams. "The Key Word Is Relevance." *Today's Education* (January 1969):14–17.

Varenne, Herve. "Culture as Rhetoric: Patterning in the Verbal Interpretation of Interaction Between Teachers and Administrators in An American High School." *American Ethnologist* 5:4 (November 1, 1978):635–649.

Wakatama, Matthew. *An Experimental Study of the Teaching of the Teaching of the Geography of Africa With Special Reference to Effects Upon the Attitudes of English Children Toward Africans.* Master of Arts Thesis, University of London, 1957.

Walker, Daniel. *Rights In Conflict: Report Submitted to the National Commission on the Causes and Prevention of Violence.* New York: Bantam Books, 1968.

Washburn, David. "A Conceptual Framework for Multicultural Education." *The Florida FL Reporter* (Spring/Fall 1972):27.

————. *Multicultural Education Programs Ethnic Studies Curricula and Ethnic Studies Materials in the United States Public Schools.* Bloomsburg, Pa.: Bloomsburg State College, 1974.

Watson, John B. *Psychology From the Standpoint of a Behaviorist.* Baltimore: Penguin Books, 1974.

Watson, Peter, ed. *Psychology and Race.* Chicago: Aldine, 1973.

Weaver, Thomas, and White Douglas. "The Anthropological Approaches to Urban and Complex Society." In *The Anthropology of Urban Environments,* edited by Thomas Weaver and Douglas White. Washington, D.C.: The Society for Applied Anthropology Monograph Series. Monograph 11, 1972, pp. 109–125.

Weinberg, David E. ed. *Ethnicity: A Conceptual Approach.* Cleveland: Cleveland State University, 1976.

Weinstein, Gerald, and Fantini, Mario. "Affect and Learning." In *Toward Humanistic Education: A Curriculum of Affect,* edited by Gerald Weinstein and Mario Fantini. New York: Praeger, 1970, pp. 16–32.

Weiss, Carol H. *Evaluating Action Programs: Readings in Social Action Education.* Boston: Allyn and Bacon, 1972.

Werner, Emily E. "Infants Around the World: Cross-Cultural Studies of Psycho-Motor Development From Birth to Two Years." *Journal of Cross-Cultural Psychology* 3, 2 (June 1972):111–134.

White House Conference on Children 1970: Report to the President. Washington, D.C.: U.S. Government Printing Office, 1972.

White, Leslie A. *The Science of Culture: A Study of Man and Civilization.* New York: Farrar, Straus, and Giroux, 1949.

————. "The Symbol: The Origin of Basics of Human Behavior." *Philosophy of Science* 7 (1941):451–463.

White, Robert W. "Motivation Reconsidered: The Concept of Competence." *The Psychological Review* 66 (September 1959):297–333.

White, Sheldon: Day, Mary Carol: Freeman, Phyllis K.; Hantman, Stephen A.; and Messenger, Katherine. P. *Federal Programs for Young Children,* 4 vols. Cambridge, Mass.: The Huron Institute, 1973. Vol. 1: Goals and Standards of Public Programs for Children.

Whiteman, M. "Intelligence and Learning." *Merrill-Palmer Quarterly of Behavior and Development* 10:3 (1964):297–309.

Whiting, Beatrice B. "Folk Wisdom and Child Rearing." *Merrill-Palmer Quarterly* 20, no. 1 (January 1974):9–19.

Wickman, E.K. *Children's Behavior and Teacher Attitudes.* New York:Commonwealth Fund, 1928.

Wilkerson, Doxey. "Compensatory Education: Defining the Issues." In *Disadvantaged Child: Compensatory Education a National Debate,* edited by Jerome Hellmuth. New York: Brunner/Mazel, 1970, pp. 24–34.

Wilson, A.B. "Educational Consequences of Segregation in a California Community." Appendix C-3. In *Racial Isolation in the Public Schools,* pp. 165–206. U.S. Commission on Civil Rights. Washington, D.C.: U.S. Government Printing Office, 1967.

Wilson, Herbert B.; Featherstone, J.; and Gillespie, Jane. *Cultural Literacy.* Tucson, Ariz.: Multicultural Education Center, 1972.

Winschel, James F. "In the Dark . . . Reflections on Compensatory Education 1960-1970. In *Disadvantaged Child: Compensatory Education a National Debate,* edited by Jerome Hellmuth. New York: Brunner/Mazel, 1970, pp. 3–23.

Wolf, Barbara A. *Equality of Opportunity Quantified: A Production Function Approach.* Philadelphia: Department of Research Federal Reserve Bank of Philadelphia, 1975.

Wrobel, Paul. "Becoming a Polish American: A Personal Point of View." In *Minorities Speak Out.* Washington, D.C.: Association for Childhood Education International, 1974, pp. 8–12.

Wylie, Richard E. "Selected Research on Intercultural-International Education." In *Overview and Research in Children and Intercultural Education Part II.* Washington, D.C.: Association for Childhood Education International, 1974, pp. 24–32.

Yeomans, Edward. *Education for Initiative and Responsibility.* Boston: National Association of Independent Schools, November 1967.

Young, Kimball, and Mack, Raymond W. *Sociology and Social Life.* New York: American Book, 1965.

Young, Lauren S. "Multicultural Education: A Myth Into Reality?" *Journal of Teacher Education* 26, no. 2 (September 1975):127–128.

Zangwill, Israel. *The Melting Pot.* Drama in 4 Acts, new and rev. ed. New York: Macmillan, c. 1914.

Zirkel, Perry A. "Self-Concept and the Disadvantage of Ethnic Group Membership and Mixture." *Review of Educational Research* 41, no. 3 (June 1971): 211–227.

INDEX

A

Accountability, 18
Achievement, 11, 18, 20, 23, 77, 82, 105
American
    Culture, 1, 11, 16
    Democracy, 3, 13, 16, 28
    Society, 2, 13, 14, 20
Anthropology, 53, 54, 101
Assimilation, 14, 32, 57, 59

B

Bicultural education, 37–39, 48, 71, 72, 89–94
Bias, 46, 72, 93, 103, 106, 121

C

Children, 20, 24, 26, 28, 30, 32, 35, 49, 53, 63, 77, 80
Colonial thinking, 17
Compensatory education, 12, 20, 35, 71, 73–86
Cross-cultural, 3, 8, 28, 50, 57, 69, 72, 101
Culture, 7, 10, 32, 39, 42, 44, 47
Culture Sense, 27, 38–40, 47, 56, 61, 101, 119, 129, 147
Cultural
    Anthropologists, 3, 7, 9, 18, 34, 50
    Anthropology, 6, 7, 32, 34, 42, 46, 51, 53, 54, 72, 145
    Deprivation, 11
    Groups, 2
    Pluralism, 23, 27, 38, 41–46, 48, 49, 53, 56, 58, 69, 95, 99–101, 106–112, 118, 129, 151
    Relativity, 9, 53–56, 101–106, 130, 151

D

Deficits, 15, 20, 27, 37, 71, 76, 78–82
Disadvantaged, 11
Diversity, 49, 58, 63, 82–85, 91, 93, 99, 110, 117, 127, 150
Dominant, 11, 15, 16, 23, 24, 28, 35, 36, 39, 49, 50, 81, 152
Dualism and dualistic, 50, 51, 107, 110, 111, 153

E

Education, 12, 15, 146
Educational institutions, 10, 12, 26, 34, 39, 106
Ethnicity, 23, 56
Ethnic groups, 1, 4, 32–38, 40, 46, 47, 57, 61, 74, 87, 88, 96, 101, 107, 116, 119, 145, 152
Ethnocentrism, 5, 13, 15, 19, 71, 104, 110, 146, 147
Environment, 8, 20, 22, 28, 36, 57, 63, 74, 78, 80, 117, 121, 125, 129

F

Family, 13, 52, 53, 76, 84
Function, 40, 46, 49, 62

G

Great American Dream, 17, 21

H

Head Start, 25, 79
Heritage, 44, 46, 47, 57, 86, 100
Holism and holistic, 10, 38, 41, 42,
    43, 50–54, 114, 117
Human
    Beings, 6
    Need, 62, 85, 86, 114
Humanistic education and theory,
    33, 41, 45, 53, 69, 101,
    112–117, 151

I

Immigrant, 11, 14, 57, 61, 107
Intercultural relations, 110

K

Knowledge, 6, 57, 88, 127, 149

L

Legislation, 15, 21, 22, 25, 37, 38,
    70, 78, 79, 87, 91–96, 106, 109
Low-income, 63, 75

M

Minority, 11, 14, 23–25, 32, 37, 39,
    49, 71, 86, 88, 107
Multicultural

Education, 20–22, 29, 37, 38, 49,
    64, 69–71, 94–101, 118,
    146, 152
Population, 35
Myths, 10, 11, 16, 61, 82

N

New pluralism, 14, 57, 61.

P

Poor and poverty, 14, 21, 23, 30,
    79–84, 106

R

Racism, 20, 26, 57, 63, 75, 95, 106
Reality, 9, 13, 21, 29, 55, 94, 121

S

Schools and schooling, 12, 16, 27,
    28, 49, 61, 75, 82, 115, 119,
    130, 151, 152
Science and scientific truth, 7–9, 15,
    17, 18
Socialization, 85, 121, 130
Standardization, 11, 15, 17, 28, 31,
    49, 62, 118
Symbols, 55, 86, 120

T

Tonal feeling, 129
    Tradition, 10, 16, 61, 71
    Transmission, 3, 10, 54, 115

U

Universal and universalism, 33, 48,
    51, 59, 105–111, 117, 149

Values, 6, 9, 12, 17, 20, 25, 29, 31,
35, 37, 40, 46, 48, 50, 56, 58,
61, 72, 83, 86, 88, 113, 117,
147, 150
Victim, 22, 80, 81, 122, 146, 152
Victimization, 122–126